The Concerned Indian's Guide to Communalism

VIKING
Penguin India

The Concerned Indian's Guide to Communalism

Edited by

K.N. Panikkar

VIKING

VIKING

Penguin Books India (P) Ltd., 11 Community Centre, Panchsheel Park, New Delhi 110 017, India
Penguin Books Ltd., 27 Wrights Lane, London W8 5TZ, UK
Penguin Putnam Inc., 375 Hudson Street, New York, NY 10014, USA
Penguin Books Australia Ltd., Ringwood, Victoria, Australia
Penguin Books Canada Ltd., 10 Alcorn Avenue, Suite 300, Toronto, Ontario, MAV 3B2, Canada
Penguin Books (NZ) Ltd., 182-190 Wairau Road, Auckland, 10, New Zealand

First published in Viking by Penguin Books India 1999
Copyright © Penguin Books India 1999

Copyright in individual articles in *The Concerned Indian's Guide to Communalism* is assigned as follows:

Introduction: Defining the Nation as Hindu © K.N. Panikkar 1999
The Tyranny of Labels © Romila Thapar 1999
The Road to Xanadu: India's Quest for Secularism © Rajeev Dhavan 1999
Hindutva and the Question of Conversions © Sumit Sarkar 1999
Perceptions of Difference: The Economic Underpinnings © Jayati Ghosh 1999
The Gender Predicament Of The Hindu Right © Tanika Sarkar 1999
The Ink Link: Media, Communalism and the Evasion of Politics © Siddharth Varadarajan 1999
Afterword © K.N. Panikkar 1999

10 9 8 7 6 5 4 3 2 1

Typeset in *Nebraska* by SÜRYA, New Delhi
Printed at Chaman Enterprises, Delhi

Contents

Note on Contributors

Rajeev Dhavan is a senior advocate practicing in the Supreme Court of India, New Delhi.

Jayati Ghosh teaches at the Centre for Economic Studies and Planning, Jawaharlal Nehru University, New Delhi.

K.N. Panikkar teaches at the Centre for Historical Studies, Jawaharlal Nehru University, New Delhi.

Sumit Sarkar teaches at the Department of History, Delhi University, Delhi.

Tanika Sarkar teaches at the St. Stephen's College, Delhi University, Delhi.

Romila Thapar is Professor Emeritus, Centre for Historical Studies, Jawaharlal Nehru University, New Delhi.

Siddharth Varadarajan is a senior editor with the *Times of India*, New Delhi.

Introduction: Defining the Nation as Hindu

For more than fifty years democratic values have managed to survive in India as the guiding principle of its political discourse, despite certain aberrations and inadequacies in their practice. Given its cultural diversity and religious plurality many were sceptical about the ability of the nascent state, which achieved freedom from the British colonial rule in 1947, to live beyond a couple of decades as a democratic nation. On more than one occasion India had reached the brink of both disintegration and authoritarianism, but its political system proved to be resilient enough to pull back successfully. The popular assertion against the Emergency of 1975 and the rejection of secessionist tendencies in Tamil Nadu and Punjab are among the familiar examples. By now, both as a political principle and as a social ideal, democracy has become integral to social consciousness, its weaknesses in practice notwithstanding.

The circumstances in which the democratic state in India was born were far from congenial for its well being. The communalization of both the Hindus and the Muslims during the latter part of the national liberation struggle had engendered intense sectarian strife and had resulted in the division of the subcontinent into two states. The unprecedented human tragedy which this entailed, reinforced religious identities and aroused communal passion. This political and social context was not ideal for the nascent Indian state to shape its polity and society; and to impart to it a secular-democratic character. Yet, such a choice was deliberately and consciously made during the interregnum between the attainment of independence and the adoption of the Constitution in 1950. While the foundational character of democracy was spelt out in the Constitution, secularism was envisioned as integral to political practice, though the term itself was not written into it till 1976.

The choice of secularism as a guiding principle of the state and society was, to a large measure, influenced by the manner in which Indian society was historically constituted. From ancient times India has been home to a large number of religious, cultural, racial and ethnic groups who migrated and settled here from different parts of the world. Over the centuries Indian society evolved and took the character of a palimpsest, enriched by the cultural and intellectual resources of its constitutive elements. Only combining democracy with secularism could preserve this texture of the society, as that alone would ensure equal rights and privileges to all, regardless of religious and cultural distinctions. Secularism is, therefore, a necessary political principle in a multi-religious society like India for the survival and successful practice of democracy. The secular-democratic character of the Constitution is a reflection of this reality, even if the political experience of the West was a useful referent.

But then what is secularism in India? The three salient principles of secularism as articulated in the Constitution, in Rajeev Dhavan's opinion, are 'religious freedom, celebratory neutrality and reformatory justice'.[1] The principle of religious freedom is not limited to the right to religious thought and belief, but covers all aspects of the faith as well as guarantees against religious discrimination. The second principle is intended to create a participatory secular state, which would *neutrally* assist and celebrate all faiths, without discriminating against any one of them. At the same time, the third principle underlines the regulatory and reformative character of the state. It is arguable that these principles are mutually contradictory and therefore secularism as envisioned in the Constitution had no chance of success. But then, the Constitution tries to harmonize these three principles without sacrificing the essence of any one of them. 'The guarantee of religious freedom was broad, but included an invitation to evolve a consensus for reform, while placing the Indian State in a positively neutral position to benignly provide support for and celebrate all faiths.'[2] The celebration, however, is intended without involvement or identity with any one religion, thus maintaining 'a principled distance, a flexible but value based relations that accommodates intervention as well as abstention'.[3] A non-religious concept of citizenship and the secular character of fundamental rights and obligations further reinforce the neutrality.[4]

Influenced by the European antecedents, almost all conceptualizations of secularism tend to focus on the relationship between state and religion. Be it Gandhiji's *Sarva Dharma Samabhava* (equal respect for all religions) or Nehru's *Dharma Nirapekshata* (equal distance from all religions) the concern is mainly about how religion is treated by the state. So is it in most of the early studies and recent debates on secularism.[5] The secularity of the state is indeed, a necessary imperative—religious partisanship of the state is antithetical to secularism—but that alone is not sufficient to ensure a secular polity and society. Secularism, as Rajeev Dhavan rightly points out, 'is not just concerned with the triumphs and failures of the political state, but also of civil society'.[6] In a multi-religious society secularism can be a living reality only if civil society is secularized by divorcing religion from public life and institutional practices. Even if theoretically well grounded and constitutionally prescribed, a secular state is hardly possible without civil society internalizing the attributes of secularism; the relationship is dialectical. To a great extent the fragility of this connection accounts for the departures of the Indian State during the last fifty-two years from the constitutionally prescribed secular ideal. Rather than the inadequacy of secularism as a concept and its inappropriateness for Indian conditions, as critics aver, this weakness is primarily a reflection of the lack of secularization of civil society.[7]

Religious tolerance is often invoked as a possible means for the construction of a secular society. Some even identify tolerance with secularism. India is secular because Hinduism is tolerant: it is non-evangelical in character and universalist in perspective. Ashis Nandy locates 'the clues to the renewal of Indian political culture in the religious tolerance encoded in the everyday life associated with the different faiths of India'. Tolerance according to him is implicit in every religion: Ashoka based his tolerance on Buddhism, Akbar on Islam and Gandhi on Hinduism.[8] Whether tolerance can be an alternative to secularism is doubtful. For tolerance is sufferance or endurance and can even turn into tyranny, when exercised by a religious majority. The 'tolerance' of Hindutva, for instance, concedes to the non-Hindus a subordinate position, devoid of rights and privileges.[9] A truly secular society, therefore, is one which does more than tolerate differences. 'It is one in which the right to be different is recognised and even encouraged; and, perforce, one whose identity is not overtly or covertly over-identified with or appropriated by the people of any one faith, persuasion or community to the exclusion of others.'[10]

In 1963 an American scholar, Donald Eugene Smith, who was the first to make a detailed study of the practice and prospects of secularism in India, had stated that the secular state in India 'has more than an even chance of survival'.[11] At that time the communal forces had not made much headway in Indian politics or gained influence in social consciousness, despite their presence in different forms for more than fifty years. Since then the situation has changed dramatically, particularly during the last two decades. Hindu communalism has spread its tentacles in civil society and also succeeded in gaining access to state power, even if briefly. In the process some of the vital principles and practices of a secular state and society have been either undermined or endangered. The essays collected in this volume seek to join the public debate made imperative by the communal initiatives taken by the government led by the Bharatiya Janata Party (BJP) during its thirteen-month term and by the social and cultural interventions of the members of the Sangh parivar, particularly the Vishwa Hindu Parishad (VHP), the Rashtriya Swayam Sewak Sangh (RSS) and the Bajrang Dal.

I

A religious concept of nation has been at the heart of communalism in India. Both among the Muslims and the Hindus such a notion struck roots in the twentieth century. Although the history of the subcontinent during the last fifty years has proved it wrong—Pakistan founded on religious grounds could not hold its constituents together—this notion has persisted and gained influence in India. Among the Hindus the foundations of this idea, both theoretically and programmatically, were laid by V.D. Savarkar and M.S. Golwalkar, in their now well-known texts, *Hindutva* (1924) and *We, Or Our Nationhood Defined* (1942) respectively.[12] What they tried to do in these texts was to demarcate India as a Hindu nation, which their disciples in the Sangh parivar are currently engaged in realizing through ideological, cultural and political work.

The ideological legitimacy and rationale for this quest is

sought, among others, in a religious interpretation of the past, a Hinduized history, which Romila Thapar describes as 'historically baseless fulminations',[13] constructed by those who have no training in the discipline and as such are not sensitive to its methods.[14] The resulting misrepresentations and falsifications are not rooted in ignorance alone, but are as much a product of ideological preference. For the Hinduized history is a deliberate construction, which seeks to valourize the Hindu in the chequered history of the nation. It traces the lineage of the nation to the ancient Hindu past, claims the Hindu scriptures as the source of all knowledge, the Indian civilization as superior to every other civilization, and ancient India's achievements in science, mathematics and other branches of knowledge as unsurpassed by other civilizations. The political history of India is interpreted as a record of the heroic Hindu resistance against foreigners and the last one thousand years as a period of continuous conflict between the Hindus and the Muslims. The entire cultural past of India is appropriated as Hindu, as evident from the claim that medieval monuments like the Taj Mahal, Qutab Minar and Red Fort are Hindu buildings. These deliberately concocted myths are being widely disseminated as authentic history through pamphlets, journalistic writings and public discourses, and as a result have received a certain social acceptability. The historian's history is in danger of being marginalized in popular discourse.

The history of Ayodhya put out by the Sangh parivar during the Ramjanmabhoomi campaign is a prime example of an alternative religious history, however false and unsubstantiated it may be, gaining ground in the popular consciousness.[15] A large number of pamphlets on Ayodhya narrating its history in the mode of religious literature were distributed or sold at pilgrimage centres and religious sites. Some of them are provocatively titled and presented: *Shri Ram Janmabhoomi Ka Romanchakari Itihas* (The Thrilling History of

Ramjanmabhoomi), *Shri Ram Janmabhoomi Ka Rakt Ranjit Itihas*
(The Blood Stained History of Shri Ram Janmabhoomi), and
so on. All of them unambiguously claimed, though without
citing any evidence, the site of the Babri Masjid as the
birthplace of Shri Ram. The question of evidence was
circumvented by asserting that the birthplace of Ram is a
matter of faith of the Hindus.[16] When the central fact is thus
placed beyond dispute, other details effortlessly follow to
reinforce the existence of the temple as an 'indisputable fact
of history'.[17] They include the demolition of the temple by
Babar's general, Mir Baqi, in 1528, and the heroic and spirited
resistance of the Hindus in defence of their faith. It is
estimated that 1,74,000 Hindus sacrificed their lives fighting
against the Mughal army to save the temple![18] Thereafter
seventy-seven battles were fought against the Muslims in which
three lakh fifty thousand Hindus laid down their lives to
liberate the temple. These 'histories' are no more confined to
popular pamphlets; they have made their entry into prescribed
textbooks in schools in BJP ruled states and those run by the
RSS.[19]

A more systematic attempt to create a Hinduized historical
common sense appears to be now on the anvil. The RSS, it is
reported, has initiated a national project to write histories of
all districts in the country, highlighting the contribution and
achievements of the Hindus and to advance their exclusive
claim to the nation. These are planned and written as local
histories, not necessarily by historians but those who belong to
the locality, instructed to reduce Hindu history into convincing
micro-narratives. When they are completed and circulated,
their easy access and familiar content is likely to influence the
popular historical consciousness more than the mega-histories
of the nation.

The religious interpretation of the past has a contemporary
political intent. It seeks to identify the non-Hindus as foreigners
and to stigmatize them as enemies by invoking a weird logic

that their ancestors were guilty of aggression, iconoclasm and proselytization. This concept of a foreigner, initially laid down by V.D. Savarkar and M.S. Golwalkar, in itself militates against the historical evolution of Indian society. For, Indian society is composed of those who came and settled here, including the Aryans, and identified their interests with that of the country of their adoption. It was precisely on this ground that a Maharashtrian intellectual in the mid-nineteenth century, Bhaskar Pandurang Tarkadkar, distinguished the Muslim rulers from the British. The only foreign rule in India, according to him, was the British colonial rule, as the British, though they ruled for about two hundred years, remained distanced from Indian society, and, more importantly, unlike the earlier rulers like the Mughals and the Turks, drained wealth out of India.[20] At any rate, as Romila Thapar argues in her essay, the present day national territorial boundaries are not co-terminus with those of the pre-colonial period: 'The territorial boundaries of today did not exist in those days and dynasties which had their origins in clans and families based on what we now call the Indo-Iranian borderlands and Afghanistan or the Arabian peninsula, can hardly be called foreign once they settled in the subcontinent and made it their home'.[21]

The communal history shares considerable ground with the colonial view of Indian society as a conglomeration of monolithic religious communities. In both, the inter-relationship of religious communities—their differences, antagonism and conflicts—provides the complete, even though monocausal, explanation for historical events. The works of James Mill and a host of Orientalist scholars had popularized 'the concept of a uniform, monolithic Hindu community dominating early history as did their Muslim equivalent in the subsequent period with the relation between the two becoming conflictual'.[22] Such a view of communities and their mutual antagonism is also central to communal history, as initially worked out by V.D. Savarkar in *Six Glorious Epochs of Indian*

History. In this influential study on Indian history which forms the blueprint for much of the Sangh parivar's Hinduized history, Savarkar conceived the entire history of India as a saga of Hindu resistance against the foreigners, beginning with the time of the Shakas till the British rule.[23] Explaining historical change only in terms of the relationship between religious communities, and that too in a monocausal manner, Romila Thapar argues, is methodologically invalid, historically inaccurate and misleading as historical explanation. History as a discipline—its quality, character and method—is, therefore, at stake, if communal historiography gains ascendancy in teaching and research institutions. Hence countering communal history as being disseminated by the Sangh parivar, is more than a political challenge; it is, in fact, a defence of the discipline itself.

II

That India is the land of the Hindus is the underlying assumption of the Hindu religious interpretation of history. By implication the members of all other religious denominations of the population, who are either descendants of migrants or converts from Hinduism, are not part of the nation, if the criteria of *pitrubhumi* and *punyabhumi* as enunciated by Savarkar in his influential text, *Hindutva*, is applied.[24] This demarcation, which is at the heart of cultural nationalism, is invoked by the Sangh parivar to consolidate the Hindu community by stigmatizing the minorities as the aggressive, alien 'other' at whose hands the Hindus have suffered in the past.[25] The RSS leader, M.S. Golwalkar, had identified both Muslims and Christians, along with the Communists, as main enemies of Hindutva. For a long time, however, the ideological and political campaign of the Parivar has been primarily against the Muslims, of which the demolition of the Babri Masjid on 6 December 1992 was one of the many unfortunate consequences. This campaign, though it has spurred many a riot in independent India and at the same time yielded handsome political dividends to the Parivar, now appears to have exhausted its mobilizing potential, as the 'historical wrongs' supposedly committed by the Muslims can no longer sustain the earlier appeal. The Parivar has, therefore, turned to the other enemy—the Christians—during the post-Babri Masjid period in order to continue to demarcate the nation as Hindu.

The last one year has witnessed well over a hundred incidents of attack on person and property of Christians all over the country. The period of this unprecedented violence coincides with the rule of the BJP-led government at the centre. These attacks are not incidental to communal conflicts to which Christians are a party, but are unprovoked physical attacks, arson and intimidation by the stormtroopers of the Parivar. Missionaries have been stripped naked and paraded through the streets, even burnt alive, nuns have been gang-raped, churches have been razed to the ground and the Bible and other religious literature has been set on fire. While the nation was outraged by this unprecedented violence against a peaceful community, the leaders of the Parivar attributed conversion as the reason for these attacks. While some of them, including the prime minister, Atal Behari Vajpayee, suggested a public debate, the others demanded a ban on conversions. The freedom of conscience and '*the right freely to profess, practice and propagate religion*' are fundamental rights of all Indians guaranteed by Article 25(1) of the Constitution. This right is not confined only to the citizens of India, but covers all persons residing in India.[26] As Sumit Sarkar points out, 'propagation makes no sense at all without the possibility of convincing others of the validity of one's religious beliefs and rituals'.[27] The freedom of belief and the right to propagate it, be it of religious faith or of atheism or of any political philosophy, cannot be dissociated from the rights of the citizen in a democracy. While conversion by force or fraud is 'contrary to the basic principle of equal freedom', the banning of conversion is both against the provisions of the Constitution and the principles of democracy.

Conversions in the past, either to Christianity or to Islam, though they aroused fears and apprehensions in some quarters, had not led to any serious social conflict. For, the change in religious affiliation has not been a sudden and total transformation but has been so gradual to be nearly imperceptible, mostly 'involving an entire group, family or kinship network, or a local community'.[28] Also, there is hardly any evidence of large-scale forcible conversions and it appears that 'in large parts of the subcontinent, certainly in the medieval times and to a considerable extent even today, the great religious traditions have been expanding at the cost, not so much of each other as in relation to a multitude of local cults and practices'.[29] Most of the conversions to Christianity took place in areas largely outside the provenance of mainstream Hinduism like the north-eastern and central Indian tribal belts. Rejecting the existing theories of conversion to Islam, Richard M. Eaton in his study on Bengal suggests that neither patronage nor social liberation account for the spread of Islam in India. For most of these conversions took place in areas far removed from the centre of power and where caste oppression was relatively weak.[30] Social liberation, however, is a powerful motive as is evident from the conversions in Kerala, where low caste aggrestic slaves converted to Islam after the abolition of slavery.[31]

From the latter part of the nineteenth century onwards, however, conversions became a controversial issue among the Hindus, who were seized by an apprehension about their declining numbers. The reason for this change Sumit Sarkar traces to 'community borders becoming simultaneously harder and more vulnerable', due to the influences of colonial modernity.[32] The *shuddhi* (reconversion) programme of the Arya Samaj, which is now being pursued as an aggressive agenda by the Parivar, was a reflection of the fear of the upper caste Hindus about the future of their community. Unlike the Arya Samaj, the Parivar pursues reconversion—*paravartan* (homecoming) in their vocabulary and often effected by use of force and material allurements—as a part of their political agenda of reappropriating those Hindus lost through the aggression of other religions.

Neither the demographic strength of the Christians—the census figures show that their population has been stagnant at around 2.5 per cent for quite some time and that during the last decade it has actually declined—nor the current rate of conversion through evangelization constitute a threat to the Hindu community. The charge of conversion, therefore, is an afterthought, a convenient pretext, to justify what appears to be a political move rather than a step in defence of religion. Moreover, most of those who became targets of violent attacks were not engaged in evangelical work, but were associated with charitable and humanitarian institutions, active among the tribals and the rural poor. For instance, Graham Staines, who was burnt alive along with his two young children in Orissa, was a medical doctor engaged in the treatment of lepers and the nuns of Madhya Pradesh who were gang-raped were running a school. They, and several others, who suffered because of the current Hindu militancy, were not known for any evangelical work. The reasons for attacks were evidently something other than religious outrage.

The BJP's electoral support has been mainly from its middle class–upper caste base which, the recent elections have shown, is not adequate to gain a majority in the Parliament. Given that the minorities and the lower castes are almost out of reach, the tribal communities are a possible social group to fill the gap. With this aim the Parivar has initiated social and religious work in tribal areas through a network of organizations known as Vanvasi Kalyan Samitis. A separate organization to establish and run schools in the tribal areas has also been set up. The secretary of the Vishwa Hindu Parishad (VHP) recently stated that about five thousand schools would be established in the tribal areas within the next one year. These welfare activities are not an end in themselves but only a means to integrate the tribals into mainstream Hinduism and thus to recruit them to the Parivar fold. The already existing Christian organizations are, however, a major hindrance in this effort, as they enjoy considerable appreciation of and support for their work from the local population. The advance of the Parivar in the tribal area is, therefore, possible only if the Christians are discredited and displaced.

Yet another reason for the antagonism is the secular position taken by several Christian organizations after the demolition of the Babri Masjid. Sensing the danger to the minorities posed by the Hindu communal upsurge, they took several initiatives to promote secularism and to sensitize people about secular values, which have understandably invited the ire of the Parivar. For instance, the Young Men's Christian Association in their annual convention in 1993 organized a special session on secularism and followed it up with several projects to advance secular consciousness in society. More recently, 'Christian groups have been prominent in many anti-war and anti-nuclear protests', and have also reached out to secular, liberal and Left formations for joint initiatives.[33]

If Hindu communalism is potentially fascist in character, the attack on the Christians holds a mirror to the possibilities of the future. The Christians have been foregrounded as another enemy, a new symbol, to demarcate the nation as Hindu. As such the violence against them is not a law and order issue created by some anti-social elements, as some seem to believe, but a profoundly political question with serious implications for the well being of the democratic republic.

III

A large number of social and cultural organizations, either sponsored by the Parivar or controlled by it, have contributed to the growth of communal consciousness. This is an outcome of a long-term dual strategy: the creation of institutional networks on the one hand, and infiltration of the existing organizations on the other. A good example of this dual strategy is the field of education, which is central to the cultural activities of the RSS. The students are recruited at an early age from the already established schools through *shakhas* held in their premises.[34] At the same time, the RSS organized schools of its own. Initiated as early as 1942, a chain of schools under the denomination of Saraswati Shishu Mandir and Gyan Bharati was established. In 1978 an all-India organization, Vidhya Bharati Shiksha Sansthan, was set up to oversee the functioning of these institutions and to further their educational programme. In 1992 the Sansthan claimed under its management 6000 schools with 1,200,000 students and 40,000 teachers. It is estimated that it has about 20,000 schools under its control now, imparting education to about fifty lakh students. The curriculum followed in these schools has a Hindu colour in many respects and the textbooks prescribed in them contain explicit communal propaganda.[35]

Following the Constitutional principles, the Indian State has generally pursued a secular educational policy. The BJP's rise to power has led to a qualitative change. Its governments, both at the Centre and in the States, have tried to impart a Hindu bias to education, as evident from the proposed new national education policy. Formulated by the RSS organization, Vidhya Bharati, it has the unmistakable imprint of a clear Hindu programme. Vidhya Bharati sought to 'Indianize, nationalize and spiritualize' education, make Sanskrit a compulsory language and to include the study of Vedas and

Upanishads in the curriculum.[36] The BJP's state governments have also taken steps to revise textbooks to privilege the Hindu, in the history, culture and traditions of India. A Hindu system of education is thus foregrounded—the Parivar promises to implement it whenever it gains the necessary political clout—and the controversy around it is likely to benefit the communal cause.

Education is a long-term investment, with slow but abiding returns. The dramatic groundswell of support Hindu communalism received during the last two decades is a result of a shift in the discourse of agencies, which play a decisive role in the formation of public opinion. Such a shift is most discernible in the response of the media to the communal cause. Despite their liberal and secular past, though not unblemished, most of these agencies either took a neutral stance or succumbed to the pressure or even identified with it. Even editors with active radical pasts and those with a strong background contributed to this transition. This change, however, is not confined to the prominence given to the communal content in the news coverage alone. Several editors and journalists have indeed tended to favour Hindu communal formations in recent years. Many of them have also provided considerable space to the reportage of communal activities and the views of communal ideologues. The journalistic virtues of fairness and impartiality are often invoked in justification. That the media will inevitably reflect the existing social and political reality is also advanced as an explanation. Yet, it is true that in recent years the corporate preference and bias of editors has been in favour of Hindu communal formations. But the real reason for this shift in the media is more fundamental. It is primarily due to the 'prevailing media epistemology' which largely determines the nature of information and the modes of its communication.[37]

The vocabulary of the Indian press, both national and regional, is replete with communal clichés and stereotypes. It generally follows a communitarian view of society, that is 'inimical to the concept of citizenship and Indianness'. Such a view was inherited from the colonial times, although its implications are qualitatively different today. Religious identity was a convenient marker employed in the newspapers of the nineteenth century. As a result individuals and groups were identified in editorials and letters to the editor by their religious affiliation, even if their contents were secular. Bhaskar Pandurang Tarkarkar who made a trenchant and secular critique of colonial rule signed his letters to the *Bombay Gazette* as 'A Hindu'.[38] Such a tendency continued to prevail even during the national movement. As Siddharth Varadarajan points out, 'print-capitalism in India was not to be the unifier of the nation, the vehicle through which the national claims would be asserted'. On the contrary, most newspapers 'suffered from the tendency of mediating nationhood by religious community'. Even when 'colonialism was challenged or excoriated, it was often from a "Hindu" or a "Muslim" point of view'.[39]

The contemporary Indian press has internalized the communal logic to such an extent that most of its news reporting and analysis suffers from an undercurrent of sectarian bias. The examples are too copious to cite. The repeated references to 'one thousand years of foreign rule', the identification of Indian civilization and culture with Hindu religion, the aggressiveness of the Muslims, the tolerance of the Hindus and so on have become accepted truths in journalism. What illustrates most acutely the sectarian partisanship of the media, however, is the reporting of the communal riots, which according to a commonly accepted code is expected to refrain from identifying the communities and the victims. This admirable principle, meant to obviate the possible retaliation and escalation of violence, is not only violated in a surreptitious manner, but also invoked to favour the majority community. In some reports, even when the fiction of not naming the community is maintained, the description of the incident, the reference to the dress of the victims, the opinion of the local residents etc. carry enough clues to make the identification possible. In others, the names of the victims are selectively reported, giving a false impression about who the aggressor is. Worse still is the adherence to anonymity when it could set off suspicion against the members of a particular community. Apart from all these, instances of newspapers inciting violence against the members of minority communities, as happened recently in Gujarat, are also not rare.[40] It appears that a Hindu press has already emerged in India, not from the portals of the RSS, but from within the liberal, even radical, milieu. As a result, the media seems to have surrendered its critical role in interrogating the implications of Hindutva's ascendancy.

The cause of secular journalism, however, is not irretrievably lost, for there are still several adherents who have refused to succumb, both within the mainstream as well as outside it. They function under severe threat and intimidation, and are even subjected to physical assault. They have managed to survive, despite inadequate public support and indifferent government protection primarily because of their conviction.

IV

The precepts and practices of Hindu communalism unambiguously foreground its political agenda—the creation of a Hindu Rashtra in which the rights of the members of other religious denominations, as M.S. Golwalkar prescribed a long time back and the thirteen months' BJP rule clearly indicated, will be considerably restricted. The implications of such a political perspective, which is fundamentally undemocratic in character, would not be limited to the minorities alone; it would impinge upon the rights of all others, regardless of their religious affiliations. Neither would it restrict only the political rights; the social and cultural rights would be equally in peril. There are enough indications of such a prospect in the social and cultural activism of Hindutva.[41]

Hindu communalism has worked through a large number of social and cultural organizations carefully nurtured during the last many years. The number and strength of these organizations with branches all over the country are difficult to ascertain, but they cover almost every field of intellectual and cultural activity—be it education, history, archaeology, music or media, the Parivar has tried to promote its own institutional network. About twenty thousand schools under different denominations, scores of publishing outfits in almost every language, committees to write the history of each district, literary associations and drama clubs, environmental groups, women's organizations, temple renovation committees and so on are a part of this network; in fact, there is hardly any area in which the Parivar has not managed to make its presence felt. Unlike the political formations, which function sporadically and intermittently, and some only at the time of elections, the presence of these organizations in civil society is continuous and uninterrupted. Their social and cultural engagements, however, are not an end in themselves, but only a means for the dissemination of the ideology of Hindutva and for furthering its political influence. If today communalism is deeply embedded in social consciousness it is to a large measure due to the cultural intervention of these organizations.

These organizations also form the channel through which the vision of a future Indian society that Hindutva seeks to usher in is transmitted and communicated. Although the social, cultural and intellectual mores they foster are not yet well co-ordinated or fully crystallized, leading to the wishful speculation in the secular camp about the tensions and contradictions within the Parivar, all of them share the essentials of the fundamental ideas of Hindutva without any ambiguity or scepticism. They all promote the hierarchy and power structure integral to Hindu tradition, uncritically reinforce and privilege the past cultural practices and valourize indegenism, even if in an opportunistic manner, over the universal. The values that they thus advance are not a product of modernity or critical-rational thinking, but emanate from obscurantism and conformity—an Indian version of Talibanism.

All organizations sponsored by the Parivar, through their social and cultural engagements, elaborate, disseminate and reinforce these values in civil society and pressurize the state to incorporate them in legislative measures. The gender perspectives and activities of the Parivar's women's wing, Rashtrasevika Samiti, are particularly important in this respect, as exemplifying the predicament of negotiating a conservative, patriarchal agenda when gender equality has already emerged as a powerful idea in society. The Samiti, founded in 1936 and meant to impart physical and ideological training to women, had for long a rather muted existence, without any major role to play in the scheme of activities of the RSS. It neither participated in mass struggles nor did much organizational work. The leaders of the RSS—an exclusive male organization till today—who entertained notions of domesticity and gender subordination for women, restricted the Samiti's work to the familial chores: to manage the homes and to rear children on values prescribed by the Sangh. In the wake of the Ramjanmabhoomi movement, however, women were brought to the forefront by forming new organizations like the Mahila Morcha, Matri Mandal and Durga Vahini and recruiting thousands of karsevikas to participate in the demolition of the Babri Masjid. Once the need for such a mass mobilization was over, 'the homebound women have been retrieved' and entrusted with 'the conservation of old and inner values'.[42]

During the past decade when the Parivar registered spectacular gains, both in organizational strength and political power, the membership of the Samiti has remained stagnant at around two lakhs in its 5000 branches. In Delhi where the BJP has been in power, the strength of the Samiti actually declined—from 2000 members in 1991 to about 1000 in 1999. In its activities the Samiti went back to its earlier limited and conservative role of sensitizing women about their feminine and domestic duties. The Samiti's programmes strongly underlined patriarchal values, opposed equal gender rights and were generally silent on gender problems. What they tried to inculcate were 'deference and obedience, conservative values like arranged marriages, good home keeping, modesty in dress and behaviour and diligent service to men and elders'.[43] At the same time the virtues of Hindu Rashtra and the misdeeds of the Muslims and the Christians were emphasized. Thus the Samiti's activities are geared to nurse its women as the repository and custodians of the essential Sangh values as well as its authentic ideology, which the other fronts had 'somewhat diluted and imperilled in the current war games over electoral power'. They are preserved as the soul of the Hindu Rashtra, trained as the defender of Hindu tradition and partners in an internal colonization over the Muslims and the Christians.[44] An obvious result of the ideological work of the Samiti is the internalization of patriarchal values by its members, which is a part of the tradition as enunciated by Manu that the Parivar wants to preserve.[45]

V

Although the roots of Hindu communalism go back to the nineteenth century and its political and social formations to the early part of the twentieth, till recently it had not made much of an impact on Indian social or political consciousness. During the last few years, however, there is a quantum leap in its influence, thus foregrounding it as a major contender for state power. This advance is not solely due to reasons internal to the history of the Parivar, its ideology, programme or organizational strength. To a large extent, it is located in the political, cultural and economic conjunctures in independent India.

Influenced both by the legacy of the national movement and the principles enshrined in the Constitution, politics in India was set on a secular-democratic course. The actual practice, however, was quite removed from the ideal; the departures were far too many, undermining the legitimacy even of the principles of democracy and secularism in the popular mind. The ruling classes and their political formations have shown no hesitation to invoke the divisive force of communalism for electoral gains and to indulge in authoritarianism to safeguard political power. Both these tendencies have substantially contributed to the growth of communalism.

During the course of this decade the demarcation between the secular and the communal has blurred considerably in the convictions and practices of political leaders and parties. A progressive decline in idealism and morality in politics during the post-independence era and the emergence of parties based on individuals rather than on ideologies and programmes have been at the root of this. The lure of power appears to be so irresistible that it has marginalized all necessary virtues of politics, be it probity or principles. The parties with anti-communal agendas and individual leaders with declared secular convictions have suddenly gone over to the communal camp. The Samata party, the Lokshakti and Telugu Desam party had earlier betrayed this tendency and the Dravida Munnetra Kazhagam has recently taken the same course. Another tendency is to appropriate the communal agenda, as the Congress party did during the Ramjanmabhoomi campaign. The failure of the secular parties to adhere to and uphold the principles of secularism and order their politics accordingly have helped to legitimize communal politics and thus further its advance. In the bargain secularism has lost much of its credibility.

A decisive moment in the advance of Hindu communalism was the Emergency of 1975, which apart from undermining the democratic texture of Indian polity, provided a major boost to the communal forces, which till then occupied only an insignificant fringe in Indian polity. They managed to infiltrate the movements opposed to the Emergency, but more importantly, became a part of the anti-authoritarian bloc during the post-Emergency period, thus gaining access, though briefly, to state power. The anti-authoritarianism, paradoxically, imparted legitimacy to a political formation which is inherently authoritarian and fascist. The opening thus gained was the beginning of the road that led to the success of the BJP in 1998. Not that there were no hurdles in between, but they were cleverly and successfully negotiated. A major stumbling block was in 1996, when in the wake of the assault on democracy at Ayodhya the secular formations thwarted the communal bid to power. Such an opposition to communalism then emerged not out of the inherent commitment of some of the centrist parties to secularism, as is now evident, but was forced by circumstances, particularly by the secular assertion in civil society after the demolition of the Babri Masjid. Between 1996 and 1998, however, a qualitative change has taken place. Many former socialists and liberals not only shed their opposition to communalism, but also became its collaborators. This political turnabout, though primarily influenced by opportunism, has yielded rich dividends to the BJP, both in terms of political power and social support.

The final thrust and momentum for the recent upsurge of communalism came from the cultural and economic crisis generated by globalization. Contrary to the expectations of the ruling classes, the integration with the global market and the entry of the transnational capital did not stimulate the Indian economy towards a better performance. Instead, globalization, which has all the accoutrements of colonization, only depressed an economy struggling to find a solution for poverty and unemployment. Take the incidence of poverty, for instance. The mid-1970s to the late 1980s was characterized by a sustained decline in poverty ratios in both rural and urban India. In the nineties with the onset of structural reforms and globalization this process has been halted and possibly even reversed.[46] The two important variables, which impinge upon poverty incidence—opportunities for productive employment and the price of food articles—have changed in a way to enhance poverty. At the same time, the economic opportunities opened up by liberalization and globalization have considerably increased the incomes of the affluent. The impact of globalization and an unfettered market, Jayati Ghosh argues, is to create 'deep and pervasive inequalities—across regions of the world, within countries, between classes and income groups'.[47] In India the disparities between the rich and the poor have never been so pronounced and visible—in consumer patterns and lifestyle. While the affluent few have unlimited choice of consumer articles and durables, none exist for the poor majority. The promise of a future El Dorado, which the ideologues of free enterprise and competition hold out, hardly help ameliorate the sufferings of the present.

A result, though unintended, of the near universal reach of the capitalist media, achieved by cultural globalization, is to bring home these inequalities and thus to foreground differences and possibilities. Paradoxically, the attempt to create a universal cultural unification and homogenization which globalization seeks to achieve in the field of culture, thus generates an acute awareness of what is denied both to the deprived and marginalized and to the aspiring and as yet unsatiated middle class. Both the idealization and celebration of consumer culture in the media and the pattern of ostentatious life of the affluent extenuate the sense of deprivation and frustration. There are indeed different ways in which these sentiments could find social and political expression, both radical and conservative. The greater social and political acceptability of Hindutva in recent times, as Jayati Ghosh suggests, 'has had a lot to do with the economic repercussions of a pattern of growth which leaves the vast majority of the population either untouched or even worse off, while generating spiralling incomes and an increasingly flamboyant lifestyle of a minority'.[48] The globalization has deepened this disparity, already inherent in the Indian path of development and the resulting discontent and frustration are directed against more vulnerable 'enemies' at home.

The politics of Hindutva has immensely gained from these adverse consequences of globalization, without, however, entering into any confrontation with it. Despite the Swedish rhetoric and an anti-Western civilizational stance, the Parivar does not oppose the neo-colonial tendencies inherent in the working of transnational capital in India. On the contrary, there are enough signs of its compromise and collaboration.[49] The nationalism that the Parivar espouses has no anti-imperialist content and is hence only 'cultural', posited in antagonistic relationship with the minorities within the country. The territorial, political and economic nationalism that the anti-colonial movement represented and advocated, therefore, has no use for the Parivar.

V

The politics of Hindutva, as the essays in this volume bring out, is primarily engaged in defining the nation as Hindu through a process of cultural homogenization, social consolidation and political mobilization of the majority community and at the same time, by stigmatizing the minorities as aliens and enemies. The character of this politics incorporates the familiar fascist traits of irrationality and coercion, as evidenced, among others, by the movement culminating in the demolition of the Babri Masjid. The homology with the ways of European fascism as described by Theodore Adorno is extremely striking:

> The objective aims of fascism are largely irrational in so far as they contradict the material interests of a great number of those whom they try to embrace . . . Since it would be impossible for fascism to win the masses through rational arguments, its propaganda must necessarily be deflected from discursive thinking; it must be oriented psychologically, and has to mobilize irrational, unconscious, regressive processes.[50]

The communal mobilization of the past two decades has mainly anchored its strategies on the irrational and the regressive, marginalizing the issues of material import and privileging the religious and the sentimental by invoking symbols associated with quotidian practices.[51] Coercion, both emotional and physical, rather than consensus has been the key to this politics, which among many other debilities, has led to an unprecedented brutalization and insensitivity in society. No better soil is needed for fascism to thrive.

June 1999   **K.N. Panikkar**

Notes

1. Rajeev Dhavan, 'The Road to Xanadu: India's Quest for Secularism' in this volume, p. 48.
2. Ibid, p. 49.
3. Rajeev Bhargava (ed.) *Secularism and its Critics*, Delhi, 1998, p. 7.
4. P.B. Gajendragadkar, *Secularism and the Constitution of India*, Mumbai, p. 53-55.
5. Rajeev Bhargava (ed.), op. cit.

6. Rajeev Dhavan, p. 36.
7. Both communalists and secular and anti-secular critics share certain common ground in this criticism of secularism, though their premises are quite different. For the opinion of these critics see Rajeev Bhargava, op. cit.
8. Ashis Nandy, 'The Politics of Secularism and the Recovery of Religious Tolerance' in Veena Das (ed.), *Mirrors of Violence: Communities, Riots and Survivors in South Asia*, Delhi, 1990, p. 85.
9. This idea is articulated by several leaders of the Sangh parivar. The most representative, however, is a statement by M.S. Golwalkar: 'Non-Hindu peoples in Hindustan must either adopt the Hindu culture and language, must learn to respect and hold in reverence Hindu religion, must entertain no idea but those of the glorification of the Hindu race and culture . . . they must cease to be foreigners or may stay in the country wholly subordinated to the Hindu nation, claiming nothing, deserving no privileges, far less any preferential treatment, not even citizen rights.' M.S. Golwalkar, *We, or Our Nationhood Defined*, Nagpur, 1947, p. 55-56.
10. Rajeev Dhavan, op. cit., p. 37-38.
11. Donald Eugene Smith, *India as a Secular State*, Princeton, 1963, p. 501.
12. For an analysis of their ideas see J.A. Curran, *Militant Hinduism in Indian Politics: A Study of the RSS*, New York, 1951; Christophe Jaffrelot, *Hindu Nationalist Movement in India*, New Delhi, 1993 and K.N. Panikkar, *Communal Threat, Secular Challenge*, Chennai, 1997.
13. Romila Thapar, 'The Tyranny of Labels' in this volume, p. 29.
14. The recent public discussion on eating beef by the Aryans is a good example. The scholarship on the subject based on sources both literary and archeological, which are aplenty, have conclusively shown that beef was part of the food of the Aryans, particularly on ritual occasions and when entertaining important guests. The Hindu ideologues scorn this scholarship without taking into account the massive evidence on which it is based. This may be good Hindutva propaganda, but points to a poor knowledge of history and its methods.
15. See K.N. Panikkar, 'An Overview' in S. Gopal (ed.), *Anatomy of a Confrontation*, New Delhi, 1991.

16. K.S. Lal, 'Ram Janamabhoomi—Some Issues', *Organiser*, October 1989.

17. Justice Deoki Nandan, *Shri Ramjanmabhoomi: A Historical and Legal Perspective*, Lucknow, n.d., p. 2.

18. For an analysis of some of these pamphlets see Gyanendra Pande, 'The Culture of History' in Nicholas B. Dirks (ed.), *In Near Ruins: Cultural Theory at the End of the Century*, Minneapolis, 1998, p. 19-37.

19. The textbooks prescribed in the BJP ruled states have tried to cast Indian history in a Hindu mould, highlighting the Hinduness of the nation. According to them the Aryans are indigenous to India and the authors of Indian culture and civilization. The schools run by the RSS undertake more explicit Hindutva propaganda. In the textbooks used in these schools, the map of India includes not only Pakistan and Bangladesh, but also Bhutan, Nepal, Tibet and Myanmar. The familiar geographical names are sought to be Hinduized: the Indian Ocean is called Hindu Mahasagar, the Arabian Sea Sindhu Sagar and the Bay of Bengal Ganga Sagar. Historical events are unrecognizably altered to underline Muslim aggression and Hindu valour. Muhammad Ghori, for instance, is said to have converted the Vishwanath temple at Benares and Bhagwan Krishna's birthplace at Mathura into mosques. He took Prithviraj to Ghazni, but Prithviraj was so brave that he killed Ghori with one arrow. For a review of these textbooks, see 'The Report of the NCERT Review Committee', Mimeographed. The other side of the coin is Pakistan naming its missiles, intended probably for use against India, as Ghauri.

20. Bhaskar Pandurang Tarkarkar wrote a series of letters in *Bombay Gazette* in July-August 1841 criticizing the British rule in India. See *Bombay Gazette*, 30 July and 10 August 1841. For an analysis of his ideas see J.V. Naik, 'An Early Appraisal of the British Colonial Policy,' *Journal of the University of Bombay*, Vols. XLIV and XLV. Nos. 80 & 81, 1975-76 and K.N. Panikkar, *Culture, Ideology and Hegemony*, New Delhi, 1995, p. 75-76.

21. Romila Thapar, p. 6-7.

22. Ibid, p. 4.

23. V.D. Savarkar, *Six Glorious Epochs of Indian History*, Pune, 1985, p. 2.

24. V.D. Savarkar, *Hindutva*, Nagpur, 1939 edition, p. 13.

25. In RSS *shakhas* this idea is conveyed through catechism. The questions are: why are Hindus alone the nation in India? Or why can't the Muslims be considered part of the nation? The answer to be memorized is: 'Unlike us—the Aryan race—the Muslims are foreigners and, therefore, not the original children of the soil: their culture, traditions and customs were alien to ours; their religious leaders, including their founder-prophet belonged to another land: their holy places lay outside our country. In negative terms, they did not accept our culture, our great men, our holy places etc. etc.' Ram Lall Dhooria, *I Was a Swayamsewak*, Delhi, n.d. p. 22.

26. P.B. Gajendragadkar, op. cit. p. 69.

27. Sumit Sarkar, 'Hindutva and the Question of Conversion' in this volume, p. 78.

28. Ibid, p. 83.

29. Ibid, p. 83.

30. Richard M. Eaton, *The Rise of Islam and the Bengal Frontier*, p. 113-36.

31. The increase of the population of the Mappilahs in the second half of the nineteenth century was mainly because of the conversions of the low castes after the abolition of slavery. K.N. Panikkar, *Against the Lord and State*, Delhi, 1989, p. 51-52.

32. Sumit Sarkar, p. 83-87.

33. Ibid, p. 100.

34. For an account of how students are drawn to the *shakhas* by the prospects of physical training, see Ram Lall Dhooria, op. cit., p. 9-17.

35. In one of the textbooks prescribed for class five, *Sanskar Saurab*, no. 3, there is a lesson on the *Kar Seva* of 1990. It narrates the martrydom of two youths from Rajasthan, the Kothari brothers, in the cause of the Mandir at Ayodha. They are projected as great heroes worthy of emulation.

36. The human resources development minister, Murali Manohar Joshi, made the new policy a part of the agenda of a meeting of the state education ministers. Although it was withdrawn in the teeth of opposition from some quarters, the minister did succeed in placing a Hindu agenda before the nation and in initiating a discussion around it.

37. Siddharth Varadarajan, 'The Ink Link: Media, Communalism and the Evasion of Politics' in this volume, p. 166.

38. *Bombay Gazette,* 30 July, 1841.
39. Siddharth Varadarajan, p. 174-77.
40. Ibid, p. 193-99.
41. During the last ten years there have been innumerable occasions when the members of the Parivar have violated the cultural rights of artists and organizations. The exhibition of Ayodhya curated by SAHMAT was vandalized, the paintings of M.F. Husain were destroyed and several artists, writers and journalists were physically attacked. The Shiv Sena threatened to disrupt the cricket match with Pakistan and stopped the screening of films it did not like, including the internationally acclaimed film, *Fire.*
42. Tanika Sarkar, 'The Predicament of the Hindu Right' in this volume, p. 142.
43. Ibid, p. 149.
44. Ibid, p. 157.
45. A Sant Samiti set up by the VHP to draft a Hindu Constitution for India suggested that the position of women should conform to the prescription in Manusmriti. Muktananda Saraswati who headed the Samiti defended sati and the prohibition against widow marriage. For the details of his ideas see his interview in *Mainstream,* 16, 23 and 30 October 1993.
46. Jayati Ghosh, 'Perceptions of Difference: The Economic Underpinnings' in this volume, p. 118.
47. Ibid, p. 112.
48. Ibid, p. 117.
49. Thomas Blom Hansen, 'The Ethics of Hindutva and the Spirit of Capitalism' in Thomas Blom Hansen and Christophe Jaffrelot (ed.), *The BJP and the Compulsions of Politics in India,* Delhi, 1998, p. 291-314.
50. Theodore Adorno, *The Culture Industry,* London, 1991, p. 129.
51. Victoria L. Farmer, 'Mass Media: Images, Mobilization, and Communalism' in David Ludden (ed.), *Contesting the Nation; Religion, Community, and the Politics of Democracy in India,* Philadelphia, 1996, p. 98-118 and K.N. Panikkar, 'Religious symbols and Political Mobilization', *Social Scientist,* Vol. 21. Nos. 7-8, July to August 1993.

The Tyranny of Labels[1]

Romila Thapar

The history of the twentieth century in the subcontinent will be remembered, among other things, for the rise of communal ideologies into a position of prominence in national politics. If in the middle of the century Muslim communalism succeeded in establishing an Islamic state in the form of Pakistan, the coming to power of a Bharatiya Janata Party (BJP) government in India at the end of the century reflects the resurgence of Hindu communalism—for at the heart of the BJP lie the organizations which are working towards the establishing of a Hindu state in India. Why there should have been a growth and a resurgence of communal ideologies has to do both with contemporary politics and with political ideologies which are based on a belief in a particular view of the Indian past. The interpretation of history is therefore central to these ideologies. Those that do not accept the particular historical interpretations foundational to a communal ideology are dismissed as distorters of Indian history. What is not recognized is that the Hindutva view of history, or its counterpart of the two-nation theory, are in effect the distortions, for they are still rooted in the colonial explanations of Indian history of the nineteenth century, and refuse to accept that historical analyses and interpretations have moved in new directions, and none of these would support either the Hindutva view or the two-nation theory.

Much of what I have to say in this essay will be concerned with recent perspectives of Indian history. My focus is on the way in which we have constructed and used the concept of communities in the history of India and more particularly in the history of the last one thousand years. This has generally taken the form of imposing on historical events the theory that Indian society consisted of two hostile, monolithic communities—the Hindu and the Muslim. Such a view does not even attempt to consider the possibility of different historical approaches to the study of communities in history. The continuing imprint of communal ideologies in our public life obstructs a diversity of views.

The viewing of Indian history in terms of two monolithic communities identified by religion has its origins in nineteenth century colonial interpretations of Indian history, where not only were the two communities described as monolithic but they were also projected as static over many centuries. This is of course not to deny that the labels were used earlier, but to argue that they were used in a different sense, and their use has its own history which has yet to be investigated in detail. My intention is to observe how those to whom we give a primary association with Islam, were initially perceived in India and the way in which such groups were represented as part of this perception. This was far more nuanced than is allowed for in the concept of monolithic communities and these nuances require exploration. The representation in turn had an impact on what have been described as the multiple new communities which came to be established. The newness was not because they were invariably alien; on the contrary they often incorporated earlier ways of community formation into the new communities. This links the first millennium AD to the second. The continuities did not have to be literal but could have been conceptual and while the nature of change

2

in some situations was new, in others it could well have followed earlier patterns.

The definition of the Muslim community extends to all those who claim adherence to Islam and the adherence is said to be demonstrated by a clearly stated belief and form of worship, which through conversion confers membership on a large body of believers, a membership which also assumes the egalitarian basis of the association. The perspective of the court chronicles of the Sultans and the Mughals was that of the ruling class and this perspective broadly endorsed the above definition and reinforced the projection of a Muslim community, a perspective in which the Hindu—as defined by such literature—was seen as the counterpart. It is as well to keep in mind that this is the current interpretation of these texts and although some of these sources may conform to the view from the windows of power, not all do so. Therefore, although sometimes carrying political and even theological weight, this view was nevertheless limited. As the articulation of a powerful but small section of society, it needs to be juxtaposed with other perspectives.

The notion of a Hindu community evolves from a geographic and ethnic description gradually giving way to religious association. The Hindu community is more difficult to define given the diverse natures of belief and worship, making it the amorphous 'Other' of the Muslim community in some of the court chronicles. The crystallization of this perception occurs when erstwhile Vaishnavas, Shaivas, Lingayats and others begin to refer to themselves as Hindus, rather than by their earlier separate labels—which in most cases is a late occurrence. Communities of the subcontinent have in the past been diverse, with multiple identities, and the attempt to force them into unchanging, static entities would seem to contradict the historical evidence. With the modern connotation of a religious community, both terms have come to include even in the interpretation of the historical past, all manner of diverse societies across the subcontinent, for some of whom convergence with the formal religion is, if at all, of recent origin.

The idea of two distinctive segregated civilizations, the Hindu and the Muslim, in conflict with each other, was assumed in colonial scholarship. References to the Hindu and the Muslim nation are common in the works of Orientalist scholars. Thus James Mill differentiated the Hindu civilization from the Muslim, which gave rise to the periodization of Indian history as that of the Hindu, Muslim and British periods. It crystallized the concept of a uniform, monolithic Hindu community dominating early history as did the Muslim equivalent in the subsequent period, with relations between the two becoming conflictual. These notions were in a sense summarized by Christian Lassen who, in the mid-nineteenth century, attempting to apply a Hegelian dialectic, wrote of the Hindu civilization as the thesis, the Muslim civilization as the anti-thesis, and the British as the synthesis![2]

Part of the insistence on the separateness of the two civilizations was the assumption that those who came with Islam had been regarded even by earlier Indians as alien, in fact as alien as the Europeans. This however was an erroneous perception of earlier historical relationships. Those associated with Islam had come through various avenues, as traders, as Sufis and as attachments to conquerors. Their own self-perceptions differed, as did the way in which they were perceived by the people of the land where they settled. For a long while in India, they were referred to by the same terms as were used in earlier times for people from west and central Asia, suggesting that their coming was viewed in part as a historical continuity. And there are good historical grounds to explain such a continuity.

The Arabs, Turks, Afghans and Persians were familiar to northern and western India, since they were not only contiguous peoples but linked by trade, settlement and conquest, links which went back, virtually unbroken, to many centuries. Central Asia was the homeland of the Shaka and Kushana dynasties which ruled in northern India at the turn of the Christian era and later of the Hunas who came as conquerors and became a caste. In Iran, the genesis of the languages spoken there and in northern India were Old Iranian and Indo-Aryan, which were closely related languages as is evident from examples of common usage in the *Avesta* and the *Rigveda*. Persian contacts with India were initially through the Achaemenids—who were near contemporaries of the Mauryas—and later through the Sassanids, closer in time to the Guptas. Territories in Afghanistan and the north-west were alternately controlled by rulers from either side of the passes. Ashokan inscriptions in Greek and Aramaic in Afghanistan attest to Mauryan rule; later dynasties with bases in the Oxus region and Iran brought north-western India into their orbit. Trading links were tied to political alliances. Close maritime contacts between the subcontinent and the Arabian peninsula go back to the time of the Indus civilization and have continued to the present.

There is therefore an immense history of interaction and exchange between the subcontinent and central and western Asia. The change of religion to Islam in the latter areas does not annul the earlier closeness. Interestingly even the Islam of these areas was not uniform, for there were and are strong cultural and sectarian differences among the Muslims of central Asia, Persia and the Arab world, differences which can in some cases be traced to their varying pre-Islamic past, and which influenced the nature of their interaction even within the Indian subcontinent.

These were contiguous people whose commercial and political relations over a long past, sometimes competitive and hostile and at other times friendly, were well recognized. Many had settled in India and married locally. One of the clauses of the treaty between Chandragupta Maurya and

Seleucus Nikator has been interpreted as a *jus conubii*, freedom for the Greeks and Indians to intermarry. Such marriages doubtless gave rise to mixed communities of new castes and practices, a process that did not cease with the arrival of Muslim Arabs and others. Similarly Indian traders and Indian Buddhist monks who lived in the oasis towns of central Asia were also to be found in ports and markets in west Asia, and were agencies of cross-cultural fertilization. Manichaeism for example drew on this and became a major religion in the early Christian era, largely because it was an amalgam of Mahayana Buddhism, Zoroastrianism, Nestorian Christianity and elements of central Asian shamanism. The dialogue between Indians, central Asian Turks, Persians and Arabs was a continuing one, irrespective of changes of dynasties and religions or of trade fluctuations. This dialogue is reflected for example in Sanskrit, Greek and Arabic texts relating to astronomy, medicine and philosophy, and in the presence of Indian scholars resident at the court of Harun al' Rashid.

The coming of the Europeans and the colonization of India by Britain was an altogether different experience. They came from distant lands, were physically different from the residents of the subcontinent, spoke languages which were entirely alien and in which there had been no prior communication; their rituals, religion and customs were alien; and above all they did not settle in India. The assumption that the west Asian and central Asian interventions after AD 800 and that of the British were equally foreign to India, in origin and intent, would, from the historical perspective, be difficult to defend.

Historically, therefore, it makes little sense to speak of the period from c. AD 1000 to the recent present as a thousand year of foreign rule. The territorial boundaries of today did not exist in those days and dynasties which had their origins in clans and families based on what we now call the Indo-Iranian borderlands and Afghanistan or the Arabian peninsula, can hardly be called foreign once they settled in the subcontinent and made it their home. Those coming from the borderlands were continuing the tradition of the Shakas, Indo-Greeks, Kushanas and Hunas, all of whom have left their imprint on Indian culture, an imprint which is acknowledged and has been internalized. Initially what was new about the Turks, Afghans and Mughals was their introduction of Islam: but even this developed an Indian version, observed by the majority of Muslims in India. Arab settlements and their intermarriage with local communities has resulted in the growth of a large number of new communities such as those along the west coast—the Bohra, Khoja, Navayat and Mappilah. Inevitably even their religion is different from orthodox Islam and is a mix of Arab Islam and the religious observances of the communities among which they settled.

Colonial interpretations of the Indian past were often contested by Indian historians, but the periodization was accepted in essentials. This was implicitly the acceptance of the idea that the units of Indian society were communities defined by single religions, requiring therefore that monolithic religious identities be sought and established in history. This view coincided with the incubation of the nation-state. All nationalisms use history, some more evidently than others. Essential to nationalist ideology was also the attempt to locate and define a national culture, often equated with that of the dominant group. Inevitably other cultures get excluded in this process. But the historian also acts as a remembrancer, reminding the society of the histories that are not always apparent up front.

When communalisms become visible on the political stage, as they were from the early years of this century, there is not only a contestation between them on the question of identity, but also a conflict with the earlier anti-colonial nationalism. The separation of the indigenous and the foreign emerges as a contentious issue and is taken back to the beginnings of

Indian history. Communal historiographies attempt to construct a religious identity into a monolithic community, claiming that only their interpretations of the past which support such a monolith are valid. Religion is sought to be restructured in order that it can be used for political mobilization.[3] There is inevitably a confrontation between historical evidence and its logic, counterpoised with resort to a fantasized past, in what are projected as conflicting histories.[4]

I would like to illustrate this by taking up one central issue, now contested, of the period prior to the modern in south Asian history. The question of identities has hinged on the definition of communities as solely religious communities, Hindu and Muslim in the main, and projected as generally hostile to each other. The assumptions have been that the Hindus and the Muslims each constituted a unified, monolithic community, and were therefore separate nations from the start, and that religious differences provide a complete—even though mono-causal—explanation for historical events and activities in the second millennium AD. The reconstruction of this history is largely based on court chronicles and texts where political contestation is often projected in religious terms, to the exclusion of other categories of texts which allow of a different reconstruction. Now that historians working on the second millennium AD are using other sources such as Sanskrit inscriptions and texts in regional languages and in Sanskrit, Prakrit and Apabrahmsa, the picture which emerges challenges the theory of monolithic, dichotomous communities.

My objection to the use of blanket terms such as 'the Hindus' and 'the Muslims', in historical readings, is that it erases precision with reference to social groups and is therefore methodologically invalid and historically inaccurate. It fails to differentiate between that which is more pertinent to religious history and that which relates to other aspects of life even if there had been an overlap in some situations. To explain the events of the time in terms only of an interaction between groups identified either as Hindus or as Muslims is misleading as a historical explanation. Some continuities in historical processes are arbitrarily broken by this usage and at the same time it is difficult to observe historical changes. Questioning the existence of such monolithic, religious communities, therefore, has extensive historiographical implications quite apart from whatever challenges it may pose to current political ideologies.

The argument that the notion of community was always defined by a single religion even in the pre-Islamic past has been countered by the evidence of sources other than Brahmanical normative texts. Such sources relate to diverse social groups and depict a different social scene. Theoretical interpretations emphasizing the nature of relationships between socially diverse groups and focusing on access to power, whether through economic or other disparities, have also changed the contours of pre-modern history. The many studies of caste, clan, village, town, language and region have encouraged a diversified view of past identities. Caste as *varna*, earlier thought to be a definitive identity, is now being recognized as intersected by identities of language, sect and occupation, perceived in the past as factors of segregation. Each individual, therefore, had varied identities, of which some might overlap, but which interfered with the consolidation of a single, monolithic, religious identity, even in societies prior to the coming of Islam.[5]

For Orientalist scholarship the construction of what came to be called Hinduism was a challenge, the religion being different from the familiar perspective of religions such as Judaism, Christianity and Islam. The latter were founded on the teachings of historically recognized prophets or of a messiah, with a theology and dogma, a sacred book and some ensuing deviations which took the form of variant sects. Yet the religious articulation which we recognize as constituting the religions which came to be called Hinduism did not

9

subscribe to these features. Of its many variant forms, some were deviations from earlier beliefs and practices but others had an independent genesis. The juxtaposition of religious sects did result almost through osmosis in similarities which introduced some common features, but the diversities remained. Hence the preference in some recent scholarship for the phrase 'Hindu religions',[6] rather than Hinduism. Because of this flexibility and decentralization, the religious identity was frequently closely allied to caste identities and since these incorporated occupation and access to resources, there were factors other than belief alone which governed religious identities. This is equally true of other religions in the subcontinent.

In the context of what we have come to label as Hindu and Muslim communities, I would like to consider briefly some facets of the initial perceptions of the one by the other. These are far more nuanced and socially graded than is allowed for in the concept of monolithic communities, and these nuances require further exploration.

The term 'Hindu' as referring to a religion is initially absent in the vocabulary of Indian languages and only slowly gains currency after it comes to be used in Arab and Persian writing. This is quite logical, given that earlier religious identities were tied to sect and caste. Membership was not of a specific religion, binding groups across a social spectrum and a geographical space, as was the case with Buddhism. Possibly this was part of the reason for the eventual rejection of Buddhism. The use of a single term to include the diversity would have been bewildering, and adjustment to this usage would have required a long period. When and why it came to be a part of the self-perception of what we today call the Hindus, needs to be historically investigated. Terms such as 'Muslim' or 'Musalman' are also not immediate entrants into the vocabulary of Indian languages after the arrival of Islam. Prior to that a variety of terms are preferred and these have their own history. The Arabs, Turks, Afghans and others are most frequently referred to variously as Tajika, Yavana, Shaka, Turushka and *mleccha*. There is therefore an attempt to associate the new entrants with existing categories and these labels are therefore expressive of more subtle relationships than we have assumed. The categories gave them an identity that was familiar and interestingly provided them with historical links, emanating from Indian connections with western and central Asia in the past. The use of these terms was at one level a continuation from the earlier past. What is striking is that initially none of these terms had a religious connotation. It would again be worthwhile to locate when this connotation was acquired in cases such as Turushka and its variants, which many centuries later included a religious identity.

Inscriptions subsequent to the eighth century AD refer to Arab incursions from Sind and Gujarat into the Narmada delta.[7] The Arabs are referred to here as Tajikas. The Rashtrakuta king had appointed a Tajika as governor of the Sanjan area of Thane district.[8] He carried out conquests on behalf of his Rashtrakuta overlord and is also recorded as granting a village to finance the building of a temple and the installation of an icon. Arab writers of this period refer to Arab officers employed by the local kings as well as settlements of Arab traders, and in both cases they had to work closely with the Rashtrakuta administration.[9]

The term Yavana was originally used for Greeks and later for those coming from west Asia or the west generally.[10] The Sanskrit word *yavana* is a back formation from the Prakrit *yona*, derived from the west Asian *yauna*, referring to the Ionian Greeks. It was used in an ethnic and geographical sense. Buddhist texts speak approvingly of the Yavanas. Some became Buddhists or were patrons of Buddhism. There was also a curiosity about Yavana society which it was said had no castes but had a dual division of master and slave.[11] A major brahmanical text of the time—the *Yuga Purana* of the *Gargi*

11

Samhita—was, on the other hand, hostile to the Yavanas,[12] even though some Yavanas declared that they were Vaishnavas. Perhaps this hostility grew out of Alexander's brutal attack on the Malloi[13] and the later resentment against Indo-Greek rulers in India patronizing what the brahmana authors regarded as heretical sects. The Yavana rulers were given the status of *vratya kshatriyas* or degenerate *kshatriyas*: those who were grudgingly given what was an apology for *kshatriya* status or those who, although born of *kshatriyas*, had not married women of an equal caste.[14] This was an example of providing a caste ranking for what was initially a ruling class which came from outside caste society. More devastating was the statement that by failing to perform the required rituals as prescribed by the brahmanical norms, the Yavanas together with various others had fallen to the status of *shudras*.[15]

Turks and Afghans are referred to as Yavanas in multiple inscriptions. This was an indication of their being from the west and to the extent that they are differentiated they are alien, but nevertheless not all that alien since there was already a status and an identity for them in the existing system. It enabled them to be included later in the scheme of how the past was conceptualized, as for example in one eighteenth century Marathi chronicle.[16] Such texts were partial imitations of the earlier tradition of maintaining king-lists, as in the *Puranas* and the *vamshavalis* or chronicles. With the establishment of Maratha power, there was the need for writing 'histories' to legitimize this power. As has been pointed out, the legitimizing of Maratha rule also required legitimizing the preceding Mughal and Turkish rule, which these texts refer to as the rule of the Yavanas.

But this was not a simple matter, for it had to conform to the *vamshavali* tradition. The earlier *vamshavalis* had linked contemporary rulers genealogically to the ancient heroes of the *Puranas*. Something similar would have to be done for these more recent Yavanas. It was therefore stated that a certain text, called the *Ramala-shastra,* contained the history of the Yavanas. We are told, in true Puranic style, that this text was first recited by Shiva to Parvati and then through Skanda, Narada and Bhrigu to Shukra, the last of whom told it to the Yavanas. It is Shiva who sent Paigambar to earth and there were seven *paigambars* or wise men, starting with Adam. This is of course reminiscent of the seven Manus with which Puranic chronology begins. The *paigambars* came to earth during the Kali-yuga. They started their own era, based on the Hijri era and different from the earlier Indian *samvat* era. They renamed Hastinapur as Dilli and initiated Yavana rule. They are thus located in time and space and provided with links to the earlier past in accordance with the established earlier *vamshavali* tradition.

The prime mover in this history is the deity Shiva and this makes any other legitimation unnecessary. Since the Yavanas had the blessing of Shiva, Pithor Raja Chauhana could not hold them back. The establishment of the Maratha kingdom also took place at the intervention of the deity. This kind of adjustment which emerges out of upper caste interests may also have been in part a response to the necessary change in the role model. Those claiming to be *kshatriyas* were now not approximating the lifestyle of their ancestors to the same degree as before, but were increasingly imitating the appearance, dress, language and lifestyle of the Mughal courts, as is evident from painting and literature. The culture of the elite had changed and there was a noticeable degree of accommodating the new. The importance of such accounts lies not in their fantasy on what actually happened, but in the fact that they provide us with a glimpse of how a historical situation was being manipulated in order to correlate a view of tradition with the problems of contemporary change. This might enable us to assess the nature of the ideological negotiation which conditioned such perceptions.

The term Shaka was the Sanskrit for the Scythians, a

people from central Asia who had ruled in parts of northern and western India around the Christian era. The reference to Turkish and Afghan dynasties as Shakas suggests a historical perception of place and people, a perception both of who the rulers were and how they might be fitted into the history of the ruled. A Sanskrit inscription of AD 1276 may illustrate this.[17] It records the building of a *baoli* and a *dharmashala* in Palam (just outside Delhi) by Uddhara from Uccha in the Multan district. The inscription, composed by Pandit Yogeshvara, dated *vikram samvat* 1333, begins with a salutation to Shiva and Ganapati. It then refers to the rulers of Delhi and Haryana as the Tomaras, Chauhanas and Shakas, the earlier two having been Rajput dynasties and the last being a reference to the Sultans. This is made clear by the detailed list of Shakas, that is, the Sultans of Delhi upto the current ruler Balban, who is referred to as a *nripati samrat* and whose conquests are described with extravagant praise. His titles mix the old with the new: *nayaka* was an earlier title and *Hammira* is thought to be the Sanskritized form of Amir. In the eulogistic style of the earlier *prashashti* tradition, Balban's realm is said to be virtually subcontinental—an obvious exaggeration. This is followed by a fairly detailed family history of the merchant in the traditional *vamshavali* style. He was clearly a man of considerable wealth. Other sources inform us that Hindu merchants from Multan gave loans to Balban's nobles when the latter suffered a shortfall in collecting revenue.[18] The identity of the Sultan is perceived as a continuity from earlier times and the identity of the merchant is in relation to his own history and occupation, and perhaps the unstated patronage of the Sultan. The sole reference to religion is oblique, in the statement that even Vishnu now sleeps peacefully, presumably because of the reign of Balban.

A Sanskrit inscription from Naraina (also in the vicinity of Delhi), dated *vikram samvat* 1384 or AD 1327 follows the same format.[19] We are told that in the town of Dhilli, sin is expelled by the chanting of the Vedas. The city is ruled by Mahamuda Sahi who is the *chudamani*, the crest-jewel of the rulers of the earth (a phrase used frequently in Sanskrit to describe a king), and is a *shakendra*, the lord/Indra of the Shakas. This may well be the rhetoric of sycophancy; nevertheless the juxtaposing of Vedic recitations to the rule of Muhammad bin Tughlaq carries its own message. The identification with the Shakas is at one level complimentary since the earlier Shakas were associated with the important calendrical era of AD 78, still in official use.

Another term is Turushka, which was originally a geographical and ethnic name. An interesting link is made with earlier Indian historical perceptions of central Asia, when Kalhana, in his twelfth century history of Kashmir, the *Rajatarangini*, uses the term retrospectively. He refers to the Kushanas of the early centuries AD as Turushkas, and adds ironically that even though they were Turushkas, these earlier kings were given to piety.[20] Here perhaps the points of contrast are the references in two twelfth century inscriptions to the Turushkas as evil—*dushtaturushka*—or to a woman installing an image in place of one broken by the Turushkas.[21] Familiarity with the Turks was also because they competed with Indian and other traders in controlling the central Asian trade, especially the lucrative silk trade between China and Byzantium and the horse trade closer home. The initial attacks of the Turks and Afghans were tied into local politics, what Kalhana refers to as the coalition of the Kashmiri, Khasa and *mleccha*.[22] The entry of the Turushkas on the north Indian scene is in many ways a continuation of the relations which had existed between the states of north-western India and those beyond.

Kalhana writes disparagingly of the king Harshadeva of Kashmir ruling in the eleventh century. He is said to have employed Turushka mercenaries—horsemen in the main—in his campaigns against local rulers, even though the Turushkas were then invading the Punjab. The activities of Harshadeva,

15

demolishing and looting temples when there was a fiscal crisis, leads to Kalhana calling him Turushka.[23] But he adds that such activities have been familiar even from earlier times. However, the looting of temples by Harshadeva was more systematic, for he appointed Udayaraja as a special officer to carry out the activities, with the designation of *devotpatana-nayaka*, the officer for the uprooting of deities.[24]

Alberuni writing soon after the raids of Mahmud of Ghazni, states that Mahmud destroyed the economy of the areas where he looted.[25] The historically relevant question would be to enquire into the degree of devastation and the memory of the disruption. An interesting case is that of the temple of Somanath associated with such a raid.[26] Curiously Bilhana, referring to his visit to Somanath later in the same century, makes no mention of Mahmud's raid. Even more interesting is the evidence of a bilingual inscription in Sanskrit and Arabic from Veraval-Somanath of AD 1264. It records the acquiring of a large area of land for the building of a mosque by a ship's captain from Hormuz, Nuruddin Firuz, during the reign of the Vaghela-Chaulukya king Arjunadeva. The mosque is referred to as a *mijigiti*—probably derived from *masjid*—and is described as a *dharmasthana*. The land was acquired through the agreement of the local *pancha-kula*, a high level administrative body whose membership included the Shaiva priests presumably of the Somanath temple, the merchants, and the elite of the area. The maintenance of the mosque was also arranged through the purchase of the estates of various temples. No mention is made of the raid of Mahmud on Somanath. Were memories surprisingly short or was the destruction of the temple exaggerated in the Turko-Persian accounts? Or were the profits of trade—doubtless the lucrative horse trade of Gujarat—of surmounting concern for the priests and elite of Somanath?[27] Or were the Arab and Persian traders from the Gulf treated in a friendly fashion, and differentiated from the Turushkas since the latter were political enemies whereas the former were contributing to local prosperity? It is interesting that they are not all bunched together and referred to as 'Muslims' as we would tend to do today.

Finally we come to *mleccha*, the most contentious among the words used. It has a history going back to around 800 BC[28] and occurs originally in a Vedic text—and is used for those who could not speak Sanskrit correctly. Language was frequently a social marker in many early societies. The use of Sanskrit was largely confined to the upper castes, and gradually the word *mleccha* also came to have a social connotation and referred to those outside the pale of *varna* society—those who did not observe the rules of caste as described in the *dharmashastras*. When used in a pejorative sense it included a difference of language and ritual impurity. The category of *mleccha* was again a well-established category but used more frequently by upper castes to refer to those from whom they wished to maintain a caste distance.

It has been argued that the term *mleccha* was essentially one of contempt for the Muslim. More recently it has been stated that the demonization of the Muslim invaders in using the term *rakshasas* for them and invoking the parallel with Rama as the protector, was part of the Indian political imagination of the twelfth century.[29] But the 'rakshasization' of the enemy—irrespective of who the enemy was—has been a constant factor with reference to many pre-Islamic enemies and going back to earlier times. To read the Ramayana into the political imagination of northern India as specific to the confrontation with the Turks, and the personification of the Turushkas as evil because they were Muslims, is to read the sources out of context and to make attributions which are not apparent.[30] Sayana's commentary of the fourteenth century AD refers to the dasas of the *Rigveda* as *rakshasas* and *asuras*. Inscriptions of this period freely use the terms *rakshasas* and Ravana for enemies who are Hindu.[31]

17

In later centuries, the reference to some Muslims as *mlecchas* was an extension of the term to include them among the many others who were denied *varna* status. This usage is more common in sources which come from the upper castes, such as Sanskrit texts and inscriptions, and was more easily used for the lower castes who were, even without being Muslim, marginalized, moved to the fringes of society and treated with contempt. The term itself included a multiplicity of peoples and jatis but generally it referred to those who were not members of a *varna*.

Nevertheless there is a marked ambivalence in the use of the term. In another Sanskrit inscription of AD 1328 from the Raisina area of Delhi, reference is made to the *mleccha* Sahavadina seizing Delhi. But he is praised for his great valour in what is described as his burning down the forest of enemies who surrounded him.[32] If in this context *mleccha* had a contemptuous meaning, it is unlikely that a local merchant would dare to use it for the Sultan. The same ambiguity occurs in earlier texts. Thus the sixth century astronomer Varahamihira states that among the Yavanas (referring to the Hellenistic Greeks), knowledge in astronomy had stabilized and therefore they were revered as *rishis* even though they were *mlecchas*;[33] and a seventh century inscription from Assam refers to one of the rulers, Shalastambha, as the *mleccha-adinatha*.[34] Thus the context of this term varied but it was generally a social marker. The identification of what were regarded as *mleccha* lands and people could also change over time.

Social markers are frequently forged by those who demarcate themselves sharply from others and this tends to be characteristic of the upper levels of society. The usage of *mleccha* is no exception. Among castes, brahmana identity has a considerable antiquity and was created out of an opposition initially to the *kshatriyas* as is evident in the Vedic corpus, an opposition which was extended to the heterodox teachings of the *kshatriyas* in the Shramanic sects, and then to the non-brahmana in general. The dichotomy of the brahmana and the *shudra* was common to virtually every part of the subcontinent. References to the coming of the *mleccha* creating a social catastrophe of a kind expected of the Kali age as described in the *Puranas* was frequently invoked whenever there was a political crisis.[35] The insistence that the brahmanical ordering of the world had been turned upside down on such occasions was repeated in brahmanical texts each time this ordering was challenged.

The social distinctions implicit in these terms applied to people of various religions. Connotations used in the last thousand years changed with time, application and context, and the mutation of meaning requires analysis. The less frequent use of Yavana and *mleccha* for Europeans had been pared down in meaning by the nineteenth century. Some uses of these terms were mechanisms for reducing social distance, others for enhancing it. A major indicator of social distance was caste. Among castes which we now identify as Hindu, there was the separation of the *dvija* or twice born from the *shudra* and even more sharply from the untouchable. Muslim society segregated the Muslim from central and western Asia and the indigenous convert. Even if this was not a ritual segregation, it was an effective barrier, and possibly encouraged the local convert to maintain certain earlier caste practices and kinship rules. At the level of the ruling class, the culture of the court influenced all those who had pretensions to power, irrespective of their religion. Further down the social scale, caste identities often controlled appearance and daily routine. Caste identity, because it derived so heavily from occupation and the control over economic resources, was not restricted only to kinship systems and religious practices. The perception of difference therefore was more fragmented among the various communities than is projected in the image of the monolithic two.

Those from across the Arabian Sea who settled as traders

along the west coast and married into existing local communities, the Khojas and Bohras of western India, the Navayats in the Konkan and the Mappilahs of Malabar, assumed the customary practices of these communities, sometimes even contradicting the social norms of Islam. Because of this their beliefs and practices were distinct even from each other, influenced as they were by those of the host community. Today there may be a process of Islamization which is ironing out these contradictions, but in the past there has been much uncertainty as to whether these practices could be viewed as strictly Islamic.[36] There have been marked variations in the structures and rules governing family, kinship and marriage among communities listed as Muslim in the subcontinent. These have quite often tended to be closer to the rules associated with the Hindu castes in the region.[37]

The process of marrying into the local community is unlikely to have been free of tension and confrontation in the initial stages. The orthodox among both the visitors and the hosts would doubtless have found the need to adapt to custom and practice on both sides that were not palatable. But their presence today as well-articulated communities speaks of the prevalence of professional and economic concerns over questions of religion. Their continuing historical existence points to the eventual adjustments of both the host and the settlers.

Even on conversion, the link with caste was frequently inherent. A multiplicity of identities remained, although their function and need may have changed. Not only was the concept of conversion alien to Indian society, but conversion to Islam remained limited in India as compared to Persia and central Asia. Possibly one reason for this was that those who introduced Islam could not break through caste stratification. If conversion was motivated by the wish for upward mobility, then even this did not necessarily follow. Conversion in itself does not change the status of the converted group in the caste hierarchy. Even converts have to negotiate a change, and the potentiality for such negotiation would depend on their original status, or else they would have to evolve into a new caste: a process which has been observed for the history of caste society over many centuries. At the same time, conversion does not eliminate diversities and there would be a carry-over of earlier practices and beliefs. Caste ranking continued to be important to marriage and occupation, for a radical change in caste ranking would have involved confronting the very basis on which Indian society was organized.

Reports as recent as a century ago point to the continuing role of caste even after conversion. The Gazetteer of Bijapur District in 1884 is an example.[38] The Muslim population was listed here as consisting of three categories: Muslims who claim to be foreign, indigenous Muslims but descended from migrants from north India, and the local Muslims. Those claiming foreign descent list their names as is usual, as Saiyid, Shaikh, Mughal, Pathan; insist that they are Urdu speaking and strictly Sunni; and many of them held office in the local administration. Like the scribes of earlier times, some had sought administrative positions in the emerging kingdoms. The second group, working in a more menial capacity, claims to have come from north Indian communities such as Jat cultivators, or from the trading communities of the west coast and identified themselves by their earlier caste names. They too maintained that they were Sunnis. Their languages varied, some using Urdu and others Marathi and Kannada, with some even preferring Tamil or Arabic.

The third group, with the maximum number in the district, was in many ways dissimilar. They were local converts, some of whom took on *jati* names that had come to have a subcontinental status and connotation, such as Momin and Kasab, but many had retained their original jati names such as Gaundi, Pinjara, Pakhali, and so on, and identified themselves by the same name which they had used prior to conversion.

The *jati* name was associated with the occupation as had often been so from earlier times. Their occupations as the poorer artisans and cultivators ranked them at the lower levels of society and tended to conform to those which they had performed as members of Hindu castes. Their Urdu was minimal because they used Kannada and Marathi. Most of them are described as lax Sunnis, not frequenting the mosque and instead declaring that they worship Hindu deities, observe Hindu festivals and avoid eating beef. The avoidance of beef may have been to distinguish themselves from untouchables who had no restrictions on eating beef. The social and religious identity of this third group would seem to be closer to that of their Hindu caste counterparts than to that of Muslims of higher castes. From the thirteenth century there was intense Sufi activity in the area, but nevertheless—or possibly because of the openness of certain schools of Sufi teaching—groups such as these could keep a distance from formal Islam. This was the larger majority of those technically listed as Muslims, who, perhaps because of their lower social status and therefore distance from formal religion, were untouched by *fatwas*.

This picture was not unique to Bijapur and can be replicated for other parts of the subcontinent. Such groups can perhaps be better described as being on the intersection of Islam and the Hindu religions. This gives them an ambiguous religious identity, in terms of an either/or situation. Were they Hindus picking up some aspects of Islam or were they Muslims practising a Hinduized Islam? Did caste identity have priority in determining the nature of the religious identity, and did these priorities differ from one social group to another?

Groups such as the third category mentioned above receive little attention from historians of religion since they cannot be neatly indexed. The same was true of their status in the historical treatment of Hinduism. The study of groups which enter liminal spaces is recent and here too there is frequently a focus on the curious religious admixtures rather than the social and economic compulsions which encourage such admixtures. But in terms of the history of religion in the subcontinent, such groups have been the majority since the earliest times and have lent their own distinctiveness to belief and to the practice of religion. On occasion, when they played a significant historical role, attempts would be made to imprint facets of the formal religion onto their beliefs and practices. History is rich in demonstrating the mutation of folk cults into Puranic Hinduism. For example, the hero who saves cattle from raiders was worshipped by the pastoralists of Maharashtra, but eventually emerges at Pandharpur, patronized by the Yadava dynasty, as the god Vitthoba, associated with Vishnu.[39] This was also one reason why belief and worship across the subcontinent, even when focusing on a single deity, was often formulated differently, except at the level of the elite who differentiated themselves by claiming adherence to forms approved of by brahmanical orthodoxy.

The evolving of Hindu religions, with specific rituals and practices often emerging from particular castes or regions, was a process which did not terminate with the arrival of Islam, nor did it turn away from Islam. The dialogue between Islam and earlier indigenous religions is reflected in various Bhakti and Sufi traditions, which have been extensively studied in recent years. Groups still further away from formal religion provide yet another dimension. Since the indigenous religions did not constitute a monolith and registered a range of variations, there was a range of dialogues. These were partly the result of such movements having a middle caste and *shudra* following, even if some of their prominent members were brahmanas. Formal religious requirements were often rejected in such groups, but not in entirety. Where a few showed familiarity with philosophic doctrine,[40] others broke away from such a dialogue. Attempts to Sanskritize the Bhakti tradition both in texts recounting the activities of the *sants* and in modern studies, have been cautioned against.

The famous *Hindu-Turk Samvad* of Eknath written in the sixteenth century in Maharashtra is the imagined dialogue between a brahmana and what appears to be a Muslim *maulana*, with an undercurrent of satire in the treatment of both.[41] The language used by each for the other would probably cause a riot today! The attempt is at pointing out the differences between facets of what were seen as Hindu and Muslim belief and worship, but arguing for an adjustment in daily life. The crux of the debate states, 'You and I are alike, the conflict is over *jati* and *dharma*' (v.60). The pre-Islamic interweaving of religion and social organization was not broken and the process of using new religious ideas to negotiate a social space continued. It is worth noting that in the seventeenth century Shivaji was writing in a political vein to Jai Singh about the grave danger facing Hindus, chiding him for his support to the Mughals and offering him an alliance. This would be an indication of the perception at elite levels being different from those at other levels and largely conditioned by factors of statecraft and political policy. Eknath's reading of the situation is a sharp contrast.

This also becomes apparent in common cultural codes symbolizing an altogether different level of communication. For example, the imagery and meaning encapsulated in the depiction of riding a tiger and therefore who rides a tiger, becomes a powerful symbol. For those who live in the forests, the tiger is the mount of the forest deity such as Dakhin Rai in the Sunderbans. For caste Hindus, the goddess Durga rides a tiger. Among Nathapanthis, the *natha* was depicted as riding a tiger and using a live cobra for a whip. In Sufi hagiography, the Sufi often rides a tiger and sometimes meets another Sufi riding a wall. At the shrine of Sabarimala in Kerala, the deity Ayyappan rides a tiger. In many rural areas there is to this day an all-purpose holy man who rides a tiger and is variously called Barckhan Ghazi or Satya-pir and is worshipped by all, irrespective of formal religious affiliations.[42] This bond, or even the subconscious memory of a bond binding a range of peoples, had no formal definition. These were not individual deviants from conventional religions. This was the religious articulation of the majority of the people in such areas. When we arbitrarily attach such religious expression to either Islam or Hinduism, we perhaps misrepresent the nature of these beliefs.

The existence of parallel religious forms, some conflicting and others cohering, has characterized Indian society. Some of these distanced themselves from all orthodoxies and attracted those who participated in what might be called forms of counter-cultures, preferring the openness of the heterodox. Their ancestry can perhaps be traced through a lineage of thought and behaviour going back to the wandering *vratyas*, the rogues with matted hair and the mendicants regarded with disapproval in an *Upanishad*,[43] the *siddhas* claiming extra-sensory powers, the Natha yogis, and some among the gurus, the pirs and faqirs. This was not invariably a confrontation with those in authority, but it was a statement of social distancing. Such distancing meant that even those who were disapproved of, were not necessarily silenced. The absence of sharply etched religious identities among such groups, gave them a universality, which was their source of strength. But it was also responsible for history neglecting to recognize their significance. This relates directly to the question of whose history are we writing?

Religious expression, if treated only in formal terms and indexed according to established religions, leaves us with a poverty of understanding. For, together with the formal there is the constant presence of the informal and of beliefs unconstrained by texts. These were often forms of legitimizing widespread popular practice which adhered neither to the formal requirements of Islam nor of Brahmanic or Puranic Hinduism. They could be, but were not invariably manifestations of peaceful coexistence, or even attempts at syncretism.

Concepts such as those of composite culture or syncretism are only partial explanations and refer to particular situations. Syncretism would apply, for example, to Akbar's attempts at reconciling variant religious activities and beliefs by propagating a religion of his own making, or to Eknath in his formulation of a dialogue between the Hindu and the Muslim. Akbar's efforts were in part a crystallization of the earlier Indian tradition where royalty bestowed patronage on a variety of religious sects, some even hostile to each other. Akbar's implicit acceptance of a religious pluralism, irrespective of how he formulated it, was significant even to the subsequent interweaving of religion and political policy, although this was not characteristic of every aspect of religion during this period.

There were aspects of life in which religion was an identifier but there were also many other aspects in which more broad-based cultural expressions, evolving over time and through an admixture of various elements, gave an identity to a social group. These are the ones which need to be investigated. Associated with this is the multiplicity of various causes for particular historical events ranging over political expediency, economic control, ideological support, social associations, religious practices and custom, the exploration of which provide variations in the ordering of priorities among causal connections.

Composite culture presupposes self-contained units in combination or in juxtaposition. In the history of Indian society such units would be *jatis*, sects, language groups and groups with a local identity, and would have a history in some cases going back to pre-Islamic times. The juxtaposition would not have been between formal religion, Hinduism and Islam—as is generally argued—since this again presupposes the notion of the monolithic community, but between variant articulations among the many constituent units of society. These units would have to be historically identified, an exercise which requires a sensitivity to the problems of writing the history of those on the intersections of varied religious expression.

The concern would be with both social dissonances and social harmonies, and a need for adjustment. Occurrences of religious conflict were not unknown, but were more frequently associated with the attitudes of formal religions for whom the conflict was rarely confined to religious factors. It arose more frequently from competing claims to patronage and resources. Perhaps the existence of the parallel, informal religions played a role, not in preventing conflict, but in ensuring that intolerance was contained and remained at the local level, as it had done even in earlier times.[44]

The relationship between segments of society, even those identified as Hindu or Muslim, would take the normal course of jousting for social space and social advancement. This would have involved diplomacy and management or on occasion conflict of a violent kind, particularly where established statuses were being challenged by newly evolved ones, using the patronage of authority. But the conflict at levels other than those of the ruling class was localized. Friends and enemies were demarcated less by religion and more by the concerns of social and economic realities. Cultural transactions and social negotiations were common but were bound by the degree of proximity to the structure of power.

To unravel the creation and modulation of religious identities is a far more complex process than the chronicling of religious activities. I have tried to argue that it is linked to social identities and historical perceptions, which in turn hinge on access to resources and power, or alternatively, to a deliberate distancing from these. I have also tried to suggest that if we move away from the notion of monolithic communities we begin to see the historical potential of understanding how identities may actually have been perceived at points in time, and their multiple manifestations and functions. Exploring the perceptions which people had of each other in the past is not merely a matter of historical curiosity, for it impinges on the construction of current identities. An insistence on seeing society as having consisted for all time of monolithic religious communities derives from the contemporary conflict over identities. Yet, historically, identities are neither stable nor permanent. Inherent in the process of historical change is the invention and mutation of identities. And the identities of the pre-colonial period would seem to have been very different from the way in which they have been projected in our times.

Readings of the history of the Indian subcontinent have been changing in many significant ways with the utilization now of a different set of additional sources and with new interpretations which are asking a different set of questions from those of the historiography of the nineteenth century. The colonial perspective of monolithic communities is being replaced by more detailed and nuanced studies of social groups and their historical articulations as well as their inter-linkages—social, religious, political and economic. The writing of history has to that extent become far more specialized, technical and professional. New sources ranging from archaeology to inscriptions and a variety of texts have been added to the data which earlier focussed largely on court chronicles. Textual criticism and the evaluating of the social context of a text and the assessing of inscriptions as data, require professional expertise. This involves more than just the knowledge of their language. Historical analyses of socio-economic data require some understanding of the formulations of the social sciences, such as a familiarity with economic theories or sociological theories. Technical expertise is also called for in reading archaeological reports and making historical generalizations on the basis of these.

The Hindutva insistence on continuing to see the last thousand years as the history of two monolithic communities in conflict is merely a continuation in endorsing the colonial historiography of the nineteenth century and using it to support a current political ideology. The research of many historians .of different schools of historical thought is now indicating a very different picture, where there are on occasion situations of contestation and on other occasions, situations of assimilation. This calls for a range of historical explanations. Inevitably this creates a divide between those who are involved in historical research and those who are merely toeing the line of the Hindutva ideology. Only the brashness of 'born-again Hindu' journalists who propagate this ideology encourages them to dismiss the research of over half a century of Indian and non-Indian scholars working on Indian history and attempt to replace it with their own historically baseless fulminations.

Yet there is an audience for this brashness. In India there are still many who believe that historical explanation is a free-for-all and every one has a right to insist on the validity of their views on the past, however ill-informed they may be. Yet the same people who know little about history but hold forth on what happened in the past and how, would hesitate to demonstrate their ignorance on matters pertaining to economics or sociology. This is paralleled in the sciences where there is the same casualness in holding forth on animal and plant behaviour, but a much greater hesitation when it comes to the properties of matter as determined by physics or chemistry.

Nor is this attitude limited to Indians in India. Some of the more pernicious views on communities and the Indian past are expressed by those Indians in the diaspora who cling even more fervently to the Hindutva ideology. This ideology provides them with a compensation for being a minority in the country of their adoption. Indians settled in the white world, however wealthy and established they may be professionally, do not command the social, cultural and political resources of the white elites among whom they live. This has

29

led some to adopt a ghetto mentality and attempt to package Hindu religion and culture in a marketable form as provided by agencies such as the Vishva Hindu Parishad, which encourages them also in the fond belief that Hindu culture has a superiority far exceeding all other cultures in age, in quality and in unbroken continuity. They are unaware that these are issues which are not now at the forefront of historical discussion. Historians are no longer concerned with evaluating cultures, or measuring longevity; they are concerned with trying to understand the making and functioning of a culture.

Since the understanding of the Indian past among such diasporic Indians is out of date, it is not surprising that their understanding of the First World is equally out of date. Many have now taken on the role of cold war warriors and defenders of McCarthyism, using the once familiar rhetoric about 'commies' and 'pinkies', and endlessly tilting at a windmill which they see as the communist bogey. The current policy of the First World of targeting Islam as the post-cold war enemy feeds into the anti-Muslim project of Hindutva.

The intervention of Hindutva from the diaspora not only finances the diffusion of a history which is no longer acceptable, but makes a bid thereby to give respectability to communal ideology in a situation where the diasporic Indian is seen as the role-model by the Indian middle class. Those who support the Hindutva ideology but are not settled in India can at a safe distance indulge in the assertion of this identity, since they are not affected by the killing of Muslims in riots, the raping of Christian nuns or the dire threats to dalits and tribals who have converted to Christianity. The intervention of groups from the diaspora in the movement for Khalistan aggravated the agony of the Punjab. The terrorized lives of Hindus and Muslims in Kashmir is a phenomenon not unrelated to organizations of south Asian origin outside the subcontinent.

The tragedy is that actually the study of the past sends us very different messages but we choose not to read them.

Indian society has always been a multi-religious, multicultural society where identities have inevitably been multiple. Such a society is not in itself secular but is conducive to the evolving of a secular society protecting the civil and human rights of all its citizens. Our history in India has been very different from that projected in the two-nation theory and the Hindutva ideology. If we can read our history with more sensitivity and insight, it would contribute to avoiding a fascist future.

Notes

1. An earlier version of this essay was delivered as the Zakir Hussain Memorial Lecture in Delhi. I would like to thank K.N. Panikkar and Muzaffar Alam for comments on an earlier draft.
2. *Indische Alterthumskunde*, Leipzig, 1845-62.
3. R. Thapar, 'Syndicated Hinduism' in G.D. Sontheimer and H. Kulke (ed.) *Hinduism Reconsidered*, Delhi, 1996 (2nd. ed.).
4. This is demonstrated in the debate over the history of the Ramjanmabhoomi at Ayodhya. S. Gopal (ed.) *Anatomy of a Confrontation*, Delhi, 1990. See especially, K.N. Panikkar, 'An Historical Overview,' p. 22-37. The pamphlet published by the Jawaharlal Nehru University historians entitled *The Political Abuse of History*, is concerned with the same issue.
5. R. Thapar, 'Imagined Religious Communities? Ancient History and the Modern Search for a Hindu Identity' in R. Thapar, *Interpreting Early India*, Delhi, 1992, p. 60-80.
6. As for example in some of the papers included in G.D. Sontheimer and H. Kulke (ed.), *Hinduism Reconsidered*, Delhi, 1996 and V. Dalmia and H. von Steitencron (ed.) *Representing Hinduism*, New Delhi, 1995.
7. R.S. Avasthy and A. Ghosh, 'References to Muhammadans in Sanskrit Inscriptions in Northern India,' *Journal of Indian History*, 1935, 15, p. 161-84.
8. *Epigraphia Indica* 32, p. 47 ff; 64 ff.
9. M. Athar Ali, 'Encounter and Efflorescence . . .' *Proceedings of the Indian History Congress*, Gorakhpur, 1989.
10. R. Thapar, 'The Image of the Barbarian in Early India' in R.

Thapar, *Ancient Indian Social Histoiy: Some Interpretations,* New Delhi, 1978, p. 152-92.

11. *Majjhima Nikaya,* 2, p. 149-92.

12. D.C. Sircar, *Studies in the Yuga Purana and Other Texts,* Delhi, 1974; D.R. Mankad, *Yugapuranam,* Vallabhavidyanagar, 1951; J. Mitchiner, *Yuga Purana,* gives a different reading.

13. Arrian 6.6 ff. Plutarch 69.

14. Manu X.20.

15. Manu X.43-44.

16. The *Caryugaci-bakhar* discussed in N.G. Wagle, 'Hindu-Muslim Interactions in Medieval Maharashtra' in G.D. Sontheimer and H. Kulke (ed.), *Hinduism Reconsidered,* p. 51-66.

17. Palam *Baoli* Inscription in P. Prasad, *Sanskrit Inscriptions of the Delhi Sultanate 1191-1526,* Delhi, 1990, p. 3 ff.

18. I. Habib, 'Economic History of Delhi Sultanate,' *The Indian Historical Review,* 1978, 4, 2, p. 291, 295. Quoted in P. Prasad, op. cit.

19. Naraina Stone Inscription. Ibid, p. 22.

20. *Rajatarangini,* I. 170; VIII. 3412.

21. Avasthy and Ghosh, op. cit.

22. Ibid. VIII. 887.

23. Ibid. VII. 1095, 1149; VIII. 3346.

24. Ibid. VII. 1091.

25. E. Sachau, *Alberuni's India,* London, 1910, p. 22 .

26. *Vikramankadevacarita,* XVIII.

27. R. Thapar, *Narrative and the Making of History,* Lecture 2: Somanath, Narratives of a History, D.D. Kosambi Memorial Lectures, University of Bombay, 1999 (forthcoming).

28. R. Thapar, 'The Image of the Barbarian in Early India,' *Comparative Studies in Society and History,* 1971, XIII, p. 408-36. A. Parasher, *Mlecchas in Early India,* Delhi, 1991.

29. S. Pollock, 'Ramayana and Political Imagination in India,' *Journal of Asian Studies,* 1993, 52, p. 1.

30. See the critique of Pollock in B.D. Chattopadhyaya, *Representing the Other? Sanskrit Sources and the Muslims,* Delhi, 1998. p. 99 ff.

31. *Epigraphia Indica,* 1, p. 26 ff.; M.K. Sharan, *Tribal Coins,* Delhi, 1972, p. 122-27.

32. Sarban Stone Inscription. P. Prasad, op. cit., p. 29.

33. *Brihatsamhita* (ed. M.R. Bhat), II. 32.

34. Bargaon Copper-Plate Inscription of Ratnapaladeva; quoted in K.L. Barua Bahadur; *Early History of Kamarupa*, Gauhati, 1966, p. 66-67.

35. C. Talbot, 'Inscribing the Other, Inscribing the Self-Hindu-Muslim Identities in Pre-colonial India,' *Comparative Studies in Society and History*, 1995, 37, 4, p. 692-715; E. Zelliot, 'Four Radical Saints in Maharashtra,' in M. Israel and N.K. Wagle (ed.), *Religion and Society in Maharashtra*, Toronto, 1987, p. 131-44.

36. For example, V.S. D'Souza, *The Navayats of Kannara*, Dharwar, 1955.

37. I. Ahmed (ed.), *Family Kinship and Marriage among Muslims in India*, Delhi, 1976.

38. Summarized in R.M. Eaton, *Sufis of Bijapur*, New Jersey, 1978, p. 310 ff.

39. A. Dandekar, 'Landscapes in Conflict: Flocks, Hero-stones and Cult in Early Medieval Maharashtra,' *Studies in History*, 1991, VII, 2, p. 301-24.

40. D.N. Lorenzen, 'Social Ideologies of Hagiography,' in M. Israel and N.K. Wagle (ed.), *Religion and Society in Maharashtra*, Toronto, 1987, p. 92-114.

41. E. Zelliot, 'A Medieval Encounter between Hindus and Muslims: Eknath's Drama-Poem Hindu-Turk Samvad' in F.W. Clothey (ed.), *Images of Man: Religion and Historical Process in South Asia*, Madras, 1982.

42. In the Sundarbans the tiger and its manifestations such as Dakhin Rai the tiger-god, Bonobibi the goddess of the forest, or Ghazi Sahib, are universally worshipped by Hindus and Muslims alike and the mythologies which accompany this worship have diverse Hindu and Muslim sources as also does the chanting at the *puja*. For an account of the continuity of this worship to this day, see S. Montogomery, *Spell of the Tiger*, New York, 1995.

43. Maitri Upanishad 7.8.

44. R. Thapar, *Cultural Transactions and Early India*, Delhi, 1987.

The Road to Xanadu:
India's Quest for Secularism

Rajeev Dhavan

I

Too many centuries have passed by for India and Indians not to know the meaning of 'secularism' or understand the importance of its implications for the subcontinent. India has been home to many people—some indigenous, some not. Some came to settle; others to conquer. Below the highest mountains of the world lie the fertile valleys of the many rivers of the subcontinent—each breeding in and around it a diversity of life and life forms, colours and seasons and cultures and faiths that suffer no parallel. Its people have not always lived together amicably. But they have constantly devised ways and means to make living together in peace possible. Its history has been a tour de force—constantly adjusting to diversity and accommodating change. This process—of which the quest for secularism is a part—will, undoubtedly, go on.

Although there was always much to fight over, till recently there was a relative abundance to share. The dominant voice of Hinduism developed a complex hierarchical caste system to maldistribute resources and structure unequal relationships.

Both its constitutive ideology and its over-structured prescriptions confronted opposition, defiance and rebellion. Its endeavour was to catch peoples' imagination so that their lives would follow suit. It presented 'life'—indeed, the universe and the cosmos—in its infinitude, locating peoples' lives in a hierarchic and cyclic understanding of where they belonged. Yet such a dispensation was not acceptable to sceptics and non-believers. Where wisdom failed, pragmatism followed. Yielding to people as much as it might have wanted people to yield to it, Hinduism preserved its hegemony precisely because it broke up into a plethora of sects, beliefs, interpretations, practices and expressions—treating each variation as part of *dharma* which adapted from place to place and *yuga* to *yuga* (epoch), but retaining an enviably tight control over resources and opportunities. In this plenitude grew rebel philosophies which abnegated 'god', rebel sects which disclaimed adherence to the faith, and rebel faiths which turned their backs on Hinduism to flower in their own right.

New people brought new faiths to establish new empires and new basis for social and political governance. Many of these ideas found native root—transforming and adapting to the circumstances as they went along. New religious ideas and beliefs were invented—combining the diverse elements of many faiths and practices.[1] Inevitably, in the struggle for resources, opportunities and supremacy, religion was suborned to the struggles amongst peoples. Wars, battles, skirmishes and tensions appropriated and exploited religion to lead the faithful into combat. This continues to happen. But, each struggle—howsoever bitter—has made permanent additions to India's ever-increasing social diversity. The wisest of Indian rulers have not been those who have answered fanaticism with bigotry, but those who have looked for principles of governance which would pledge people together rather than divide them. In our times, the subcontinent was savagely dismembered along communal lines, leaving it to the rulers and peoples of the partitioned parts to pick up the pieces. A new quest for secularism began, which will carry over into the next millennium.

II

Even the most homogenous societies have to look for ideas to deal with differences between and amongst people. The quest for secularism begins when it is no longer possible or desirable to satisfy the demands emanating from diversity from within the conspectus of any one particular faith or tradition. Resisted by orthodoxy and supported by oppressed minorities, secular principles develop over time. Imposed coercively, they may fail to elicit support. Projected as consensus, they are as fragile as the forces that uphold or oppose them. We are concerned here not just with compromise solutions which will purchase peace, but more lasting issues of principle to create justice amongst all peoples of all persuasions.

In all this, law plays a critical role in giving objective expression to secular practices, concretizing their existence in a seemingly autonomous status, stating them in explicit terms and rendering them enforceable. 'Law' is indeterminably 'Janus faced'. It seeks to satisfy both the powerful forces which create it as well as the ideals of justice which it claims to fulfill and from which it derives legitimacy.[2] We are not just concerned with the 'law' declared by the State, but also those innumerable rules in civil society which are clearly understood to be binding in their effect as a consequence of the many subtle and coercive mechanisms through which a society calibrates compliance to social norms.[3] Likewise, secularism is not just concerned with the triumphs and failures of the political State but also of civil society. A State may be secular in form, but people in that State may be intolerant, tyrannical and cruel to people not of their persuasion. Conversely, a State may be constitutionally linked with a church or faith, but located in a tolerant society. The secular capacity of a people needs to be tested at all levels. A secular State in an intolerant society is at best—and that too, not always—a progressive symbol. An intolerant State in a secular society is an aberration. Both situations can be volatile, breeding dangerous consequences for the future. Between these involuted extremes lie many tolerant and intolerant variations.

There is a considerable difference between a merely tolerant society and a secular one. Toleration may simply be an act of necessity—a concession rather than an acceptance of another's right. The 'toleration of difference' is writ large over many social and legal systems. The Hindu *dharmasastra* itself had no other choice but to co-exist with stubborn customs (*sadachara*) and conceded that *dharma* must change from *yuga* to *yuga*. Roman law distinguished *ius civille* (law for citizens) and *ius gentium* (law for others). Canonical law used the doctrine of *factum valet* to accept contrary customary practices as irredeemable facts from which there was no escape. Islamic jurists recognized the importance of *hadith* (tradition), *ijma* (consensus) and equity (*istihsan*) to mould the law.[4] Difference cannot be wished away. It has to be assimilated into law and social practice. We are still a considerable juristic distance away from an acceptance of the principle of equality which implicitly guarantees the right of people to be different, and not be discriminated against for being so. But although equality was an important breakthrough in the evolutionary quest for secularism, in some societies—not the least post-Civil War America—the acceptance of equality, too, may have been drawn out from necessitous circumstances. Toleration founded on necessity is concessionary in nature—not an entitlement, but a gift by the 'them' to the 'not-them'. Beyond such necessitous circumstances lies the domain of secularism. A truly secular State or society is more than one which tolerates difference. It is one in which the right to be different is recognized and even encouraged; and, perforce, one whose identity is not overtly or covertly over-identified with or appropriated by the people of any one faith, persuasion or community to the exclusion of others.

The diagram below attempts to typologize variations in secular and non-secular approvals to deal with differences between people.

Applicable both to States and civil society, this diagrammatic explanation does not necessarily seek to present a continuum along its two axes.[5] Thus, a State or society which is uncompromisingly fundamentalist and wholly intolerant (i.e. Box A/1) has no place in a chart on secularism. Equally, it may be argued that a regulatory and reformist State or society (as that configured in Column F) does not belong at the end of a continuum of increasing tolerance towards religion. Yet, it receives place at the end of that 'continuum' precisely because intimations of such reform are supposed to enable a consensus for change by democratic dialogue under relatively non-coercive conditions. The distinction between 'intolerant', 'tolerant', 'egalitarian' societies and those which guarantee 'religious freedom' does not merit further explanation. Some faiths require the positive help of the State to survive. Indeed, this is precisely how the institutions of the faith have been strengthened by land and other endowments by the State.[6] Along with respect for religious freedom and support for all faiths has also grown a new attitude to religious faiths which 'requires' them to respond—if not yield—to modernity, gender justice and reform. States and societies have been broadly classified as 'theocratic' and 'non-theocratic'. Theocratic societies have been broadly identified as those which are uncompromisingly 'fundamentalist', those with strong 'Church—State' links and those where such links may be formal and ceremonial. Non-theocratic States may be 'strictly neutral' and refuse to recognize religion in its dealings, or be generally supportive of all faiths but dealing with all religions

RELATIONSHIP BEWEEN RELIGION, SOCIETY AND STATE

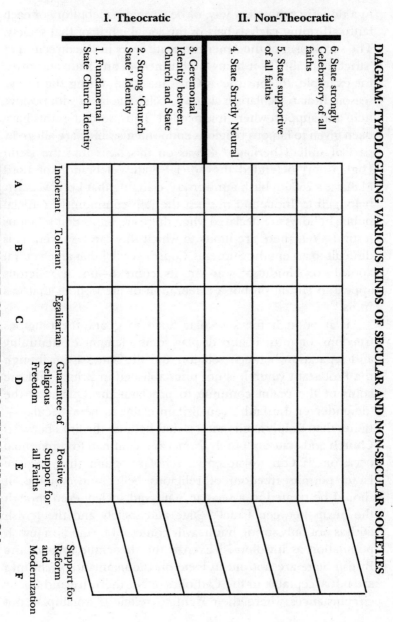

DIAGRAM: TYPOLOGIZING VARIOUS KINDS OF SECULAR AND NON-SECULAR SOCIETIES

I. Theocratic

II. Non-Theocratic

1. Fundamental State Church Identity
2. Strong 'Church State' Identity
3. Ceremonial Identity between Church and State
4. State Strictly Neutral
5. State supportive of all faiths
6. State strongly Celebratory of all faiths

A Intolerant
B Tolerant
C Egalitarian
D Guarantee of Religious Freedom
E Positive Support for all Faiths
F Support for Reform and Modernization

EXTENT AND NATURE OF ATTITUDE TO RELIGIOUS FREEDOM

in a non-discriminatory way, or be strongly celebratory of each faith, affirming each as part of the social fabric of that society. The secularism of the American State veers in the direction of 'strict neutrality'[7]—it being no business of any State authority, for example, to construct a Christmas tree during the festive season. Indian secularism claims to celebrate faiths with positive help and support where it is needed. Thus, several grants have been given to famous religious endowments which are allegedly part of India's heritage.[8] It was on this basis that the Delhi High Court defended the official State celebration of Lord Mahavir's 2500th birth anniversary, claiming that Lord Mahavir belonged to India and not just the Jain community.[9] Official public holidays are declared when there are important religious festivals. Yet, there are limits to which this can be taken. It is difficult to accept the Supreme Court's verdict that an electoral appeal to 'Hindutva' was—in its context—not a religious appeal to Hinduism but a celebration of the wonder that was India.[10]

Is it enough for a secular State to guarantee religious freedom, or must it also display some element of neutrality and separation between religion and the State? Even though the Protestant Church is not disestablished in Britain and the coins of the realm continue to proclaim the Queen as the 'defender of the faith', can Britain claim to be a 'secular'—rather than simply a tolerant—society because the links between Church and State are purely formal and confined to ceremonial occasions?[11] Can we accept a scholarly claim that because Israel permits freedom of religious belief and worship, it should be treated as a secular State and society even though the nexus between Israel's State and society and the Jewish faith is not only strong but heavily contested by the non-Jewish population as invidious?[12] Even if the theocratic links of the British State are not put in issue on the mainland, such links are not acceptable to the Catholics of Northern Ireland under circumstances where their right to religious worship is not curtailed and discrimination against them is on the decline. It is not just the nature of the link between Church and State that is important to determine the 'secular' credentials of any society or State, but also the manner and extent to which such links are viewed by those who live in that society. The more such links are critiqued, contested and rejected as unacceptable, the less plausible that society or State's claim to be considered a secular society or State.

All this is of considerable significance to contemporary Indian debates. In their best re-statement for a tolerant India, the Bharatiya Janata Party (BJP) and its fundamentalist allies project a future Indian *ram-rajya* (the perfect reign of Lord Rama) in which Hinduism would be the official religion of the realm but equality of treatment and opportunity and religious freedom would be guaranteed to all. Such a projection is heavily contested and discounted by minorities and secularists as both a false promise as well as unacceptable. India's Muslim population is almost a 100 million strong—making India's Muslim contingent the third largest in the world after Indonesia and Bangladesh. Its Sikh, Buddhist and Jain populations have important shrines in India. Indian Christianity falls in a unique class of its own. Hinduism itself is not a monolithic or homogenous faith but one which breaks into thousands of faiths and practices, each distinct form the other. The idea that India or the Indian State belongs exclusively to a group or entity called the Hindus, or any one sect or section of them, is eminently unacceptable. A secular India is not just one in which there is a genuine non-discriminatory toleration of the religions of others, but one which is not appropriated by one faith to the exclusion of others.

The colonial and imperial expansion of the western nations of the last four centuries was inextricably linked with an arrogant, racist and condescending attitude in which Christianity was politically transformed and appropriated to serve the purposes of empire. More than half the peoples of the world were liberated from imperialism on the basis of the right to self determination. It would be wholly unsatisfactory if the aftermath of that liberation was to clothe the 'liberated' nations with immutable religious identities. Using the same demand of the right to self determination, various peoples and groups within the new nation States could, and do, demand independence and the right to secede. The extent to which they succeed depends on the extent of support they get from the powerful nations of the world. Thus, German and European support had a lot to do with Croatia's demand for independence in 1991. If this pattern is followed any and everywhere, the map of the world would be in constant flux, at the mercy of those who are economically and politically strong enough to contrive change. States would be constantly partitioned amidst conditions of chaos. Going beyond the minimalist agenda that the rights of minorities should be protected, secularism is an alternative to the continuous politically inspired religious balkanization of the world. While such a re-drawing of the political map may be necessary in some cases, rather than continue the imperialist agenda of continuously re-writing the political map of the world along religious lines, the secular approach is to increase religious toleration, maximize religious and cultural diversity and preserve the neutrality of the State and governing processes of any society. Eventually, this must be a goal for the whole world—the practice of which must commence and take root in the sovereign states which compose the family of nations. The world and the State do not belong to any one group; nor should it be permitted to do so. In a choice between 'balkanization' and 'secularism', the latter is to be preferred.

It is very easy to view the future of world as a 'clash of religious civilizations'[13] and leave it at that. It is infinitely more difficult to preserve the pluralistic diversity of the world, increase religious tolerance and equality towards all faiths, and seek to separate Church and State from the dangerous propensities that have made the twentieth century one of the bloodiest centuries of all time. However, secularism is not a stagnant ideal, but a vector along which a society will move in its own way. Each society has to view its circumstances and evolve its own answers along this vector.

III

India's contemporary quest for secularism is firmly located in its post-colonial predicament following the aftermath of the empire. Too much can be made of the policy of 'divide and rule' of the British, too little may have been learnt from its implications. As trade gave way to empire and revenue collection to governance, the British devised a common administration to exact revenue and keep the peace; and a unified court system culminating in provincial High Courts in India and the Privy Council in London to provide for civil and criminal justice.[14] Convinced that they were dealing with a lesser 'oriental' people who needed to be introduced to Christianity, modernity and the 'accidental' way of life, the British burdened the Indian psyche with a self-reinforced bias against itself and its own ways.[15] To the burden of 'occidentalism' was added the influence of Benthamite utilitarianism.[16] Within the limits and needs of the empire, India soon became the laboratory of many modernist experiments.

From a legal point of view, a seemingly contradictory policy was developed. On the one hand, it was decided that it was more consistent with 'justice, equity and good conscience' that natives should be governed by their own personal and customary laws as recognized and modified by British Indian courts.[17] On the other hand, it seemed more convenient and progressive to create a uniform civil and criminal code by which all persons in India would be governed. The product of this all-embracing codification were the Anglo-Indian codes of the nineteenth century, which continue to govern Indians today; and will continue to do so into the next century.[18] However, while these codes covered civil and criminal procedure and the law relating to property, contract, trust and fiduciary and commercial relations, they kept clear of the personal law and social practices of the natives. Although several successful and unsuccessful attempts were made by the British to reform various invidious social practices (such as sati, dowry, child marriage, infanticide and the like), such social reform was later left to be devised by Indians for themselves. In time, the British Raj settled for a holding operation to keep the 'imperial' peace; and amended their criminal law and censorship to enable this.[19] This tri-focal legacy—to (i) recognize and give effect to traditional laws, practices and customs, (ii) develop a powerful system of modern law courts and administration and (iii) assume a superior reformist posture within the framework of a 'holding' operation to keep the peace—continues to ambiguate the policies of India's present rulers.

If the law of British India entrenched identities, the policies of the Raj politicized them. As the movement to gain 'independence' gathered ground, it was more conducive to the British to give a political identity to various communities by promising them separate representation. This began by 'communal' nomination to government councils under the Indian Councils Act 1892 and continued till India was partitioned in 1947. A policy of 'separate representation', founded on distinct and 'separate electorates', was readily included in the Indian Councils Act 1909. Once the ball was set rolling, Indians themselves negotiated with each other in these terms. The Lucknow pact of 1916 accepted a division of spoils on the basis of communal electorates. By 1928, the Nehru report's proposal of joint rather than separate electorates was rejected by leading Muslim politicians. Despite Gandhi's

44

interventions, the Communal Award of 1932 was accepted as the basis for the Government of India Act 1935 whereby separate electorates were guaranteed to Muslims, Europeans, Sikhs, Indian Christians and Anglo-Indians.[20] The politicization of religious communities was complete. The leaders of various communities, as indeed the communities themselves, were drawn into the vortex of claiming political power for themselves.[21] The British knew that what they were doing was wrong. The Montagu–Chelmsford Report protested that such an approach was invidious. In 1930, the Indian Statutory Commission (better known as the Simon Commission) recalled the words of the Montagu–Chelmsford Report which they paraphrased as follows:

> Such communal electorates . . . were opposed to history . . . (T)hey perpetuated class division . . . (T)hey stereotyped existing relations . . . (and) constituted a very serious hindrance to the development of the self governing principle . . .[22]

Yet, the lessons of history gave way to the politics of empire. No number of speeches, resolutions and protests were of any avail. The moving finger of imperial politics had written; and, having writ moved on. It is idle to speculate on the counter-factual possibilities of history to ask whether the Cabinet plan of a quasi-confederal government was workable or whether it was Nehru or Jinnah who irritated 'Partition' into being.[23] One thing was clear: the politicization of religious communities paved the way for new kinds of warring demands which often did not admit to consensus solutions or compromise. It was under those brittle circumstances, and under the shadow of the cataclysmic events of Partition, that the Constituent Assembly drafting India's Constitution was confronted with the task of resolving the highly charged demands of overtly politicized communities into a Constitution. Since tragedy stalked the events of Partition, the tone of the demands was initially less full-throated than it might have been. Yet, the undercurrent behind the demands was comparatively clear. The minorities sought a constitutional compensation for their loyalty. This 'compensation' consisted of comprehensive guarantees to protect the individual and group rights of the minorities.[24]

Although the Constituent Assembly is correctly revered for its insight, pragmatism and sagacity, it had a seamier side which has been glossed over by those who have written about its deliberations; and, no less, by the small cabal which guided its deliberations. If the Drafting Committee was cheekily referred to as the 'Drifting Committee', it was to express the angst with which some members viewed it.[25] Looked at from this angle, its deliberations were like a political auction in which bids were made, accepted, rejected or ignored. At the very initial stage when three drafts were made of the proposed chapter on Fundamental Rights, K.M. Munshi's draft was skilfully prioritized over the Ambedkar and Harnam Singh versions. The record of the Constituent Assembly displays a tussle between many factions. The results of the compromises are self evident from the text of the Constitution.[26] Proceeding from the universal sublime to the strangely particular, the religious freedom articles contain a specific provision that '(t)he wearing and carrying of *kirpans* shall be deemed to be included in the profession of the Sikh religion'. The same Article throws open 'Hindu religious institutions of a public character to all classes and sections of Hindus' and sweepingly clubs the 'Sikh, Jaina (and) . . . Buddhist religion(s) . . .' as 'part of the Hindu religion'.[27] The Swami Narayans were justly annoyed with the Supreme Court's attempt to declare that they were in fact Hindus even though they protested that they were not![28] The Constitution abolishes 'untouchability' and makes it punishable as an offence. The 'socialist' lobby was able to include the prohibition of *begaar* or forced labour as enforceable fundamental rights, but the rest of the socialist agenda was relegated to the unenforceable Directive Principles. Unable to resolve the hotly contested issue of cow slaughter, a compromise was evolved, that this issue be housed in the chapter containing the Directive Principles of State Policy which were unenforceable in a court of law but allegedly important to the business of the nation.[29] A similar exercise was undertaken over the vexed issue of the 'uniform civil code' which, in the Indian context, is concerned solely with the reform of personal laws; and, more often than not, is in our times politically pointed in the direction of the Muslims to embarrass them over the reform of Muslim Personal Law.[30] It was only on 16 June 1949 that the contentious issues over separate or joint communal electorates were resolved by declaring that there would be a common electoral roll. But, whilst special electorates were abolished for the imperially selected Muslims, Christians and Sikh communities, such electorates were retained for the Anglo-Indians, Scheduled Castes (SC) and Scheduled Tribes (ST).[31] Provisions were also made for ameliorative programmes for the SC and ST; but, as if to concede the caste based demands of the 'Other Backward Castes' (OBCs), the possibility of preferential treatment for the OBCs—who were primarily identified on the basis of caste—was left open.[32] Years later, the demand of the OBCs was politicized in the 1980s to wholly alter and de-stabilize Indian politics.[33] At the end of the Constitution making process, the 'minority' faiths were not entirely appeased even though cultural and linguistic demands of the 'Urdu' speaking people and others as well as the autonomy of the Christian schools were duly protected as enforceable cultural and educational rights. Special areas—including Kashmir—were demarcated for special treatment.[34] What emerged from these constitutional endeavours was an accommodating secular compromise at a time when—in the aftermath of Partition— such a compromise seemed improbable. Today, even the possibility of such compromises evolving is doubtful.

47

Contemporary India has not been able to satisfactorily quell disputes over a medieval mosque which was ignominiously destroyed in 1992.[35] If India were to start a new Constitution-making process afresh today, it is doubtful if a common text would emerge.

The Constitution makers had done well. It would be a tremendous disservice to their efforts to point to their compromise solutions without acknowledging the overall secular design of the Constitution which can be summarized as articulating three salient principles: (i) First, and foremost, is the principle of 'religious freedom' which expansively covers not just the right to religious thought and belief, but every aspect of the faith including its beliefs and rituals as also freedom from discrimination on grounds, *inter alia*, of religion, race, caste, place of birth or gender.[36] (ii) The second secular principle of 'celebratory neutrality' and the depoliticization of religion underlying the Constitution was devised to create a participatory secular State which would neutrally assist and celebrate all faiths in addition to generally not discriminating amongst them. Accordingly, there was nothing to prevent the State from giving financial and other assistance to all faiths, but no persons could be compelled to pay taxes which were specifically appropriated 'for the promotion or maintainence of any particular religion or religious denomination'. Such assistance could also be given to religious denominational schools who, in turn, could not then compel anyone to partake in religious instruction or discriminatingly, refuse to admit persons not of that denomination.[37] (iii) The third salient feature of India's secular State was social welfare and reform, with an accent on a 'regulatory and reformative justice'. The Constitution was self-professedly regulatory and reformative in nature. Apart from the usual restraints that religious freedom could be curtailed on grounds of 'public order, health and morality' and that the 'economic, financial, political or other secular activity' of a religion could be regulated, there was a strong specific and general reformatory element. The Constitution specifically permitted the State to provide for 'social welfare and reform'; and, more specifically, abolished untouchability, threw open all Hindu, Jaina and Sikh temples for all castes and sections of that community, prohibited discrimination by the State and those financially assisted by, or linked to, the State on grounds of religion; and, generally pointed in a reformatory direction in the matter of gender justice, the uniform civil code and cow slaughter—by placing these and other issues in the Directive Principles of State Policy.[38]

What do we make of these three principles underlying the secularism of the Indian Constitution? Are they not contradictory? Is not the 'third' principle (which espouses the regulation and reform of religion) contrary to the 'first' principle of religious freedom? And, if the 'third' principle unfurls its agenda of regulation and reform, will this agenda not run foul of the 'second' principle of 'celebratory neutrality' towards all faiths ? If all faiths are to be celebrated, which parts of the same faiths are to be undermined to enable regulation and reform? Jumbled up as opposing and contradictory, these questions can never yield satisfactory answers. The initial pride of place must be given to the 'first' principle so as to maximize genuine claims to religious freedom, ensure equality of all faiths and increase and expand toleration towards plural diversity. But this 'first' principle does not stand on its own to the exclusion of all else. It has never been anybody's case that religious freedom should be unlimited in its scope and design. The usual 'plimsoll line' approach indicating the limits below which no faith can go is the time-honoured formula of 'public order, health and morality'. The contours of such a formula are—in our times—usually eventually determined by judges. However, in the Indian context, the Constitution makers specifically empowered the State to generally ordain or assist in the reform of many unjust religiously sanctioned social practices, customs and laws. This is the essence of the regulation and reform oriented 'third' principle which was intended to be much more cautious in its emphasis as it was wide in its empowerment. The 'third' principle did not represent some demoniac deification of modernity which would eclipse all religions into obsolescence.[39] Both State and society were enjoined to develop a consensus for social change. The 'third' principle of secularism was certainly not devised to arm political Hindu fundamentalists to chastise Muslims for not making their law 'gender just', or vice versa. It was expected that a sense of fraternity would animate the interpretation of the 'third' principle and guide its implementation.

India's Constitution was an elegant response to its sensitive and somewhat unparalleled post-colonial solution. The guarantee of religious freedom was broad, but included an invitation to evolve a consensus for reform, while placing the Indian State in a positively neutral position to benignly provide support for and celebrate all faiths.

IV

Although it is fashionable to criticize Prime Minister Nehru for the many ills that plague us today, in 1950 there were few doubts that the way forward was to transform Indian society through planned development. The goals of this projected change were technological transformation, modernization, economic growth and poverty alleviation through a powerful State machinery to liberate people from the bondage of their past to fulfil their future 'tryst with destiny'.[40] Nehru was not really saying anything new. This was happening all over the world. Modernity was held up as the Holy Grail, indicting Indians as others for lagging behind.[41] 'Salvation' was alleged to lie in instrumenting change through a powerful model of 'law and development'. New laws would replace old traditions.

New bureaucracies would create plans. The people for whom such plans were to be made were expected to do their bit and change their lifestyle, social practices and attitudes. This is not the place to enter into controversies over the naïve instrumentalism[42] of this approach or its crippling effect in forcing Indians to look down upon themselves. All this was avidly accepted by India's 'western' educated middle class who thought they had an edge over others because they were already halfway there. Neither Nehru nor anyone else thought that these prescriptions meant—or could ever mean—that India would give up its colourful diversity. But, there was a fear that casteism, communalism and traditional linguistic and other identities could tear India apart. The pain of Partition was too fresh to elude memory.[43] No less, the new Republic of India had brought people from various Provinces and Princely States together into a single political entity after a very long— if not the first—time. Consequently, a broad and strongly reformist and vastly over-written Indian secularism may have been brought into play to declare 'war' on all or any forms of divisiveness.

The reality was more forbidding than the posture. Although Nehru made strong Cassandra-like warnings about the fissiparous tendencies that plagued India's future, yet his discourse on 'change' was democratic—seeking to move towards reform through consensus. Nehru's government first tackled those areas of reform directly ordained by the Constitution (e.g. the abolition of untouchability) and then moved on towards the wider goal of creating a more integrated and modern society. When a demand was made to create the state of Andhra Pradesh on a linguistic basis, Nehru strongly opposed it—ostensibly because it would lead to the balkanization of India, but no less because it was in respect of the Nizam's dominions in Hyderabad where a strong communist movement was gaining ground. Yet, Nehru succumbed to this demand eventually, realizing that a claim of linguistic diversity strengthened rather than weakened the polity.[44] When the Hindu Code Bill ripened for its final rites of passage through Parliament, Nehru's government encountered strong resistance; and backed off to enact an incomplete codification of Hindu law in which the property relations of the joint family were left relatively untouched.[45] Although various Congress state governments of Nehru's era set about to control religious endowments, this was done with a lightness of touch. The social reform legislation of the period used criminal law techniques and penal measures to exact social change. It had too many design faults to be wholly effective.[46] Nehru's regime extolled diversity but was fearful of too much of it. Its policies had inadvertently, willy nilly, adopted a strong seemingly uncompromising reformist posture which was later misunderstood, attacked and ridiculed as pseudo-secularist.

Nehru's approach to secularism was a political response to confront India's contemporary challenges. Proud of India's diversity which he portrayed in his *Discovery of India* and *Glimpses of World History*, Nehru had not even imagined that this plural richness would be put at risk by his more general project to modernize India.[47] India was both colourfully diverse as well as modern. Any concept of secularism had to be built around this vision. It was for the courts to develop a juridical concept of secularism and define its content. The Supreme Court was already at loggerheads with Nehru's government over political censorship and land reform.[48] At first, it also appeared to be resistant to some of the other initiatives of the government of the day. In 1951, it refused to allow a distribution of seats along caste lines to masquerade as affirmative action.[49] In 1954, in the *Srirur Math* and connected cases, Justice B.K. Mukerjea, an expert on the law relating to Hindu religious endowments, tried to give the widest possible meaning to freedom of religion to protect all the essential practices of a faith, striking down insensitively intrusive regulatory provisions.[50] But this 'essential practices' test was double-edged. It was left to the court to decide what an 'essential practice' was, and who could claim to be its custodian. After some sensitive decisions, including upholding a religion's power to ex-communicate its adherents,[51] many questionable decisions emerged from the Court. In this, a leading role was played by Justice Gajendragadkar who was determined to extend the regulatory control of the State over religious endowments and practices. Without abandoning the 'essential practices' test, the courts—especially the Supreme Court—deprived the Khadims of the Durgah Committee of Ajmer many of their traditional rights,[52] refused to accept the rights of those traditionally linked with the Nathdwara temple in Rajasthan,[53] threw open both temples and mosques for worship, told the Swaminarayans that they were, in fact, Hindus even as they protested they were not,[54] permitted the exclusion of non-Gowda Saraswat brahmins from certain ceremonies of a public temple,[55] proclaimed that the Jains had lost their right to manage a temple which had been taken over by the Raja of Udaipur and enabled its statutory takeover,[56] made the role and functions of the traditional *archakas* of a temple purely secular in nature,[57] informed the Muslims that, on the basis of the Court's reading of the texts and the advice of a Hindu pandit, 'cow sacrifice' was not an essential practice of the Muslim faith,[58] pronounced that the 'tandava' dance was not a significant part of the faith of the Anand Margis,[59] found that the practice of *pinda* and *shradh* were integral to the Hindu faith,[60] and stated that praying in a mosque was not crucial to the Muslim faith because they could pray anywhere, 'even in the open'.[61] A similar pattern followed in the Court decisions on State control of schools and colleges run by religious denominations.[62] Slowly, but surely, such institutions have been brought under a rigorous State and statutory control. At times, the Court has been called upon to diffuse difficult situations such as those concerning the shifting of

Muslim graves[63] or cow slaughter,[64] the right to proselyte a faith or to resolve the aftermath of the destruction of the Babri Masjid in 1992.[65] Some of its solutions—including the reasoning underlying them—have been questionable, insensitive in their formulation and excessive in permitting more regulation of religious institutions and practices than should be expected in a secular society which guarantees religious freedom.

Although State control of Hindu religious endowments can be traced back to a British formula of 1863 by which the custodians of these endowments were declared to be 'trustees' and the State had the limited rectificatory 'default power' to issue instructions, or temporarily take over, where there was mismanagement of the institutions and defalcation of funds.[66] However, since 1950, there has been an increasing tendency in India to take over important temples and run them through bureaucrats and statutory boards, whilst including some of the adherents of the denomination in the management of the endowment. The most widely publicized among them was Governor Jagmohan's takeover of the temple at Vaishno Devi in Kashmir.[67] The 'Jagmohan' model—if it can be called that—is defended on the basis that the State manages such institutions much better than those traditionally associated with them. On this basis, the famous Vishwanath Temple at Varanasi has also been placed under a Board. In a series of recent judgments,[68] the Supreme Court has not just condoned such takeovers, but defended them as being consistent with the true interpretation of Hinduism. What is happening is not the temporary intervention of regulatory control by the State. Religious endowments are being nationalized on an extensive scale. The affairs of the Sikh community were placed within a statutory framework in 1925, with awkward results.[69] Several statutes of various States have brought many religious and charitable trusts and societies under State ownership and strict bureaucratic control.[70] The concept of State run religious institutions sits uneasily with either the idea of religious freedom or the concept of a positive and supportive secular State. The strength and continuity of religious faiths rests on such faiths creating viable institutions which keep the faith alive and responsive to pressures, demands and challenges from both within and without the faith. No doubt, crooks, thieves and layabouts have lumpenized many religious institutions; however, it is not for the State to take over institutions, but for the communities to find the appropriate answers.

But if the regulation of religious institutions has been one part of the State programme, reform has been the other. One important area of reform has been the issue of the uniform civil code.[71] Many of the religious personal laws of various communities are unjust and discriminatory—especially to women. What is to be done about them? Involved here are delicate issues of marriage, divorce, children, guardianship, adoption, succession and the multiple ownership of many forms of property. One possible solution was to codify all personal laws and merge them under a uniform civil code. A small step in this direction was to provide a 'secular' law of marriage, divorce, guardianship and succession which could be opted for by adherents of any or every faith.[72] 'This preliminary optional solution' is not enough. Society and its pressures take over. The social status quo remains. The second alternative is the 'Fundamental Rights' (or the Article 13) solution. If we accept that 'personal laws' are laws (under Article 13 of the Constitution), they have to be subjected to rigorous scrutiny under the Fundamental Rights chapter. Thus, if personal laws are discriminatory to women, they would have to be tested against the doctrine of equality; and then struck down if found to be discriminatory or unreasonable. But this 'Fundamental Rights' (or Article 13) solution is pre-eminently a court-oriented solution, leaving it to the judges to determine what is fair and what should be eliminated from the personal laws as unfair. Unfortunately, the judges have lost courage and backed away from the 'Fundamental Right' (or Article 13) solution. Finding technical refuge in the impossible distinction that 'personal laws' were not like other 'customary laws' and therefore outside the remit of the Fundamental Rights chapter,[73] the courts shied away from being lumbered with the responsibility of making personal laws fair, just and non-discriminatory. This takes us to the third or 'statutory' solution which seeks to reform all or any of the personal laws by enacting legislation to that effect. Few religions like to be told that they need to be reformed—still less by outsiders. Perhaps that is why the goal of 'personal law' reform was more neutrally described in Article 44 of the Constitution in terms of achieving a 'uniform civil code' (UCC). But reference to the 'uniform civil code' complicates rather than clarifies the issue. It grows out of a nineteenth century dream to codify all laws in the manner of the later Justinian of Roman law or the Code Napoleon. But codification may simply be consolidatory rather than reformative. A reformative uniform civil code of personal laws does not just require all personal laws to be stated in the form of a statute, but seeks to radically transform— and not just rewrite—them. Such a goal sets up a competition amongst personal laws, with the State asking: 'Which is the fairest of them all?' Nor is the task of finding a common denominator from all of them any easier. The British Raj made an elaborate codification of all but the personal laws. After some evangelical attempts to reform some practices such as sati, *thugee*, infanticide or child marriage, the British administration backed off—acceding to native Indian requests to change the Muslim law relating to *waqfs* or the Hindu law on the Gains of Learning to correct unacceptable decisions of the Privy Council.[74] It was under pressure from Muslims that the government enabled the *shariat* to displace the application of customary laws in certain areas in 1937;[75] even though such support was not fully forthcoming for the legislation which made 'dissolution of marriages' possible under circumstances outside the *shariat*.[76] Under the British regime, tentative steps were taken to initiate the enactment of a reformist Hindu Code. After Independence, the legislation to create a Hindu Code was confronted by political controversy. Eventually a truncated 'code' was enacted, amidst opposition, in 1955-56: this dealt with the laws related to marriage, adoption and maintainence, guardianship and succession.[77] But, the law relating to the joint family remained intact. So India today portrays the awkward position that a woman can be prime minister of India but not the head of a Hindu joint family! But, if the 'uniform civil code' was once a serious constitutional objective, it has now been trivialized into becoming a tragic farce. Politics has taken over. Hindu politicians, who are not really concerned about personal law reform, use the idea of the uniform civil code to chastise Muslims for not emulating the Hindu example. The accusation concentrates on 'sexual' matters; and, in particular, the right of the Muslim male to have four wives and divorce them at will. That Muslim jurisprudence is a lot more delicate in its response to such issues is overlooked. The cause celebre came when the Supreme Court subjected Muslim spouses to the 'secular' law of maintainence in the Criminal Procedure Code[78] and Rajiv Gandhi's Congress government promptly responded with a separate legislation exclusively for Muslims.[79] This initiative was seen as preferential treatment for Muslims and inimical to secularism. Matters became more highly charged than necessary. In the end, the solution was awkward, but not entirely unsatisfactory. The issue of the 'uniform civil code' will remain with us for a long time. The political arm of the State is as paralysed as the powers that control it. The judiciary refuses to be drawn into finding a solution. It is for the various communities to devise appropriate reforms for their adherents under non-contentious conditions. When they are persuaded to do so, they will, no doubt, be aware that they are free to draw inspiration from their own inventive and rich traditions as well as those of others. But politics has perversely blocked and obviated such a simple solution. As long as the issue of the 'uniform civil code' remains a Hindu weapon to beat the Muslim and other communities into embarrassment, no further progress can take place.

Over the last twenty years of this century, India's politics has been intensely communalized along religious lines. This is an offshoot of the general 'lumpenization' of all aspects of India's polity and social life generally, whereby, according to the official Vohra Report, governance has been taken over by hoodlums—no less disguised as politicians as anyone else.[80] It is these lumpen elements in various social groups and political parties who have whipped up Hindu sentiment as political emotion. Once in power, governments elected on such platforms have been as inept and corrupt as any other. But a politically nurtured communalism has gained ground as a tactic—exploiting every possible event as an issue to excite and exact support. The story of the Babri Masjid, which is alleged to be built on Lord Rama's birthplace, is only one such story which resulted in the four-century-old Masjid being razed to the ground in 1992, with the connivance of the BJP in power in the state of Uttar Pradesh and the Congress in power at Delhi. Even after the Masjid was destroyed, Prime Minister Narsimha Rao established a pro-Hindu status quo which was unfortunately validated and blessed by a split decision of the Supreme Court.[81] Whilst the Supreme Court has made brave declarations on secularism and validated the imposition of Emergency Rule on BJP state governments after the chaos that followed in those states, following the destruction of the Masjid,[82] it has been skilful, but irritatingly vague, in its non-elucidation of the meaning of secularism.[83] Meanwhile, in 1998-99, attacks were made on Christians in Gujarat, Orissa, Maharashtra and other states.[84] While commissions and committees have been appointed to investigate the problem, most governments and political parties have been slow to defend the minorities for fear of electoral repercussions.[85] No State can be neutral or aloof in these circumstances. To do so is itself violative of the most elementary principles of toleration in a civilized society. Populism of this nature which feeds on religious mal-sentiment gets caught in its own frenzy to excite awkward situations into brinkmanship and violence.

V

'Secularism' has been declared part of the basic structure of the Indian Constitution and was inserted along with socialism into the Preamble of the Constitution during the Emergency in 1976.[86] But what does it mean? We must return—as inevitably as we started—to the various debates on Indian secularism. Some doubt whether it exists. Others proclaim that it is no more than a spurious invitation to an over-rationalized modernity.[87] Others ask: 'What is wrong with this kind of modernity?'[88] After all, the resistance to modernity itself is born out of the discourse on modernity. It has been argued that Indian secularism clumsily rests on an imperial concept of communities which is outmoded, subversive and irrelevant.[89] Conversely, a plea had been made to retain a framework of communities[90] between, amongst and around those for whom an egalitarian justice must be created. Indian secularism has been found wanting as not effecting a proper separation of State from Church when compared with its American counterparts.[91] If some governments and political parties have been criticized for not protecting innocent religious communities; others have been assailed for being over-partisan in extending help to disempowered minorities for political reasons. The discussions on secularism continue—more often than not as unsavoury exchanges rather than in the spirit of democratic dialogue.

Yet, more than simply a word which invites esoteric academic discourse, secularism is an important aspect of the discourse on power on States and society in India. To begin with, it has a special significance as a response to the problems of post-colonial India. The makers of India's Constitution did not intend secularism to be seen as a modernizing whirlwind—sweeping away all 'irrational' beliefs and practices that lay in its path. Nor did they intend to create a State which stood wholly aloof from the rich cultural diversity of India. Moulded as a positive and participatory entity, India's secular State was designed to celebrate all faiths and also enjoined to eliminate some specially invidious practices sanctioned by the religion in question. The larger questions of social reform had been left open to be worked out as they emerged. The carnage that followed Partition, when social fervour was diverted to communal savagery, is a reminder of what has happened, and can happen. We live in no less unsettled times. New fundamentalist pressures have tried to cash in on and exploit raw communal nerves for political, social and economic advancement. The BJP's White Paper on Ayodhya[92] declared that some kind of historical revenge was due to Muslims. And if such a stance is taken, can the Buddhists complain about Hinduism? What form will such a revenge take? Will it be the destruction of 'Muslim' monuments? Will Muslims be asked to leave? If so, where will they go? Or will the Muslims, along with many other communities in India, remain second class citizens within a Hindu India? Or, will India be partitioned again along politically communalized religious lines? Where will all this end? Abjuring such derisive and vicious alternatives, the Indian answer seems to lie within a yet-to-be-fully-explored concept of 'secularism' which goes beyond toleration to guarantee equality and freedom of religion; and to deny the appropriation of State and society by any one particular faith. This is only a framework requiring many inconsistencies and contradictions to be worked out.

However, India's quest for the basis of a viable secularism cannot just be located in the tawdry politics of our time. Not just a nation-State, the subcontinent of India houses a complex civilization, with a dazzling array of cultures and traditions. It is of a kind that does not exist anywhere else in the world. Like Europe, it has many languages. Like the rest of the world, it houses many faiths and traditions. Yet it eludes description precisely because it is large and contains multitudes. How does one script a Constitution for a civilization? Or devise principles of governance for a singularly unique and varied people? It is like devising a Constitution for the world. The 'concept' of secularism as it is evolving in India is not just an answer to the problems created by an imperial legacy, but responds more globally to the predicament of a veritable civilization which eludes self-definition. The three ingredients of India's secularism—namely religious freedom, celebratory neutrality and reformatory justice—have a universal significance. If there be a Xanadu, the road to Xanadu must surely lead to peace and justice, of which secularism is a part. In a shrinking world, all societies have to strive to be secular; but some societies, like ours, have to be more secular than others. And, in a sense, they lead the way for the rest.

Notes

1. In this essay, I am not really concerned with the creation of new 'syncretic' faiths which are abstracted from the existing one [see C. Stewart and R. Shaw (ed.) *Syncretism, Anti Syncretism*, London, 1994]. India is replete with genuine examples of such abstractions. Akbar's attempts to create a new faith (*Din-i-elahi*) is a political—as opposed to a social—example of the attempt to create such a syncretic faith. But, syncretic faiths are not just born out of a conscious desire to 'sink differences'; they also emerge as practices of various faiths merge with each other.
2. The phrase 'Janus faced' is taken from D. Washbrook, 'Law State

and Agrarian Society in Colonial India,' *Modern Asian Studies* 7 (1981). But I am suggesting that such a 'double' faced system of laws does not just exist in colonial societies, but all societies where a 'law' or legal system seeks to simultaneously speak for its political masters in the language of justice. This contradiction creates 'indeterminacy' in the law to leave open the possibility of the 'rule of law' being what E.P. Thomson (in *Whigs and Hunters*, London, 1975) calls a 'mixed blessing' to become the possible situs of struggle.

3. I take this expanded view of law from B. Malinowski's *Crime and Custom in a Savage Society*, London, 1959, p. 55, 67-8. India's *dharmasastra* is very much a 'social law' supported and enforced by a range of social mechanisms.

4. On the *dharmasastra* see generally R. Lingat, *The Classical Law of India*, Berkeley, 1973, p. 176-206, on custom and the changing nature of law; on custom in the *dharmasastra* see also P.V. Kane, *History of the Dharmasastra*, Poona, 1941, Vol. III, p. 825-55; on the doctrine of *factum valet* see J.D.M. Derrett, 'Factum Valet: Adventures of a Maxim', *International and Comparative Law Quarterly* 7 (ICLQ) (1958) p. 280-302. On the development and sources of Muslim law see J. Schacht, *An Introduction to Islamic Law*, Oxford, 1964; N.J. Coulson, *A History of Islamic Law* Edinburgh, 1964; *Mulla's Principles of Mahomeddan Law*, Bombay, 1994, p. 22-24.

5. Some may—as we shall see—demur that religious freedom cannot co-exist with a reforming modernism (column F). Nor, arguably, should the State distort faiths by positively supporting all faiths (column E). By the same logic the most secular State may not be celebratory in nature (column 6). I have indicated my sense of the range; and deliberately placed column F on a differently angled trajectory.

6. Grants have played a great role in the development of all faiths throughout the world. In a secular State, grants would have to be given evenhandedly to all. This could become a difficult exercise. Since 1950, Indian dispensations in this regard have been sporadic rather than systematic. Note, the converse situation of religious institutions being asked to pay for their upkeep by the State or to charge pilgrims a 'fee' (see Ram Chandra v. West Bengal AIR 1966 Cal. 164; Modi Das v. Sahi AIR 1959 SC 942) on the basis

that such a levy is for a secular activity.

7. The concept of 'neutrality' stems from the non-'establishment' clause in the American Constitution. See generally L. Tribe, *The Constitutional Protection of Individual Rights*, New York, 1976, p. 812-885; G.R. Stone, Louis M. Seidman, Cass R. Sunstein and M. Tushnet, *Constitutional Law*, New York, 1996, p. 1531-1626.

8. Grants have been given for the restoration of religious monuments which suffered riot damage (see K. Raghunath v. Kerala AIR 1974 Ker. 48). But even outside the exigencies of riots, restorative or renovative grants have been made to temples, such as Lord Jaganatha's temple in Orissa (see Bira Kishore Deb v. Orissa AIR 1975 Orissa 8).

9. Suresh Chandra v. Union of India AIR 1975 Delhi 162.

10. Ramesh Yeshwant Prabhu v. Prabhakar (1996) 1 SCC 130.

11. For interesting examples which tax British ingenuity see S.H. Bailey, D.J. Harris and B.L. Jones, *Civil Liberties: Cases and Materials*, London, 1995, p. 578-612.

12. See Gary J. Jacobson, 'Three. Modern Examples of Secular Constitutional Development: India, Israel and the United States,' *Studies in American Political Development* 10 (1996) p. 1-58.

13. Samuel P. Huntington, *The Clash of Civilizations and the Remaking of the World Order*, New York, 1996.

14. On the 'modernization' of the Indian legal and administrative system and its displacement of the traditional system see M. Galanter, *Law and Society in Modern India*, Oxford, 1989, p. 15-53, 92-100. By this process the personal law was transformed to suit 'modern' 'imperial' needs [on which see R. Dhavan, 'Dharmasastra and Modern Indian Society: A Preliminary Exploration,' *Journal of the Indian Law Institute* 34 (1992) p. 515-540].

15. Cf. James G. Carrier (ed.) *Occidentalism: Images of the West*, Oxford, 1995.

16. For a glimpse of the Benthamite influance see Eric Stokes, *The English Utilitarians in India*, Oxford, 1957.

17. On the origins and use of this formula in India see J.D.M. Derrett, 'Justice, Equity and Good Conscience in India,' *Bom L.R.* 64 (Journal) (1962) 129 and 145.

18. See Whitely Stokes, *The Anglo India Codes: Volume I, Substantive Law; Volume II: Procedural Law*, Oxford, 1887.

19. Once again, the 'rule of law' came into play to project a 'neutral' image of colonial aims. Under the aegis of keeping the peace, a powerful system to control public order and impose censorship was built up—especially to deal with religious tension and to put down dissent (see R. Dhavan, *Only the Good News: On the Law of Censorship in India*, Delhi, 1987, p. 25-91, 274-339. On British attempts at social reform through law and Indian reactions see C.H. Heimsath, *Indian Nationalism and Hindu Social Reform*, Princeton, 1964.)

20. For the constitutional background see B. Shiva Rao, *The Framing of India's Constitution: A Study*, Delhi, 1968, p. 459-472.

21. Indeed, it has been powerfully argued by Benedict Anderson (in *Imagined Communities*, London, 1991) that 'nationalism'—as we know it—is a modern phenomenon, using modern methods to create 'imagined' communities by drawing inspiration from the past. *A fortiorari*, 'communal' identities flow from similar efforts (see G. Pandey, *The Construction of Communalism in Colonial North India*, Delhi 1990). Both Muslim and Hindu identities came to discover and use 'nationalism' for self definition [see C. Jaffrelot, *The Hindu Nationalist Movement in India*, New York, 1996; Mushirul Hasan (ed.) *Islam: Communities and the Nation: Muslim Identities in South Asia and Beyond*, Delhi, 1998, and more generally the many views in G.D. Sontheimer and H. Kulke (ed.) *Hinduism Reconsidered*, Delhi, 1987]. This is not to detract from the wider argument that 'nationalist' thinking is inextricably linked to colonial discourse (see P. Chatterjee, *Nationalist Thought and the Colonial World*, London, 1986).

22. *Indian Statutory Commission* (known as the Simon Commission) (1930) Cmn. 3568; Vol. 1 pr. 147 p. 137.

23. This controversy was awakened with fervour with Ayesha Jalal's *The Sole Spokesman, Jinnah: the Muslim League and the 'Demand for Pakistan'*, Cambridge, 1985. This thesis finds support from a distinguished Indian jurist (see H.M. Seervai, *Partition of India: Legend and Reality*, Bombay, 1989). What principle of 'causation' do we use to analyse these events? The best that can be said is that Nehru did not create the situation that led to Partition, but may have blundered in his tactical diplomacy.

24. See B. Shiva Rao (*supra* n. 21)—particularly Chapter 25 at p. 741-780(on minorities). Indeed, many matters shuffled back and

forth from the 'Fundamental Rights' Committee to the 'Minorities' Committee, and vice versa (*infra* n. 26).

25. Comment of N. Ahmed: (1949) XI Constitutional Assembly Debates 973 (25 Nov)—see generally R. Dhavan, *The Constitutional Assembly and Human Rights* (forthcoming).

26. See B. Shiva Rao (*supra* n. 21), p. 107-118 (on how the Constituent Assembly worked) and p. 257-281 (on the discussion on religious and minority rights in the Assembly). More generally, on the practice exploited out of the constitutional text see R. Dhavan, 'Religious Freedom in India,' *American Journal of Comparative Law* 25 (1987), p. 209-254.

27. see *Constitution of India* art. 25 (2), Explanation 1 and II.

28. Yagnapurushdasji v Muldas AIR 19 66 SC 1119; and note the comments of M. Galanter, *Law and Society in Modern India*, Delhi, 1989, p. 237-258; J.D.M. Derrett, 'The Definition of a Hindu,' 2 *S.C.J. Journal*) (1966) 67.

29. See *Constitution of India*, Art. 48 (on animal husbandry and cow slaughter). The status of the Directive Principles of State policy is that they are unenforceable in a court of law but fundamental to the governance of the nation (see Art. 37 of the Constitution). In the fifties, the court merely used the Directive Principles as an aid to interpretation. After the Fundamental Rights case [Kesavananda v. State of Kerala (1973) 4 SCC 225], their presence has been greatly emphasized to include some of them as part of the enforceable right to 'life and liberty' of the Constitution. By this route, the Directive Principle on 'universal education' till the age of fourteen years has been rendered enforceable. However, the controversial Directive Principles dealing with cow slaughter (Article 46) or the uniform civil code (Article 44) have been less emphatically stressed for judicial implementation.

30. *Constitution of India*, Article 44.

31. See *Constitution of India*, Article 325 (on the general electoral roll) and Articles 330-334 (on reserved seats for Scheduled Castes, Scheduled Tribes and Anglo-Indians—initially for ten years, but decennially extended till the year 2000 AD).

32. See Constitution of India Article 15 (3), (4); 16 (3) (4) (4A), 335 of the Constitution.

33. A great controversy started in 1990 on reservations for jobs and posts in the Central Government. This affirmative action was

resisted by the competing privileged. Riots ensued, resulting in the fall of Prime Minister V.P. Singh's government and the famous Mandal case [Indra Sawhney v. Union of India (1992) Supp. 3 SCC 217]—see further R. Dhavan, 'The Supreme Court as Problem Solver: The Mandal Controversy' in V.P. Panandiker, *The Policies of Backwardness*, Delhi, 1997, p. 262-332. Attention is drawn to other articles in the book as well.

34. See *Constitution of India*: Art. 370 (on Kashmir), 371 (on Gujarat and Maharashtra), 371A (on Nagaland), 371B (on Assam) 371C (on Manipur), 371F (on Sikkim), 371G (on Mizoram), 371H (on Arunachal Pradesh), 371I (on Goa). Indian federalism has thus yielded to regional considerations and India's plural diversity.

35. Neither the courts (see M. Ishmail Faruqui v. Union *infra* n. 61), nor legislation [see the *Religious Institutions (Prevention of Misuse) Act* 1988, which generally prohibited politicizing religions; and the *Places of Worship (Special Provisions) Act* 1991, which tried to diffuse the Babri Masjid and other temple controversies] have had even a symbolic effect. In future, it may not be possible to even pass legislation of this nature.

36. See *Constitution of India*, Article 14 (equality), 15 (2) (3), 16 (2), (non-discrimination) 17 (abolition of untouchability), Articles 25-26 (religious freedom, subject to limitations), Article 29-30 (right to language and culture).

37. The fact that the State may have to be involved in religious matters is foreshadowed in Art. 16(5) of the Constitution. Neutrality is maintained to assure non-discrimination where the State gives a grant to an educational institution [Article 28 and 29 (2)]. The clause dealing with non-taxation for specific religious purposes (Article 27) does not prohibit grants by the State to religious institutions and causes.

38. More specific to religious freedom and secularism, the reformist element can be seen in the Constitution of India Article 14 (equality), 15(1), (3), 16(2) (gender equality), 15(2), 25(2) (non-discrimination in public places), 17 (abolition of untouchability), 25(1), 26 (regulatory control of religious affairs), 25(2) (general and specific empowerment for reform), 44 (uniform civil code), 45 (compulsory education for all women including presumably 'the girl child'), 48 (animal husbandry and cow slaughter), 15(4), 16(4) (affirmative action), 330-342 (special provisions for certain communities).

39. There has been a tendency in recent discussions on secularism (as, for example, by Ashis Nandy and T.N. Madan, *infra* n. 87) to lay a far greater emphasis on the reformist modernity of the secular dispensation of the Constitution than is warranted. Such a construction reinforces a fundamentalist approach.

40. Taken from Nehru's famous speech on the night of 14 August 1947 when India got Independence.

41. Foreign scholars seem to have tried to assuage Indian sentiments by paying tribute to the modern inventiveness of Indian 'tradition' (see L. Rudolph and S. Rudolph, *The Modernity of Tradition: Political Development in India*, Chicago, 1967). E. Said's *Orientalism* (New York, 1979) is surely right in drawing attention to the emotional and intellectual effect of people being disparagingly portrayed as inferior orientals.

42. For a summary of the literature on the 'instrumental' dimensions of law and development and how the standard American export models of law and development came to be abandoned, see R. Dhavan, 'Law as Concern: Reflecting on Law and Development,' in Y. Vyas, *Law and Development in the Third World*, Nairobi, 1994, p. 25-50.

43. The fear of India not being able to hold together may, in hindsight, seem exaggerated, but was a genuine fear at the time. We have just to turn to contemporary accounts of Partition to range its impact (for an example see Mushirul Hasan, *India Partitioned: The Other Face of Freedom*, Delhi, 1995).

44. See S.K. Agarwala, 'Jawahar Lal Nehru and the Language Problem,' in R. Dhavan (ed.) *Nehru and the Constitution*, Delhi, 1992, p. 134-60.

45. For an account of Hindu codification see Archana Parashar, *Women and Family Law Reform in India*, Delhi, 1992, p. 77-183. For a foreign scholar's contemporary estimate of the changes made by the 'Hindu Code' see J.D.M. Derrett, *Hindu Law, Past and Present*, Delhi, 1957.

46. See R. Dhavan, 'Kill them for their Bad Verses: Criminality, Punishment and Punishing Social Crimes in India,' in R. Shankardass (ed.) *Punishment in India*, forthcoming, Delhi, 1999.

47. I have taken a much more charitable view of Nehru's secularism in my long 'Introduction' to R. Dhavan (ed.) *Nehru and the Constitution*, Delhi, 1992. Even if Nehru's *Glimpses of World*

History (Oxford, 1981) and *Discovery of India* (Oxford, 1981) appear to be greatly over-written, Nehru was genuinely committeed to celebrating India's diversity.

48. See State of Bihar v. Kameshwar Singh AIR 1952 SC 252; and more generally H.C.L. Merrillat, *Land and the Constitution,* Bombay, 1970 (on land reform); and Romesh Thapar v. Madras AIR 1950 SC 124; and Brij Bhushan v. Delhi AIR 1980 SC 129 (on the early censorship cases). Both these cases gave rise to constitutional amendments to reverse the Supreme Court's decisions.

49. Madras v. Champakam Doraijan AIR 1951 SC 226; Venkataramana v. State of Madras AIR 1951 SC 229. Later the Court was concerned about 'caste' being the basis of affirmative action (see the eclectic decision in Balaji v. Mysore AIR 1963 SC 1649; Chitralekha v. Mysore AIR 1964 SC 1823), but realized in the Mandal case (*supra* n. 33) that caste could not be ignored in any determination of the beneficiaries of affirmative action schemes in India.

50. Commissioner HRE v. Sri Lakshmindra (1954) SCR 1005; Mahant Sri Jagannath v. Orissa (1954) CR 1046; Ratilal v. Bombay (1954) SCR 1055. Justice B.K. Mukedee's Tagore Law lectures were on the *Hindu Law of Religious and Charitable Endowments,* Calcutta, 1952.

51. Saifuddin Saheb v. Bombay AIR 1962 SC 853; and note the comments of J.D.M. Derrett (1963) 12 *ICLQ* 693.

52. Durgah Committee Ajmer v. Syed Hussain AIR 1961 SC 1402.

53. Tilkayat Shri Govindlalji Maharaj v. State of Rajasthan AIR 1963 SC 1638.

54. This arises out of the provisions of Art. 25(2) of the Constitution. It was in this context that the Swami Narayans protested they were not 'Hindus' (see the Yagnapurushdasji case *supra* n. 28); on the opening up Muslim mosques, see Sarwar Hussain v. Additional Civil Judge AIR 19 83 All 251.

55. Venkararamanna v. Mysore AIR 1958 SC 255.

56. Rajasthan v. Sulanmal AIR 1975 SC 706 where the Court also went into pronouncing on tenets of Jainism.

57. E.R.J. Swami v. Tamil Nadu AIR 1972 SC 1586.

58. Mohd. Hanif Qureshi v. Bihar AIR 1958 SC 231, A.H. Qureshi v. Bihar AIR 19 61 SC 448.

59. Jagdhishwaranand v. Police Commissioner, Calcutta AIR 1984 SC

51. But note the courageous stance of The High Court in Commr. v. Jagdishwaranand AIR 1991 Cal. 263. where Justice Ruma Pal took the view that the Supreme Court had not explored the issue adequately.

60. See R.M.K. Singh v. State AIR 1976 Patna 198. *Quaere.* Are those who do not perform those essential rites not 'Hindus' in the eyes of the law? Can the Court say—as it did in S.P. Mittal v. India AIR 1983 SC 1—that followers of Sri Aurobindo do not adhere to a faith but only a philosophy?

61. M.Ishmail Faruqui v.Union of India (1994) 6 SCC 360 (the Babri Masjid case); see further R. Dhavan, 'The Ayodhya Judgement: Encoding Secularism in the Law,' *E.P.W.* 29 (1994), p. 3034-40.

62. Denominational schools have had to struggle to defend their constitutional viability. Note the leading judgements in Bombay v. Bombay Educational Society AIR 1954 SC 561; In Re Kerala Education Bill AIR 1958 SC 956. St. Xaviers Colleges v. Gujarat AIR 1974 SC 1389; St. Stephens College v. University of Delhi AIR 1992 SC 1630. See generally R. Dhavan (*supra* n. 26) 231-245. The extent of protection and autonomy to be given to such schools is now before the Supreme Court of India.

63. Ghulam Abbas v. U.P. AIR 1983 SC 1268; Abdul Jalil v. Uttar Pradesh AIR 1984 SC 882.

64. *supra* n. 58.

65. On the right to proselyte a faith see the controversial decision in Stainislaus v. State of Madhya Pradesh AIR 1977 SC 908. For details of the Babri Masjid case see M. Ishmail Faruqui v. Union *supra* n. 61.

66. For the background see R. Dhavan, 'The Supreme Court and Hindu Religious Endowments: 1930-1975,' *JILI* 20 (1978), 52 102, esp. p. 57-63.

67. On aspects of the Vaishno Devi case when it reached the Supreme Court see Bhumi Nath v. State of JK (1997) 2 SCC 745.

68. Sri Adi Visheswarn of Kashi Nath v. U.P. 91997, 4 SCC 606 (on the takeover of the Vishwanath temple). For the other important recent cases which consolidate the state's regulatory control and takeovers of religious endowments, see also Sri Sri Lakshmanna v. A.P. (1996) 2 SCC 498; A.S. Narayana v. State of A.P. (1996) 9 SCC 5 48 and by way of follow up at (1997) 5 SCC 376; Pannalal v. State of A.P. (1996) 2 SCC 498; Shri Jagannath

Puri Management Committee v. Chantamani Khuntia (1997) 8 SCC 422.

69. The Sikh Gurdwara Act 1925 was designed by the British to keep the Sikhs apart. Instead, for decades the statutory framework proved to be a cementing force; see Rajiv Kapur, *Sikh Separatism: The Politics of Faith*, London, 1984.

70. The sweep of control is increasing—see for example the *Andhra Pradesh Charitable and Hindu Religious Endowment Act* 1966 (as amended) which virtually takes over crucial aspects relating to the working of all public charitable trusts.

71. The objective of a 'uniform civil code' is to be found in Article 44 of the Constitution. For the background to this controversy see Archana Parashar, *supra* n. 45 p. 201-263.

72. The 'secular option' is provided by the Special Marriage Act 1954, the Indian Succession Act 1956 and the Guardianship and Wardship Act 1890, in addition to provisions like S. 125 of the Criminal Procedure Code 1973 for providing maintenance to wives and children—on which see Shah Bano's case (*infra* n. 78). In some areas the personal law obviates the exercise of the secular option.

73. Ahmedabad Women's Action Group (AWAG) v. Union of India (1997) 3 SCC 573 and the decisions cited there.

74. The Gains of Learning Act 1930 was passed when the Privy Council declared in Gokul Chand v. Hukam Chand (1921) 48 IA 162 that the salary of a civil servant belonged to the 'joint family' which invested in his education. Likewise after the Privy Council ruled in Abul Fatah v. Rusumoy (1994) 22 IA 76 that *waqfs* (trusts) which were ultimately dedicated to God were invalid in Muslim Law. The Mussalman Waqf Validating Act 1913 was passed to reverse this decision.

75. See Muslim Personal (Shariat Application) Act 1937.

76. See the Dissolution of Muslim Marriage Act 1939.

77. Thus, the truncated 'Hindu' code consists of the Hindu Marriage Act 1955, the Hindu Succession Act 1956, the Hindu Adoption and Maintenance Act 1956 and the Hindu Minority and Guardianship Act 1956. For an interesting review of Hindu Law immediately following this codification see J.D.M. Derrett, *A Critique of Modern Hindu Law*, Bombay, 1970.

78. See Mohd. Ahmed Khan v. Shah Bano Begum AIR 1985 SC 943.

79. Rajiv Gandhi's government successfully introduced the Muslim Women (Protection of Rights on Divorce) Act 1986 which grants maintenance rights for larger sums to divorced Muslim women from the husband and his family. The view that a summary procedure is not available under this Act is also, perhaps, incorrect [Noorjahan (1988) Cr.L.J. 2826 (Bom.)].

80. The Vohra Committee's Report was an internal report on the extent of extra-Constitutional control over Indian governance. For details, and on the litigation that followed, see Dinesh Trivedi v. Union of India (1997) 4 SCC 306.

81. M. Ishmail Faruqui v. Union (1994) *supra* n. 61.

82. S.R. Bommai (*infra* n. 83).

83. The Supreme Court's statements on secularism are collected in S.R. Bommai v. Union of India (1994) 3 SCC 1; and M. Ishmail Faruqui (the Babri Masjid case, *supra* n. 61). These statements are ambiguous, equivocal and without any centrality and direction.

84. Christian communities have been mercilessly attacked in Gujarat, Maharashtra and Orissa in 1998-99. The murder of Revd Staines—an Australian priest—led to the appointment of the Justice Wadhwa Commission to investigate the incident. While the Wadhwa Commission Report on Orissa is awaited, 'people's' reports have been published on the incidents in Gujarat (see Report of the All India Fact-finding Team of the All India Federation of Organization for Democratic Rights, *And Then They Came for the Christians: A Report to the Nation*, Delhi, 1999; K.M. Chenoy, *Report of the Citizens' Commission: Violence in Gujarat*, Delhi, 1999, flowing from an initiative of the National Alliance of Woman.

85. Do government commissions make a difference? In 1998, the eminently sensible Report of the Srikrishna Commission on the Bombay riots was rejected. Justice Ranganatha Mishra's Report on the riots of 1984, following Prime Minister Gandhi's assassination, was pro-Congress and pro-government. Various other reports including those on Mallegaon (1967), Ranchi-Hattia (1967-68), Gorakhpur (1967 and 1969), Ahmedabad (1969), Bhiwana (1970) and Jamshedpur (1979) have been ignored.

86. This was done during the Emergency (1970-71) by the Constitution (Forty-Second Amendment) Act 1976. More generally on the spurious nature of this Amendment see R. Dhavan, *The Amendment:*

Conspiracy or Revolution, Allahabad, 1976. The Indian debates on 'secularism' are legion and range from India's deviation from the true 'secularism' (*infra* n. 91) to attacks on its modernity (*infra* n. 87). If secularism is a site for a plural diversity [see Rustom Bharucha, 'The Shifting Sites of Secularism: Cultural Politics and Activism in India Today,' *EPW* (24 January 1998) p. 167-80], it is also a vehicle for a strong reformism, if not a political ideology (*infra* n. 88). In this essay, I have projected secularism as an eminently sensible 'consensual' basis for governance with justice.

87. See Ashis Nandy, 'The Politics of Secularism and the Recovery Religious Tolerance' in Veena Das (ed.) *The Mirrors of Violence*, Delhi, 1990, p. 69-93. T. Madan, 'Secularism in its Place,' 46 (1987) *Journal of Asian Studies* p. 747-59.

88. Achin Vanaik, *Communalism Contested: Religion, Modernity and Secularism*, New Delhi, 1997. But Vanaik seeks both to gather the political faithful to fight for the new 'political ideology of secularism' as well as advance the superior normative claims of this ideology. This is a plea to liberate people to move towards the 'secular city' [see H. Cox, *The Secular City* (New York, 1990)].

89. For an interesting and insightful approach see Kum Kum Sangari: 'Politics of Diversity: Religious Communities and Multiple Patriarchies,' 30 *E.P.W.* (1995) (23 and 30 December) p. 3287-3300; 3381-3389. Apart from this distinctive approach, there is a more general view that the 'majority–minority' framework generates invidious politics, undermines equality between and amongst communities and creates a vested interest in entrenched identities. But there is a difference between a 'community' identity and a 'communal' identity. Equally, identification with a community should not obviate the quest for a just order (see A.G. Noorani, 'Muslim identity: Self Image and Political Aspirations,' in Mushirul Hasan, *supra* n. 21, p. 121-138).

90. Approaching this question from another angle see Rajeev Bhargava 'Why Must We Retain the Majority–Minority Framework,' 1997.

91. For this earlier approach which sought to compare 'our' secularism with 'theirs', see V.P. Luthera, *The Concept of a Secularism in India*, Oxford, 1964; D.E. Smith, *India as a Secular State*, Princeton, 1963.

92. See BJP's White Paper on Ayodhya (Delhi, 1993).

Hindutva and the Question of Conversions

Sumit Sarkar

I

Pokhran blasts apart, it seems likely that the Bharatiya Janata Party-dominated rule at Delhi might come to be remembered above all for the concerted campaign that has been carried out against Christians. The targeting of a minority community is not new: the Sangh parivar has always needed one or more enemy Others to consolidate into an aggressive bloc the 'Hindu community' which it claims to represent and seeks to constitute. What is largely new is that over the past year Christians seem to have displaced Muslims as the primary target.

The epicentre, so far as the number of incidents is concerned, has been BJP-ruled Gujarat, where already in August 1998 a fact-finding team sent by the Nishant theatre group, Delhi, saw many villages sporting the banner: 'Vishwa Hindu Parishad welcomes you to Hindu Rashtra's village'. The earlier attacks were widely spread out, and not confined to the Dangs tribal area. Particularly gross incidents included that of Samuel Christian, whose body was exhumed from Kapadvanj cemetery (Nadiad district) on 8 July and thrown outside the Methodist church, and the attack on a century-old Christian girls school at Rajkot on 20 June, where amidst slogans of 'Jai Shri Ram', copies of the New Testament were torn out from the hands of students and 300 of them burnt. Already by August 1998, the All India Catholic Union had compiled a list of thirty-three incidents in various parts of Gujarat, most of them during the preceding six months. The targets were mostly Christians, but also included some Muslims—for they had certainly not been left off the hook altogether. Thus at Bardoli scores of shops owned by Muslims were burnt after an inter-religious marriage between a Muslim boy and a Hindu girl, and large numbers of Muslims of Randhikapur (Panchmahals) and Sanjeli (Godhra) had to flee their homes following a couple of cases of similar inter-religious love affairs. (The Gujarat government's reaction was characteristic, and revealing: it set up a police cell to 'monitor'—i.e. harass and discourage—inter-religious marriages. The same government has disbanded an earlier police cell that had been set up to investigate atrocities against women.)[1]

Then, during Christmas week, no doubt to teach Christians a lesson for having had the temerity to organize a most impressive peaceful countrywide protest and shut-down of missionary schools on 4 December, there came the obviously concerted, planned attack on Christian Dangs. Between 25 December and 3 January, twenty-four churches, three schools, and six houses or shops were burnt, destroyed or damaged, and nine Christian tribals suffered serious injuries. 'The only lights visible that black Christmas night, and the nights to come, were infernos of churches.'[2]

Incidents in other states have been more sporadic, but in some cases even more horrifying. On 23 September there was the gang-rape of four nuns at Jhabua, Madhya Pradesh. B.L. Sharma, former BJP MP and currently central secretary of the Vishwa Hindu Parishad, claimed that this was a result of the 'anger of patriotic youth against anti-national forces . . . the direct result of conversion of Hindus to Christianity by the Christian priests.' The subsequent assurance by VHP general secretary Giriraj Kishore that his organization was not condoning rape did not improve matters, for he demanded that 'foreign missionaries should be removed from the country'.[3] And then in the last week of January 1999 came the burning alive at Monoharpur, Orissa, once again amidst slogans of 'Jai Shri Ram', of the Australian missionary doctor Graham Staines and two of his children. Staines had left the comforts of First World life to serve for forty years the lepers of this obscure village in India.

The sheer horror of the Staines murder, and the almost unbelievable fortitude, dignity, and deeply moving Christian forgiveness with which his widow received the news, evoked powerful and widespread emotional reactions both in India and abroad. 'Serve lepers, do not burn those who serve them', ran the banner carried by some schoolchildren at a protest demonstration in Delhi on 30 January, one of many throughout the country. Quite unusually, the initiative for protest rallies often came from students generally aloof from politics, as at Delhi colleges like Miranda or St Stephens. The prime minister claimed that he was hanging his head in shame, and the intensity of reactions seems to have forced a certain retreat for the time being for the organizers of the anti-Christian tirade. But scattered incidents of violence and intimidation are still being reported, and there are also signs that a systematic campaign of lies and distortions concerning Christians is being disseminated through leaflets and brochures. Some of these—usually those without press-lines—are crudely slanderous, and threaten open violence against Christians. Others present what might appear at first sight cogent arguments against missionary activity, often claiming to quote from respected national figures.

Let me give one example, from a pamphlet of the more

'sober' kind. *Seva ki ar me church ka sharayantra* (Church conspiracy under cover of service) by Dr Ravindra Agarwal (Hindu Manch, Delhi, Sivaratri, 1999), carries, very prominently on its inside cover, the Hindi translation of a passage from Gandhi which seems to justify the current anti-missionary campaign. I checked up the reference, and found that it is indeed there in the Mahatma's *Collected Works*, Volume XLVI, p. 27-28, nor is the translation unfair. In an interview dated 22 March 1931 given to the *Hindu*, Gandhi apparently stated that if in self-governing India missionaries kept on 'proselytizing by means of medical aid, education, etc., I would certainly ask them to withdraw. Every nation's religion is as good as any other. Certainly India's religions are adequate for her people. We need no converting spiritually.' The crunch comes when we look at the entire article, which was first published in *Young India*, 23 April 1931. Here Gandhi began with this passage, but went on to add that, 'This is what a reporter has put into my mouth . . . All that I can say is that it is a travesty of what I have always said and held.' He offered a corrected version, where he explained that, 'I am, then, not against conversion. But I am against the modern methods of it. Conversion nowadays has become a matter of business, like any other.' The modifications he made in the rest of the quote are equally interesting: 'Every nation considers its own faith to be as good as that of any other. Certainly the great faiths held by the people of India are adequate for her people. India stands in no need of conversions from one faith to another.' As striking, and utterly in contrast to Hindutva tenets, is the list he went on to offer of India's 'great' and 'all-sufficing' faiths: 'Apart from Christianity and Judaism, Hinduism and its offshoots, Islam and Zoroastrianism are living faiths.' The article ended with a characteristic plea for 'living friendly contact among the followers of the great religions of the world and not a clash among them . . .'

An anti-Christian campaign in India necessarily has to

base itself on the question of conversions. This is in partial contrast to Hindu–Muslim relations, for between Hindus and Christians there are no memories of communal violence or Partition, nothing that really corresponds to issues like *go-korbani* (cow sacrifice) or music before mosques that have sparked off so many riots at least from the 1890s onwards.[4] It is not at all accidental, therefore, that the so-called mild face of the BJP, Vajpayee, had recourse to this ploy when he visited Gujarat just after the Christmas burnings of churches and called for a 'national debate' on conversions, thus adroitly hinting that Christians are ultimately responsible for their own woes. And this in spite of the fact that C.P. Singh, Director-General of the Gujarat police, had categorically declared on 6 October that the charges being made of forced inter-religious marriages and conversions were baseless, and that it was rather 'the activists of the Vishwa Hindu Parishad and Bajrang Dal who were taking law into their own hands which posed a serious danger to peace in Gujarat'.[5] As for Staines, he had been a doctor, not an ordained priest, and could not have baptized anyone even if he had wanted to. A delegation of religious leaders of various communities that went on a pilgrimage to Monoharpur recently found that there was not a single Christian among the eighty inmates of Staines' leprosarium.[6] Conversion through force evidently requires the complicity of sections of the state apparatus, and, whatever may or may not have happened occasionally under colonial rule, in today's circumstances—and most obviously in the BJP's Gujarat bastion—it is clearly absurd to think that such support could ever come the way of Christian missionaries.

Actually some information is available about who exactly is doing forced conversions in the Dangs: '. . . since the past few months, and more extensively in the first fortnight of January, tribals (of Goghli and surrounding villages) were being bundled into jeeps and taken to the *garamkund* (hot springs) at Unai for a *shuddhikaran* (purificatory bath). Then they were driven to Swami Aseemanand's ashram, to state that they have "reconverted" to Hinduism!'[7]

What is worrying is the confusion the question of Christian conversions can still evoke, even among well-intentioned and progressive people. There are very few who would not condemn the Staines murder, yet this could be accompanied by something like a sotto voce 'but' about conversions. Thus even Swami Agnivesh, well-known champion of so many progressive causes, welcomed Vajpayee's call for national debate, and, while stating that 'individual freedom is the key to the modern outlook', declared that he was 'indignant at conversions'.[8] The Hindu Manch pamphlet I have cited quotes with great glee a report from *Indian Express*, 7 January 1999, headlined 'Gandhians blame conversions, seek total ban'. The statement apparently comes from two senior Gujarat Sarvodaya workers, one of whom, the eighty-two-year-old Ghelubhai Nayak, claimed that way back in 1948 Sardar Patel had sent him to the Dangs to counter possible Christian conversions there.

In logic and law alike, one would have thought, there is little scope for doubt or confusion here. Article 25(i) of the Fundamental Rights chapter in the Constitution defines the 'Right to Freedom of Religion' quite categorically: 'all persons are equally entitled to freedom of conscience and the right freely to profess, practice and propagate religion'. Propagation makes no sense at all without the possibility of convincing others of the validity of one's religious beliefs and rituals. Freedom of choice, in religion or for that matter in politics or anything else, and therefore freedom to change one's beliefs, is surely in any case integral to any conception of democracy. Conversely, conversion by force or fraud is contrary to the basic principle of equal freedom.

Yet, in an admittedly specific and isolated judgement, a Supreme Court judge has recently defied common sense by declaring that the right to propagate does not include the right to convert, and it is pointless to deny that doubts about this subject have come to be accepted as somehow 'natural' by many. But it is always the 'natural' that stands in need of the most rigorous questioning, and I feel that a little historical exploration might help. In what follows, I look first at the question of conversions and its changing meanings and forms across time, trying to investigate when, under what conditions, and how it became such a contentious issue. My closing section will come back to current events, and ask why the Sangh parivar has chosen such a tiny minority as prime target, and what developments might be helping to make such targeting appear plausible.

II

Let me begin by raising two preliminary questions, one of logic, the other of semantics.

What conditions, or widely held assumptions, are necessary before conversions can become a contentious issue, and arouse widespread and violent passions? Clearly, religious communities need to have become crystallized, come to be seen as having firm and fixed boundaries, so that the crossing of borders becomes a dramatic, one-shot matter. Such developed 'community-consciousness', however, is a necessary, but not sufficient, condition for the development of what twentieth century Indian English has come to call 'communalism': when, obviously, conversions become controversial on a qualitatively higher scale. This requires not just the transition from 'fuzzy' to 'enumerated' communities to which Sudipto Kaviraj drew our attention some years back in an influential essay, but the further assumption of inevitable, and over-riding,[9] conflict of interests, such that, in a kind of zero-sum game, the gain of one community is thought to invariably involve the loss of the other.

It needs to be emphasized that this distinction between

developed community-consciousness and communalism is important precisely because tendencies exist that virtually equate the latter with any firmly-bounded religious identity. These operate from two diametrically opposed points of view. Pradip Datta has recently made the very perceptive point that communalism is distinctive among ideologies in its refusal to name itself.[10] There is rather the constant effort at identification with religious community, as well as, for Hindu-majoritarian communalists, with nationalism. Consider for instance the very term 'Hindutva', which literally means no more than 'Hindu-ness', but has come to be the self-description, from the mid-1920s onwards, of a much more specific and narrow ideology.[11] And here extremes sometimes meet, for if secularism gets equated with anti-religion, the implication becomes that communalism can be countered only by exposing religion as 'superstitious' or 'irrational'. Once, again, in effect, 'communal' is being collapsed into 'religious community'. Operationally, such hostility to religion has been rare within Indian secularism, for here the term has really been synonymous with anti-communal policies and values, rather than being anti-religious or even particularly rationalist. Anti-secularist polemic however frequently makes such an equation for its own purposes. Paradoxically, when combined with rejection of Hindutva as within an influential current intellectual trend, 'communal' and 'community' once again tend to get collapsed into each other, except that then a sharp disjunction is postulated between 'modern' and 'pre-modern' communities, 'religion-as-ideology' as contrasted to a somewhat romanticized 'religion-as-faith'.[12]

The sense of outrage evoked by religious conversion, thirdly, can be greatly intensified and made to appear much more legitimate if the loss can be given a 'patriotic', or 'national', colour. This, of course, has been the special advantage enjoyed by Hindu majoritarianism, particularly after 1947. Sangh parivar justifications of recent outrages against

Christians are replete with instances of such an equation.

One needs to note also the very effective semantic ploy through which it has come to be widely assumed that Hinduism is near-unique among religious traditions in being non-proselytizing: conversion to other faiths therefore is a loss that cannot be recuperated, and so particularly unfair. This at first sight seems to fit in well with the common-sense view that one can become a Hindu by birth alone, since caste (whether in the *varna* or the *jati* sense) is crucial to Hinduism, and your caste status is hereditary. But certain ticklish questions arise as soon as we enlarge the time-perspective: where did all the Buddhists of ancient India go, for instance? And how did Hindu icons and myths spill over into large parts of South-East Asia? More crucially, one needs to recognize that, across centuries but in accelerated manner with modernized communications, brahmanical Hindu rituals, beliefs and caste disciplines have spread across the subcontinent and penetrated and sought to transform communities with initially very different practices and faiths. It has somehow become conventional to describe the processes here by anodyne terms like 'Sanskritization' or 'cultural integration', but they really amount nevertheless to what with other religious traditions would have been termed 'conversion'. There is also much historical data about the spread of specific varieties of Hindu traditions, like for instance Chaitanya bhakti from central and western Bengal into Orissa and the uplands of Jharkhand. A whole battery of terms was developed, in fact, from the late nineteenth century onwards as expansion directed towards marginal groups and tribals became more organized: 'reclamation', *shuddhi* ('purification'), 'reconversion', *'paravartan'* ('turning back', the term preferred by the Vishwa Hindu Parishad today). Common to all these labels is an insistence that all that is being attempted is to bring people back to their 'natural' state: which, for all the targeted groups, is always assumed to be being Hindu in a more-or-less

81

Sanskritized manner. Semantic aggression can hardly go further.

But if shifts in religious allegiance are obviously nothing new, their forms are likely to have changed over time. The precise meanings of 'conversion' need to be historicized.

The thrust of much recent historical work has been towards the destabilization of assumptions of continuous, firmly-bounded identities. This is in significant contrast to the bulk of earlier historiography, which had tended to essentialize terms like Hindu or Muslim, and then gone on to emphasize either the moments of synthesis, or (in the communal variant) perennial conflicts.[13] One need not go as far in the questioning of pre-colonial identities as some colonial discourse analysts would want, to agree that the absence of modern communicational networks (developed roads, railways, telegraph lines, the printing press, etc.) must have greatly hindered the formation of stable and tight countrywide religious blocs. Trends in medieval Indian scholarship seem to be moving in a similar direction, through a more rigorous probing of the rhetorical aspects and precise implications of texts that at first sight seem to indicate a high level of religious conflict and persecution. (Selective nineteenth-century translations from some of these, notably by Elliot and Dowson, had greatly contributed to communalization.) Thus Persian chronicles boasting of wars against infidels and desecration of temples—or for that matter a text like the Vilasa copper-plate grant describing in lurid but highly formulaic terms the Kali-yuga ushered in by Muhammad bin Tughlaq's destruction of the Kakatiya dynasty in Andhra—are being recognized to have been in part legitimizing devices. (The same temples, for instance, seem to be getting destroyed again and again, as Romila Thapar has shown recently in an as yet unpublished paper about Somanath.) Again, 'Hindu' texts, in Sanskrit or regional languages like Telugu, use, overwhelmingly, ethnic rather than religious terms (Turushka, most commonly) to describe the kingdoms and armies we have become accustomed since the nineteenth century to call 'Muslim'.[14] All this does not mean, of course, that there were not many instances of conflicts and acts of violence and persecution wholly or partly 'religious' (though even the meaning of that term is not entirely transparent, or impervious to change), amidst much everyday coexistence and commingling of practices. But their generalization into mass communal ideologies with a subcontinental reach was unlikely.

In an important discussion of processes of Islamization in medieval Bengal, Eaton has tried to draw out the implications of this relative absence of firmly-bounded communities for the question of religious conversions. Use of the term itself, he argues, becomes 'perhaps misleading—since it ordinarily connotes a sudden and total transformation', whereas the changes could have 'proceeded so gradually as to be nearly imperceptible'.[15] Like other secular-minded historians, Eaton rejects the theory of large scale forcible conversion, since the regions that became massively Muslim—east Bengal and western Punjab—were also those furthest away from major centres of Muslim politico-military power. He discounts also the view that Islam attracted converts from lower castes primarily by virtue of its egalitarian tenets, for these were also the areas where brahmanical penetration—and therefore structures of caste oppression—had been relatively weak. By implication, Eaton's account draws attention to the possibility that in large parts of the subcontinent, certainly in medieval times and to a considerable extent even today, the great religious traditions have been expanding at the cost, not so much of each other as in relation to a multitude of local cults or practices. Conflicts in pre-modern times would have been considerably reduced, further, by the slow, phased nature of the transition. Here Eaton distinguishes three heuristic moments, of 'inclusion' of Islamic cult figures within the local cosmologies, 'identification' of some of these with indigenous objects of worship, and finally (and perhaps often mainly in the nineteenth century), 'displacement' through which Islam became 'purified' through reform or purging of non-Islamic beliefs and practices.[16] One might add that pre-colonial 'conversion' was probably not so much a matter of individual and one-shot choice, as of slow changes involving an entire group, family or kinship network, or local community—which would once again reduce the potentials for conflict.

Three major changes, which began to take effect roughly from the latter part of the nineteenth century onwards, seem particularly relevant for understanding why conversions started becoming so much more controversial.

The first was the tightening of community boundaries: there has come into being a broad consensus about this among historians, despite continuing differences regarding the extent of novelty involved here, or in the precise weighing-up of causes.[17] Within the broader framework of developing politico-administrative, economic, and communicational integration, particularly important inputs probably came from colonial law, and from census operations. In matters of so-called 'personal' or 'family' law, the British had decided in the 1770s that they would administer according to Hindu or Islamic sacred texts and in consultation with brahman pandits and Muslim ulema: differentially, in other words, for the two major religious traditions. In many everyday situations, therefore, one had to declare oneself a Hindu or Muslim (or a member of any of the other religious communities that had come to develop 'personal' legal systems of their own). While superficially not dissimilar to Mughal practice, there was a significant change in so far as Mughal courts had never tried to penetrate deep into lower levels through the kind of systematic hierarchy of appellate jurisdictions that British rule developed over time. Disputes must have been often decided at local or village levels according to diverse customary standards that would have had little to do with textual (or 'religious') principles. Colonial 'personal' law centralized, textualized, made operationally much sharper the boundaries between religious communities, and probably enhanced also to a significant extent the influence over the rest of society of high caste and Muslim elites. The impact of the census from the 1870s onwards is more obvious, and has been repeatedly emphasized in recent academic discussions. Census operations necessitated the drawing of sharp distinctions, of religion, caste, language, or whatever else the administrators had decided on as worthy of being counted. Enumerated communities made for mutual competition, complaints about unfair representation in education, jobs, administration or politics, stimulated fears about being left behind in numbers games. That census procedures often involved the imposition of order, rather than simple recording of realities on the ground, becomes clear, for instance, from the amusing instance in the 1911 census of a 35,000-strong community of 'Hindu-Muhammadans' in Gujarat, so termed by a Bombay census superintendent confounded by the inextricable combination of multiple practices, beliefs, and even self-definitions. The latter was pulled up sharply by his superior, census commissioner E.A. Gait, who ordered the location of 'the persons concerned to the one religion or the other as best he could'.[18]

Colonial modernity helped to tighten community bonds: it has been less often noticed, however, that it also stimulated forces that made them more fragile. What was coming into existence by the late nineteenth and early twentieth century was a situation conducive for the growth of not one, but many community-identities: religious, caste, linguistic-regional, anti-colonial 'national', class, gender, in interactive yet often conflictual relationships with each other.[19] Among the many merits of Pradip Datta's just-published work is the way he has been able to bring together these interlocking narratives, in an effort to view 'communal formations . . . as part of a field in which they have to perforce relate to other collective identities (other than its binary in "Hindu" or "Muslim"), such as class, gender, or caste affiliations.'[20]

Signs can be discerned, thirdly, of the beginnings of a discourse of individual rights. The direct influence of western liberal and radical ideologies, while not negligible, was no doubt confined to relatively few, but there was also the fallout from certain institutional developments. Colonial justice, while shoring up religiously-defined community norms in personal law, simultaneously enlarged upto a point 'the freedom of the individual in the marketplace' in land and commercial transactions.[21] British Indian definitions of criminal liability, too, came to be theoretically based on notions of 'an equal abstract and universal legal subject'—though once again only to a partial extent, for there were many accommodations in practice with existing social hierarchies.[22] Equality before the law, promised in much-cited official documents like the Queen's Proclamation of 1858, was often severely tempered by white racial privilege. But then promises simultaneously held out and broken tend to whet appetites, and such a dialectic came to operate, though of course in widely different and at times even contradictory ways, both with respect to attitudes towards their foreign overlords of a growing number of Indians, and lower-caste (and/or class) resentments about indigenous hierarchies of privilege and exploitation.

Even more significant initially, perhaps, were developments relating to gender. It has been argued recently that the nineteenth-century legal reforms and debates around women (sati, women's education, widow remarriage, age of consent, polygamy) may have been significant above all for their unsettling effect. The concrete achievements of social reform were not very substantial, but, along with the intense debates around them that became possible though the coming of print, they did contribute to a 'destabilising and problematising (of) the old order'. For legality now clashed with religious prescription,[23] a small but growing number of women took to education violating customary prohibitions, and even conservative defenders of the old rules and norms had to use increasingly a new language of the woman's own consent.[24] Indian reformist efforts at social change through colonial legislation, though much resented by many nationalists, helped to constitute 'an excess that gave the woman, at least notionally, a sphere of personal rights outside the rule of the family and community.'[25]

I am arguing, then, that the heightened late- and post-colonial tensions around conversions have to be related to community borders becoming simultaneously harder and more vulnerable. Let me try to illustrate through a few sample instances of conflict (or its absence), relating in the main to Christian conversions.

While Christian proselytization throughout tended to focus primarily on tribals and lower castes, the Scottish missionary Alexander Duff in the Bengal of the 1830s and '40s tried out an alternative strategy of targeting elite Indians through higher education, public debates and individual contacts. There were some spectacular individual conversions in upper-caste households, like Krishnamohan Banerji and Madhusudan Dutta, and in 1845 a major controversy burst out in Calcutta around Umeshchandra Sarkar and his wife, aged fourteen and eleven, defying family elders to become Christians. The sharp differences in educated high-caste Calcutta society around social and religious reform (notably the ban on widow immolation) were suddenly forgotten as Radhakanta Deb, leader of the conservative Dharma Sabha, Debendranath Tagore, inheritor of Rammohan's Brahmo mantle, and even the Derozian Ramgopal Ghosh joined hands to float a Hindu Hitarthi Vidyalay to rescue education from the clutches of missionaries. The terms of argument as defined by Akshoykumar Dutta, Brahmo editor of *Tattvabodhini Patrika* who had a considerable rationalist reputation, were particularly interesting: 'Even the women within the household have started to turn Christian! Will we not wake up even after this terrible event?'[26] Individual conversion was felt to be a threat to family order. Resentment and fear among propertied Hindus was compounded in 1850 by the passage of the Disabilities Removal Act which sought to protect the right of inheritance of converts.

At a different and more obscure level, spread of Christianity among peasants occasionally aroused zamindar hostility. Landlords seem to have felt that converted tenants became less amenable to their demands, for in missionaries they had found an alternative source of authority and patronage. Cultivators and fishermen of Rammakolchoke, a village to the south of Calcutta, were fined ten rupees each in the late 1820s and beaten with shoes by their zamindar for turning Christian. There were clashes in 1840 at Bohirgacchi near Krishnanagar (Nadia), and in a Barisal village in 1846 Hindu zamindars seized the lands, implements, cattle and even clothes of twenty-nine Christian families and destroyed their huts. The converts had to take shelter among Muslim neighbours.[27] Diligent work on missionary archives and local official records would probably reveal many other instances. The missionaries were no doubt motivated primarily—and in many cases perhaps solely—by desire for conversion, and would not have been pro-peasant or socially radical on principle. Their presence could still be a resource for the underprivileged, as for instance when French Catholic missionaries of the Pondicherry-based Societe des Missions Etrangeres helped agricultural labourers beaten up by landlords in a court case at Alladhy in 1874-75, an incident which seems to have stimulated a wave of mass conversions in that area.[28] It needs to be added that there were occasions when missionary lobbying provided important inputs in moves towards pro-tenant legal reform, as in the run-up to the Bengal Tenancy Amendment of 1859, or in early twentieth century Chota Nagpur where according to the census report of 1911 'the agrarian legislation, which is the Magna Carta of the aboriginal, is largely due to their influence.'

It is true that there can be a nationalist position, abstracted from considerations of social justice, which might find in such pro-peasant missionary interventions evidence only of efforts to consolidate colonial power through dividing the Indians.[29] But then what are we to make of a substantial section of foreign missionaries in Bengal during the 1850s, headed by Reverend James Long, who took a public stand against fellow-white indigo planters before and during the 'Blue Mutiny'? Long even went to jail, accepting responsibility for publication of the English version of Dinabandhu Mitra's play *Neeldarpan* exposing the horrors of indigo, which had been translated by another Christian, Michael Madhusudan Dutta. Long has been deservedly immortalized in Bengal folk memory by a popular ditty:

Neel-banare sonar bangla korlo je chharkhar
Asamaye Harish molo, Longer holo karagar.

(The indigo monkeys have been ruining golden Bengal.
Harish died before his time, Long has been sent to
jail.)

Prior to around the turn of the century, Christian proselytization among the poor—as distinct from the rare but spectacular conversion of prominent men—does not seem to have become a central upper-caste (or *ashraf*) intelligentsia concern. Much of the expansion, in the nineteenth century as well as often later, was in outlying areas, largely untouched by mainstream Hinduism and Islam. The element of competition and conflict entered much later, with Hindu 'reconversion' efforts. In an interesting analysis of Christian conversion in Nagaland, Richard Eaton suggested that this could even provide a 'paradigm of how previous aboriginals of India might, in

89

earlier epochs, have acculturated to Hinduism, Buddhism or Islam.' As he argued later about medieval Bengal, the role of political coercion seems to have been negligible, despite the racial affinity between missionaries and colonial rulers. The great leap in Naga conversions took place *after* Independence, and there is also a significant lack of correlation between presence of foreign missionaries and spread of Christianity.[30] Much more decisive was the association of Christianity with the spread of literacy and effective modern medicine, processes that were greatly accelerated from the Second World War and the Kohima campaign onwards. The missionaries came as 'emissaries of the high culture of the plains bringing the written word to the forest', in a region of shifting cultivation, no written script, or town life—not unlike, in other parts of the subcontinent earlier, Brahmins, Buddhist monks, Muslim judges and holy men. There were in addition elements of skilful adaptation of Christianity to indigenous traditions, establishing links with existing Naga notions of a supreme divinity, for instance: once again, a parallel suggests itself with processes of 'Sanskritizing' kinds.[31]

The last quarter of the nineteenth century was marked by a surge in the number of Christian conversions, so much so that it has been described in mission histories as the era of 'mass movements'. Whole families, villages or sub-castes came over en masse in a manner that possibly reduced the aspect of conflict at local levels, but heightened fears elsewhere.[32] Repeated famines could have had something to do with this— the phenomenon of 'rice Christians', relief work by missions accompanied by baptisms, at times of small children, which embarrassed many Christians at times. But, in some areas at least, there were also links with lower caste/class discontent, as among the pariah agricultural labourers of Chingleput and North Arcot in the early 1890s where Methodist and Free Church of Scotland missionaries actively fostered efforts at empowerment directed against oppressive mirasidars.[33]

Developments like these may have had something to do with Vivekananda's powerful pleas, in course of and after his travels in south India, for the upliftment of untouchables—with which he often linked up the danger otherwise of Christian conversion.

Three processes began coming together from around the turn of the century to raise high-caste Hindu fears about conversion to a qualitatively higher level. The competitive logic of numbers made possible by census enumeration acquired greater saliency through the gradual spread of representative institutions. In regions where the major religious communities had been revealed by census operations to have roughly equal numbers (like, notably, Bengal and Punjab), even small changes through conversions came to be perceived as ominous. There were in addition clear signs of a rapid growth in lower-caste affirmations, in part stimulated by the census bid in 1901 to fix caste rankings. There was a quantum leap in the number of caste associations and of publications by or on behalf of lower-caste groups, seeking in the main upward mobility of a 'Sanskritizing' kind, but also going in at times for quite a lot of anti-brahmanical and anti-caste rhetoric. An additional imput was provided by British divide-and-rule moves like Gait's abortive suggestion in 1910 to list separately in the coming census lower castes denied brahman services and entry to temples. The resultant compound of resentment and anxiety was best articulated by U.N. Mukherji's very influential text, *Hindus: A Dying Race* (Calcutta, 1909), which skilfully used some census data and predictions to develop a horrific vision of Hindu decline as contrasted to Muslim growth and strength.[34]

Mukherji pinpointed subordinated castes to be the Achilles' heel of Hindu society, and his suggested remedies amounted therefore to a kind of organized and limited Sanskritization from the top at brahmanical initiative. In practice, particularly in northern India as spearheaded by the Arya Samaj, the concrete response to the fear of declining numbers so vividly expressed by Mukherji took the form of the *shuddhi* movement to 'purify' or 'reconvert' marginal groups. Social upliftment efforts, which in strict logic could have been directed towards all subordinated lower castes and untouchables, became in practice exercises in policing and modifying the borders between religious communities. The major targets of *shuddhi*—the Rahtia Sikhs around 1899-1900, the Malkana Rajputs of the Mathura-Farrukhabad region immediately after the collapse of the Non-Cooperation-Khilafat movement in 1922—became precisely groups among whom syncretistic practices had been most prominent,[35] and *shuddhi-sangathan*, in tandem with their Muslim counterparts, *tabligh* and *tanzim*, became a principal source of acute Hindu-Muslim tension and violence in the mid-1920s.

If Sikhs, initially, and then on a far more intensive scale Muslims, were the dominant 'Others' of *shuddhi*, Christians were not being entirely forgotten in this fast-developing Hindu communalist discourse which was simultaneously tending to build bridges between reform-oriented Aryas and their old, at one time very bitter, Sanatanist rivals. Danger of Christian conversion in the wake of missionary famine relief work had been one factor behind the Arya interest in the Rahtias, treated as virtual outcastes by other Sikhs.[36] A central text of the mid-1920s *shuddhi* movement, Swami Shraddhananda's *Hindu Sangathan: The Saviour of the Dying Race* (1926), while fulsomely acknowledging indebtedness to Mukherji in title and initial chapter, modified the latter's thesis by giving far greater centrality to conversion as the central cause of Hindu decline, and by somewhat unexpectedly giving almost as much space to Christians as to Muslims in its polemic. Conversion in any case had to be made into the key grievance in a movement directed towards 'reconverting' through purification, and Shraddhananda's chapter entitled 'The Causes of Decline in Number' announced, in bold headlines, 'the first cause' to be the 'conversion to other religious faiths'. Sections followed about Muslim and Christian conversions by 'force' and 'means other than force', with the author trying to use a bit of intra-Christian polemic (a German Protestant diatribe against Jesuits and the Inquisition) to establish his argument about Christian coercion and trickery. (Not too convincingly, it must be admitted, since all the instances are confined to sixteenth century Goa.)[37]

Anti-conversion sentiments received a major stimulus from Savarkar's very far-reaching and influential definition of 'Hindu' in 1923 as those who uniquely combined *pitribhumi* and *punyabhumi*, fatherland and holy land. Through a very effective appropriation of nationalism by Hindu majoritarianism, indigenous origin of religious (or by extension, other) beliefs, practices, or institutions was made into the supreme criterion of value. It became easy to brand Muslims and Christians as somehow alien, unpatriotic by definition—a charge particularly effective against Christians in the colonial era due to their religious affinity with the foreign rulers.

The aggressive Hindu-nationalist ideological-political bloc that had come to be constituted by the mid-1920s (Savarkar's 1923 text and the foundation of the RSS in 1925 providing the obvious benchmarks) also tended to be socially conservative, even though reformist strands had contributed significantly to its makings at times. The point can be made clearer through a glance at the precise ways and extent to which much-hated conversion—or more generally the presence of alternative proselytizing religious structures—could contribute towards empowerment of the downtrodden in Hindu society. Here it is easy to both exaggerate—or downplay. Proselytization, most of the time, seeks new adherents, not social justice except perhaps as means towards that end, and it would be absurd to portray Christianity (or Islam or Buddhism) as having been consistently egalitarian in its this-wordly impact. Conversion again seldom guaranteed equal treatment, for it is well known that caste prejudices and hierarchies have often persisted among converts to Christianity or Islam, despite theoretical principles of equality in the eyes of God or Allah. Yet an instance from the history of the lower-caste Namashudra movement in central and south Bengal in the early twentieth century suggests that a degree of empowerment was possible through missionary presence—even where that presence did not lead to significant conversions. The metrical biography of Guruchand Thakur (1847-1937), leader of the dissident Vaishnava Matua sect which constituted the core of the Namashudra upthrust, explains in vivid detail the circumstances that led the Matuas to seek the assistance of the Australian Baptist missionary C.S. Mead—striking an alliance that proved very fruitful for the Namashudras in their quest for educational facilities, service jobs, and eventually political advantages. The Namashudras wanted to start a high school at Orakandi, Faridpur (the centre of their movement), the poem explains, because landlords and moneylenders constantly tricked illiterate peasants like them in everyday matters of rent or debt-payment receipts. They encountered stiff opposition from the local high-caste Kayasthas, who were afraid that their sharecroppers and servants would no longer work for them if they became educated. That, they are reported to have argued, would disrupt the age-old principles of *adhikari-bheda* (hierarchy), as enshrined notably in the Ramayana. The biography explains that it was such *bhadralok* hostility that made Guruchand accept the offer of financial and other assistance from Mead, and it is also very careful to emphasize that the motives were entirely pragmatic, to get money for the school and also obtain access to British officials. The Namashudras were quite satisfied with their Matua faith founded by Guruchand's father Harichand Thakur, and very few of them turned Christian.[38]

The Christian conversions issue fell somewhat into the background in the 1930s and '40s, with communalism turned into an obsessively Hindu-Muslim affair, culminating in the blood-baths of 1946-47. That it had not vanished, however, was suddenly revealed by a near-explosion on the floor of the Constituent Assembly on 1 May 1947 in course of debates on the fundamental right to religious freedom. Many members objected to freedom of religion extending to the right to propagate, with Purushottamdas Tandon even declaring that 'most Congressmen are opposed to this idea of "propagation". But we agreed to keep the word "propagate" out of regard for our own Christian friends.' And once again the social dimensions of the issue got exposed, particularly in a speech by Algurai Shastri, who listed among the 'unfair means' adopted by Christian missionaries the utilization of 'bhangis and chamars': 'disputes between members of such castes as the sweepers or the chamars on the one side and the landlords or some other influential members on the other have been exploited to create bitterness among them. No effort has been made to effect a compromise. This crooked policy has been adopted to bring about the conversion of the former.'[39] Eventually the right to propagate—in effect, to convert—was not rejected, but, if the memory of the already-cited Gandhian opponent of conversions is to be trusted, this was because such a ban 'would make reconversion difficult'.[40]

It is worth recalling also that along with promotion of highly Sanskritized Hindi and cow protection, the fight against Christian missions was made into an early plank of Jana Sangh activity in the early 1950s as Hindutva forces sought to regain the ground lost after the murder of the Mahatma. In November 1954 the Jana Sangh organized an anti-foreign missionary week in Madhya Pradesh. Much had started being made of insurgency in largely-Christian Nagaland: then, as often now, what was conveniently forgotten is that many so-called 'secessionist' and/or 'terrorist' movements have had nothing to do with religious minorities (e.g. the predominantly high-caste Hindu ULFA), while relatively little can be understood about the deeper reasons behind such movements by simplistic 'foreign hand' explanations. The Madhya Pradesh Congress reacted to the Jana Sangh agitation in what had already become a strong base of the Hindu Right in a manner quite characteristic—and always in the long run disastrous. It tried to outflank its rival by becoming more 'Hindu', a move conditioned also by the strong presence of very similar elements within its own members and leaders. (The Mahakoshal Congress was the one provincial unit which had supported Tandon, the leader of right-wing Hindus within the Congress, against Nehru in 1951). The Niyogi Commission it set up to enquire into Christian missionary activity is still repeatedly and reverentially cited by Sangh parivar spokesmen and publications, for it suggested a ban on conversions unless explicitly proved to have been entirely voluntary—passing the onus of proof in effect on missionaries and converts. The Jana Sangh-led Madhya Pradesh government of 1967-68 did actually implement some of these recommendations, and imposed a strict test for proving voluntary choice on Christian converts. Under the post-Emergency Janata government with a strong Jana Sangh component, the destruction of some churches in the then Union Territory of Arunachal became the occasion for a law (1978) which made erection of places of worship subject to administrative permission in that region. A private bill to ban conversions was also moved in December 1978, and was supported by Prime Minister Morarji Desai, but had to be dropped in the face of Christian and other opposition.[41] Vajpayee's suggestion for a 'national debate' on conversions is therefore not a liberal proposal put forward by a good man fallen among unfortunate associates, but part of a well-thought-out Sangh parivar strategy.

Till the recent anti-Christian campaign, the Vishwa Hindu Parishad may have been associated in the public mind primarily with Ramjanmabhumi and the onslaught on Muslims culminating in the destruction of the Babri Masjid. But at the time of its foundation in 1964, and for quite some time after it, the main thrust had been directed primarily against Christian proselytization in tribal areas (the North-East, Madhya Pradesh, south Bihar). Significantly, those who figured prominently at the inaugural meeting of the VHP at Bombay included, along with the RSS boss Golwalkar and RSS *pracharak* S.S. Apte (who became the first general secretary of this new affiliate of the Sangh parivar), Brahmachari Dattamurti of the Masurasram, which had been carrying on *shuddhi-sangathana* work with a pronounced anti-Christian slant ever since its foundation in 1920.[42] The *ahcara samhita* drawn up by the VHP in 1968 included *paravartan* (turning back, i.e. reconversion) among the basic *samskaras* of the Hinduism it was trying to redefine— which amounted really to a major innovation, and indicated once again the centrality of this motif for this branch of Hindutva. There was thus a continuity with early-twentieth century *shuddhi*, but also some departure. Early Arya *shuddhi* had had a measure of reformist, anti-caste (or at least anti-untouchability) thrust critical of orthodox practices, and had at times served as a channel for upward mobility for subordinated groups irrespective of the question of reconversion. But *paravartan* is intended solely 'for those who have left Hinduism for foreign creeds like Islam and Christianity', and is not envisaged 'as a means of removing untouchability'.[43]

Christophe Jaffrelot gives some details of VHP anti-Christian work among tribals of the Chattisgarh region of Madhya Pradesh, which has been channeled through the Vanavasi Kalyan Ashrama, set up already in 1952 by an ex-official of the government tribal welfare department with RSS affiliations. The class linkages are particularly interesting: the major patrons of the organization have included the Maharaja of Jashpur; his son Dilip Singh Judeo, who combines landed property with industrial entrepreneurship, and became a RSS full-timer in 1992; and tendu-leaf magnate Lakhi Ram Aggarwal, RSS activist since 1946. Of late, Judeo has extended his activities to Chota

Nagpur, organizing a 'Ghar Vapsi' (home-return) movement there. A *Times of India* report dated 21 December 1997 described some of the fallouts of the intense anti-Christian activities headed by men like Judeo in South Bihar: seventeen cases of murder or assault of priests between 1992-97, including the stripping of the principal of a Dumka missionary school, with the SDO a benign spectator of the scene (2 September 1997), and the beheading in a Hazaribagh forest of a priest who had been helping tribals in some land ceiling cases.

The Meenakshipuram (Tirunelveli) mass conversions to Islam of thousands of dalits in February 1981 inaugurated an era of intense targeting of Muslims for well over a decade. But it is clear that the Sangh parivar has always had the anti-Christian arrow also in its armoury, and a quick switch in emphasis proved no problem at all after the formation of the BJP-led coalition in Delhi.

III

But why target the Christians, who are after all a tiny minority, stagnating in number, despite many dire predictions, at around 2.5 per cent of India's population?

Part of the explanation could be crudely pragmatic. Central government responsibility would be difficult to reconcile with wholesale campaigns against Muslims, a minority numbering well over a hundred million. There would be the possibility of large-scale violence, difficulties with coalition partners for some of whom Muslim electoral support remains important, and international repercussions. There is also, obviously, the desire to target and embarrass Sonia Gandhi, as foreign-born and Christian.

But there might be two deeper and more significant reasons. Despite swadeshi rhetoric, concessions to multinationals have gone ahead at unprecedented speed under

BJP rule. Yet many aspects of globalization remain uncomfortable for a political tradition reared on crudely nationalist, indigenist values. There is a need for surrogates that could reconfirm nationalist credentials without seriously disturbing the liberalization agenda. Both the Pokhran and anti-Christian campaigns, it might be suggested, fulfil this need. What could be more convenient for the Sangh parivar than giving to residual anti-imperialist sentiments a purely religious-cum-culturalist twist, targeting Christians, not—at least with any real seriousness—multinationals?

And the foreign origin charge does carry a certain plausibility among many with respect to Christians, despite the absurdity of characterizing thus a religion which in parts of the South is almost 2000 years old, older in fact than most living varieties of Hinduism. The plausibility derives in large part from fairly deep-rooted traditions, quite common also on the Left, of seeing Christianity and white missionaries invariably as agents of western imperialism, and Indian Christians as always collaborators with colonial rule.

No doubt there have been numerous instances of such anti-imperialist sentiments a purely linkages and complicities—but then British rule in India surely depended to a much greater extent on a far larger number of non-Christian Indian collaborators and dependent allies: notably, the bulk of princes, zamindars, government officials, most of them of high-caste Hindu origin. In more general terms, Christianity, like any major tradition, has included within its (highly variegated, quite often mutually conflicting) fold any number of diverse tendencies. One remembers the Inquisition, the many iniquities condoned or committed in the name of converting 'heathens' in the colonial world, numerous instances of crude cultural arrogance and Eurocentrism, the bitter hostility displayed towards so many progressive causes from the French Revolution down to the Spanish Civil War. Nor should one forget the lunatic-fringe Christian fundamentalists of America today. But dissident readings of Christianity have also been central to innumerable movements of the oppressed. Two obvious examples would be late-medieval European peasant movements, and Black slave culture in the USA. Even the ideals of modern democracy, and socialism of a kind, originated in significant part through a 'Puritan' revolution in seventeenth century England.

Today, particularly, the churches have been changing in quite striking ways, above all through the spread of 'Liberation Theologies' that have contributed substantially to many movements for radical change in Latin America and elsewhere. Christian groups have been prominent in many anti-war and anti-nuclear protests, and numerous other undeniably progressive initiatives. Small gains in the direction of somewhat greater social justice may have been earlier the largely unintended fallout of Christian proselytization efforts in India. Today, there is ample evidence of far greater awareness of such issues among many—though of course very far from all—Christian activists in India. There is also a welcome tendency, in face of brutal attack, not to retreat into sectarian or fundamentalist shells, but to build bridges through dialogue and joint work with secular, liberal, and Left formations.

Let me suggest in conclusion that it is precisely these aspects of contemporary Christianity that arouse the greatest anger and fear among adherents of Hindutva. I cannot think of more convincing evidence for this assertion of mine than that provided unwittingly by Arun Shourie in his *Missionaries in India*, the publication of which in 1994 preceded the large-scale campaign against Christians by just a few years. Shourie might seek to frighten his readers by citing occasional grandiose plans of some conservative or fundamentalist Christian groups to evangelize the globe in honour of the new millennium, but he is surely intelligent enough to realize that this is no more than absurdly arrogant tall talk. (It has been denounced as a 'residual western colonial mindset' by a devout Christian like the Revd Valson Thampu, who has also demanded the elimination from mission work of 'western triumphalist notions').[44] Shourie's book however provides ample signs that what has really worried him are developments like Liberation Theology. 'Today, spurred by the new "Liberation Theology", the Church is spurring movements among so-called Dalits, etc. But many of the leaders . . . patronised by way of helping "Dalits" speak with poison in their tongue. They advocate hatred by encouraging, projecting, assisting "Dalit" leaders', Shourie argues, and says movements are being fostered that 'would certainly disrupt Hindu society'.[45] Right at the beginning of his book, Shourie has stated his central assumption: 'I believe that the interests of India as a whole must take precedence—overwhelming precedence—over the supposed interests of any part or group, religious, linguistic or secular . . . the movements which are currently afoot ostensibly to "liberate" and "empower" those groups may well break India . . . those who foment them . . . ought to be dealt with using the full might of the State.'[46] What Shourie does not explain is how and by whom 'the interests of India as a whole' are to be determined, whether, given the anti-democratic measures he clearly envisages, such alleged 'interests' could not become a ideological cover for the special interests of a dominant minority of high caste Hindus.

Notes

1. *Communalism Combat* (Mumbai), ed. Javed Anand and Teesta Setalvad, October 1998. It may be added that for students of history, and political activists of a now-dying generation, the names of some of these places have a particular resonance: Kapadvanj, Rajkot, above all Bardoli, all, once upon a time, famous centres of Gandhian movements.
2. Francis Gonzalves (Vidya Jyoti, Delhi), 'Grisly Christmas for Christians in Gujarat,' *Communalism Combat*, January 1999.

3. *Hindu,* 29 September 1998; *Times of India,* 1 October 1998. [These and subsequent newspaper references are taken from the invaluable collection of press clipping circulated by the *Communalism Combat* group, *Saffron Army Targets People of the Cross, Resources for Secularism 3* (Mumbai), September 1998].

4. Christian propaganda against 'idolatry' might seem to provide a similar issue, and no doubt there have been many instances, particularly in the colonial era, of such campaigns being very aggressive. But then so many Hindu reform movements have also condemned image-worship, notably the Brahmos and the early Arya Samaj.

5. Interview with Teesta Setalvad, *Communalism Combat,* October 1998.

6. Rev. Valson Thampu, *Read the Scriptures, Mr Shourie (Asian Age,* 11 April 1999).

7. Francis Gonzalves' report in *Communalism Combat,* op. cit. At a meeting in Delhi in February, the well-known sociologist Ghanshyam Shah gave a very similar account of forcible 'reconversion'.

8. 'Why Fear a Debate about Conversions?', *Communalism Combat,* January 1999.

9. In the sense of being considered more vital than, say, anti-colonial struggle, economic development, or ideals of democracy or social justice.

10. 'Unlike fascists, no one claims to be a communalist . . . The nature of communalism encourages itself to be overwritten by other narratives.' Pradip Kumar Datta, *Carving Blocs: Communal Ideology in Early Twentieth-century Bengal,* Delhi, 1999, p. 7.

11. I find unsatisfactory also the very common definition of communalism in terms of phrases like 'politicization of religious identity', or 'political use of religion'. Politicization can take many different forms: thus in the Non-Cooperation-Khilafat movement of 1919-22 there was intense mobilization of both Muslims and Hindus through what may crudely be called 'political use of religion', and yet that was the highest level of Hindu-Muslim unity ever achieved in the anti-colonial struggle. The crucial distinction lies in the assumption of inevitable conflict.

12. The ablest statement of such views, which have become a prominent trend also within late Subaltern Studies, is Ashis

Nandy, 'The Politics of Secularism and the Recovery of Religious Tolerance,' in Veena Das, (ed.) *Mirrors of Violence: Riots and Survivors in South Asia,* Delhi, 1990. For a fuller exposition of my views on this and related themes, see Sumit Sarkar, 'The Anti-Secularist Critique of Hindutva: Problems of a Shared Discursive Space,' *Germinal,* Journal of Department of Germanic and Romance Studies, Delhi University, Volume I, 1994, as well as my *Writing Social History,* Delhi, 1997, Chapters 1, 3.

13. See the perceptive criticism made by Richard Eaton of Dineshchandra Sen's interpretation of the Satya Pir cult of medieval Bengal in his *History of Bengali Language and Literature,* Calcutta, 1954. Sen had described this cult to have been a synthesis produced by a situation where 'two communities mixed so closely, and were so greatly influenced by one another'. This, Eaton points out, 'postulated the more or less timeless existence of two separate and self-contained communities in Bengal, adhering to two separate and self-contained religious systems, "Hinduism" and "Islam".' Richard M. Eaton, *The Rise of Islam and the Bengal Frontier, 1204-1760,* Delhi, 1994, p. 280.

14. Thus Cynthia Talbott states that the sample of c. 100 Telegu inscriptions (c.14th-17th century) she has studied do not use religious labels at all while describing invasions and wars. Cynthia Talbott, 'Inscribing the Other, Inscribing the Self: Hindu-Muslim Identities in Pre-Colonial India', *Comparative Studies in Society and History,* Volume 37, 1995. See also Brajadulal Chattopadhyaya, *Representing the Other? Sanskrit Sources and the Muslims,* Delhi, 1998.

15. Eaton, op. cit., p. 269.

16. Eaton, op. cit. 113-119, 268-290.

17. Chris Bayly's essay on the 'pre-history' of communalism which sought to question 'the facile assumption that intercommunal violence, specifically violence and contention between Hindus and Muslims, was a product of the colonial period alone' by drawing attention to many such clashes between c. 1700-1860, still rejected 'any unilinear or cumulative growth of communal identity before 1860. Indeed, one may very well doubt whether there was ever an identifiable "Muslim", "Hindu", or "Sikh" identity which could be abstracted from the particular circumstances of individual events or specific societies.' C.A.

Bayly, *Origins of Nationality in South Asia: Patriotism and Ethical Government in the Making of Modern India,* Delhi, 1998, p. 44, 233.

18. Census 1911, Volume I.i (India: Report), p. 118.
19. The half-century between c. 1875-1925 was marked by the formation of the Congress (1885), the Muslim League (1906) and the Hindu Mahasabha (c.1915), a plethora of caste associations, the development of strong regional nationalisms in Bengal, Maharashtra, Andhra, Tamil Nadu and elsewhere, the foundation of the All India Trade Union Congress (1920), and of early women's organizations like the Bharat Stree Mahamandal (1910), the Women's Indian Association (1917), and the All India Women's Conference (1927).
20. Datta, op. cit., p. 9.
21. D.A. Washbrook, 'Law, State and Agrarian Society in Colonial India,' in Baker, Johnson and Seal, (ed.), *Power, Profit and Politics,* Cambridge, 1981, p. 650, and passim.
22. See the recent study of Radhika Singha, *A Despotism of Law: Crime and Justice in Early Colonial India,* Delhi, 1998. The quotation is from Singha, p. viii.
23. Sati, so long a supreme sign of Hindu womanly virtue even if operationally practised only by a few, became a crime, while widow marriage, condemned by respectable Hindu society, was made legal.
24. The petition against Bentinck's banning of sati in 1829, along with scriptural exegesis, also argued that Hindu widows immolated themselves 'of their own accord and pleasure'.
25. The above paragraph summarizes the important argument recently put forward in several papers by Tanika Sarkar. See for instance her 'The Feminine Discourse: A Candid Look at the Past and the Present,' in Rukmini Sekhar, (ed.) *Making A Difference: A Collection of Essays,* Spic-Macay, New Delhi, 1998. Quotations are from this essay.
26. Ajitkumar Chakrabarti, *Maharshi Debendranath Tagore,* Calcutta, 1916, 1971, p. 110-111, and passim.
27. G.A. Oddie, *Social Protest in India: British Protestant Missionaries and Social Reforms, 1850-1900,* Manohar, 1979, p. 114-116.
28. Henriette Bugge, *The French Mission and the Mass Movements,* in G.A. Oddie, (ed.) *Religious Conversion Movements in South Asia: Continuities and Change,* Curzon, Surrey, 1997, p. 105.

29. The census passage I have just quoted, incidentally, figures in Arun Shourie's recent violent polemic against Christianity *Missionaries in India: Continuities, Changes, Dilemmas,* New Delhi, 1994, p. 23. For him this is a telling argument proving that Christian conversion is motivated uniquely by 'worldly benefits', and forms part of a deep-rooted Western conspiracy.

30. The proportion of Christians among Nagas was only 17.9 per cent in 1941, but rose to 66.7 per cent in 1971, while 'The Semas . . . never had a missionary among them until 1948, which was *after* the steepest climb of conversion had already taken place for that group.' Richard Eaton, 'Conversion to Christianity among the Nagas: 1876-1971,' *Indian Economic and Social History Review,* XXI, i, January-March 1984, p. 17-19.

31. Ibid, p. 32, 43, and passim.

32. The number of Protestants in Madras Presidency shot up from c. 75,000 in 1851 to 300,000 by 1891; while converts of the Jesuit Madurai Mission, 169,000 in 1880, had become 260,000 in 1901. There was a sharp upturn also in north India, after a long period of very slow growth. 'Native' Christians in the North-West Provinces and the Punjab numbered only 2000 in 1852 and 5000 ten years later, but 40,000 in the Punjab alone in 1901. Bugge, op. cit. Avril Powell, 'Processes of Conversion to Christianity in Nineteenth-century North-Western India,' both articles in Oddie, ed. *Religious Conversion Movements,* p. 97, 17.

33. Oddie, *Social Protest,* op. cit., p. 128-46.

34. Datta, *Carving Blocs,* op. cit., Chapter I (*Hindu Unity and the Communal Common-sense of the 'Dying Hindu'*); Sumit Sarkar, 'Identity and Difference: Caste in the Formation of the Ideologies of Nationalism and Hindutva,' *Writing Social History,* Delhi, 1977, Chapter 9; Sarkar, 'Identities and Histories: Some Lower-caste Narratives from Early Twentieth-century Bengal' (Paper presented at a conference in Osaka, January 1999, forthcoming).

35. Thus the 1911 census described the Malkana Rajputs as a group that claimed 'that they are neither Hindus nor Muhammadans, but a mixture of both. Of late some of them have definitely abjured Islam.' Op. cit. p. 118.

36. J.T.F. Jordens, *Swami Shraddhananda,* Delhi, 1981, p. 52-53.

37. Shraddhananda Sanyasi, *Hindu Sangathan: Saviour of the Dying Race* (n.p., March 1926), p. 14-20, and passim. The once-standard

Arya-reformist themes of 'perversion of the Aryan social polity' and 'child marriage and degradation of women' are mentioned, but only as second and third causes of Hindu decline, well after conversions.

38. Mahananda Haldar, *Sri Sri Guruchand Charit*, Calcutta, 1943, p. 100-110.
39. *Constituent Assembly of India Debates*, Volume II, p. 483, 492.
40. *Indian Express*, 7 January 1999, cited in Rabindra Agarwal. *Seba ki ar me . . .*, op. cit.
41. Christophe Jaffrelot, *The Hindu Nationalist Movement and Indian Politics, 1925 to the 1990s: Strategies of Identity-Building, Implantation and Mobilization (with special reference to Central India)* Paris, 1993; p. 163-5, 224, 287. The Hindu Manch pamphlet of Agarwal ends with an extract from the Niyogi Commission Recommendations of 1956.
42. Eva Hellman, *Political Hinduism: The Challenge of the Visva Hindu Parishad* (Uppsala, Sweden,1993), p. 70-71.
43. Ibid, p. 110-111.
44. Thampu, op. cit.
45. Shourie, op. cit., p. 201, 235.
46. Ibid, p. 3.

Perceptions of Difference: The Economic Underpinnings

Jayati Ghosh

F rom Bosnia to Brazil, from Sumatra to Sierra Leone, and from Mumbai to Manhattan, some of the main news stories are now depressingly similar. They are stories of growing divisions between social groupings determined by often shifting notions of identity based on race, language, religion or ethnic group; of increasing intolerance periodically boiling over into violence; of new hatreds and resentments justified by an imagined past of irreconcilable differences. In fact, what can be observed in India as a resurgence of seemingly archaic medieval loyalties and renewed aggression towards those categorized as 'the other' is a reflection of a much wider global trend.

The international context

Historians of the future may find it remarkable that the last decade of this century, which has been marked at one level by such an onslaught of globalizing and centralizing economic forces, and the geopolitical creation of a world more unipolar than ever before, has also witnessed the emergence of greater social divisions and more violence across the world. After all, unipolarism is supposed to bring with it more stability, even if it is otherwise unequal and unfair. And the current hegemony of the ideology of capitalist globalization, as well as the cultural homogenization that is under way, are supposed to create at least some uniformity of understanding and aspiration among very different societies and peoples.

But on second thought, perhaps historians may not be so surprised at this congruence of what appear to be very divergent tendencies. For it is possible to identify links between them, not least because the actual operations of integrated and 'globalized' markets do not necessarily unify and homogenize the world (except in the most trivial sense) but instead tend to aggravate and perpetuate inequalities.

Consider some of the more obvious effects of the most recent phase of capitalist globalization. The first point relates to just how limited growth has been for large sections of the world's population. Purely in terms of geographical distribution, around 1.7 billion people (more than one-fourth of the world's population) live in countries in which average incomes have actually fallen over the past decade or more. By contrast, the number of people living in countries where average incomes have risen in real terms is slightly less than that, at below 1.3 billion. In seventy countries per capita incomes are less than they were in 1980, and in forty-three countries (many of which are in the continent of Africa) such incomes are less than they were in 1970.[1]

Over the course of the 1990s, average incomes have fallen by a fifth or more in thirty countries, in the formerly socialist countries of Eastern Europe and the former Soviet Union, in sub-Saharan Africa, and now even in some parts of South-East Asia. Countries like Russia have experienced historically unprecedented declines in average living standards, which have in turn precipitated major social disintegration and a collapse of demographic indicators, pointing to severe crisis. Even in several countries in which average incomes have risen, including those in Asia, worsening distribution has meant that there are many more poor people in terms of absolute numbers than two decades ago.

The inequalizing nature of the process currently in operation is revealed most dramatically in the worldwide gaps between rich and poor, which have widened even faster in the recent past. The gap in per capita income between industrial and developing worlds has more than tripled between the 1960s and 1990. Between 1960 and 1991, the income share of the richest 20 per cent of the world's population rose from 70 per cent to 85 per cent, while the income share of the poorest 20 per cent of population fell from 2.3 per cent to 1.4 per cent. In fact, the income shares of more than 85 per cent of the world's population actually fell over this period. The ratio of shares of the richest quintile group to the poorest group doubled from 30:1 to 60:1.

This has also been reflected in the growing concentration of assets. Thus, today the net worth of the world's richest people, the 358 dollar billionaires, is equal to the combined incomes of the poorest 45 per cent of the world's population, that is 2.3 billion people, who are likely to hold assets worth even less than this. All of these inequalities are estimated to have grown over the past decade. Similarly, international production has become increasingly concentrated, with a few giant multinational corporations now dominating productive activity in most sectors.

One of the important reasons why economic growth related to the globalization process has been so iniquitous is because it has effectively been jobless, in that the employment generation involved in income-generating activity has been insufficient to meet the needs of the growing world population.

Labour requirement per unit of output has actually fallen not just in most activities, but for gross production. This has meant very high rates of open unemployment in Europe and disguised or unrecorded unemployment in countries like the US and Japan, high unemployment rates despite rapid economic growth in some Asian countries, and absolute falls in aggregate employment in parts of Latin America and Africa as well as in the crisis-ridden economies of East Asia. Such unemployment not only reflects the most tremendous human and social waste, but also leads to much greater social frustration and resentment among job seekers.

This is also a process that has been termed 'voiceless', because it denies true democratic voice to large sections of the population. This does not only refer to the authoritarian governments which have been associated with high economic growth. The unfettered functioning of markets in their desired fashion may actually require some degree of lack of democratic voice, simply because they involve growing inequalities. The denial of social and political participation goes hand in hand with the economic disenfranchisement of marginalized groups and social exclusion. In fact this is a tendency which is not confined to authoritarian politics, but is spread across many so-called democratic societies in both developed and developing worlds.

Similarly, the pattern of globalization has been relatively rootless, in its largely unthinking elimination of various forms of social, cultural and economic identity. This is related to its celebration and encouragement of the market-driven '*homo economicus*', working out all costs and benefits in rational choice-theoretic terms. One of the saddest and yet most frightening aspects of recent capitalist expansion is precisely this: that it reduces human nature to its most narrow and self-seeking aspect, and defines its goals in the most individualistic and ultimately non-creative way. As a result it has been able, through the sheer force of the economic incentives offered

110

and the pressures created, to mould societies and people in this restricted image, whereby potentially vast motivations are squeezed into the straitjacket of purely material and commercial aspirations. Thus it is that paradoxically, the process of capitalist globalization becomes simultaneously the celebration of economic self-interest; and inequalities are sought to be justified and made acceptable by holding out the slender hope that every individual has a chance to gain by winning out over his or her peers.

It also has operated to create a most extraordinary cultural sameness, a sort of hybrid 'McWorld' which has come to dominate the imagination and aspirations of especially the youth across the world. Even in Asia, a continent previously marked by diversity and the strength of local customs, the homogenizing influence of this one cultural pattern is now strongly evident, most markedly in the urban areas. At one level, to the casual observer, the victory of American culture over the minds and hearts of Asian youth has never seemed so complete. Technological changes and media spread have combined to disseminate the American Dream and to make it the common aspiration of middle classes everywhere.

This has made this universal culture of the last decade of this century the unabashed celebration of consumerism. It is most often presented, at least by its votaries, as the widening of choices and the proliferation of variety and difference. Consumers can supposedly choose between many different models of cars, between a range of food and clothing, and so on, and the logic of market processes ensures the continuous expansion of such choices. But this perception of individual consumer choice is illusory, for it is predicated on a prior limitation imposed by the nature of investments, and by the determination and manipulation of the enormous advertising industry. Indeed, the myth of diversity of consumer choice blurs two crucial points: the type of genuine choice offered, which is often quite restricted because certain things are

111

simply ruled out by the market, and the alleged independence of people's wishes in the face of a multi-billion dollar advertising industry.

It has been argued that the amazing ability of Disney et al. to colonize world culture stems from the age-old dichotomy between hard and easy, slow and fast, complex and simple. 'The first of these oppositions is bound up with amazing cultural achievements, while the second corresponds to our apathy, weariness and lethargy. Disney, McDonald's and MTV all appeal to the easy, fast and simple.'[2]

Thus we have the combination of an attempt at universal cultural unification on the basis of the least common denominator, combined with the fact that economic globalization and unfettered market functioning create deep and pervasive inequalities—across regions of the world, within countries, between classes and income groups. As mentioned earlier, these inequalities encompass gaps in wealth, income, access to productive employment, opportunities and a whole range of other material and social conditions. And they are made the more painful for those who are deprived, by the constant display of the advantages of being better off, emanating from both media imagery and actual consumption patterns of the wealthy.

The tensions and insecurities brought about by these widening inequalities cause people to seek refuge in particularities: political separation, regionalist demands, revanchist cultural movements, and so on. This may explain why so many people appear to have become so susceptible to social tendencies that tend to identify and blame some real or imagined 'other' for the harrowing gap between aspiration and reality. Because the real perpetrators of the problem appear too large or too remote to be confronted at all, antagonistic energies are diverted to those nearer home and easier to fight. Thus any social group that can somehow be treated as the 'other' becomes the object of hatred and violence. Imperialism paradoxically welcomes such diversion of the aggression borne out of frustration, not only because it divides those who would otherwise be arrayed against it, but because it creates a miasma of confusion about what the real problems are and who are the real culprits.

In India, we are familiar with the growing potency of fundamentalist and communalist tendencies and the support for such divisive forces even among the youth. We are also being made sickeningly aware of the grotesque forms that such reaction can take, whether in the burning of unprotected missionaries in Orissa, or in the insidious dislocation of Muslim families from homes and property in Mumbai, or even in the patriarchal violence against women that is growing within households. But these depressing tendencies are not confined to India; indeed, they find echo in reports of similar acts of open or repressed violence from other parts of Asia and from all over the world.

Thus, in Indonesia, the response, especially in the wake of severe economic crisis, is taking the form of Islamic reaction against Christians and growing antagonism between the Javanese and other groups on other islands. In Malaysia increasing friction between ethnic groups is observed, along with attacks on migrant workers. In Latin America the streets of the cities are no longer safe either for residents who can be mugged, or even for homeless street children who can be randomly shot at by self-styled vigilante groups. In Africa, the intense struggle over sparse resources among those at the bare margin of material survival has found expression in tribal conflicts which are then abetted and given greater credibility by imperialist powers keen to retain control over precious mineral and other assets. Everywhere in the developing world, small-scale violence is on the increase, and in some countries it has unfortunately been matched by large-scale violence as well.

Nor is the so-called developed world immune from such

113

tendencies. Religion-based militaristic extremist groups have been turning more violent in the US in recent times. Neo-fascist forces have gathered strength almost everywhere in Europe, and attacks on immigrants are growing apace. In the formerly socialist countries of eastern Europe, the expression has been in the form of the emergence of more petty nationalist identities, in a process that shows no hint of ending. In some parts of the world, most recently in the Kosovo region of Yugoslavia, the blatant interests of imperialist powers in stoking such separatist feelings and encouraging strife are now apparent.[3]

Of course, there are always some cultural roots to such social divisions, and it would be foolhardy to ascribe all social ills to material processes. But the role of economic alienation in generating perceptions of more fragmented and divided sociocultural identities cannot be denied. Even as the unifying forces of globalization expand and, octopus-like, attempt to swallow up other cultures, they sow the seeds of divisiveness and suggest this unity's own disintegration. This explains the paradox that the most prominent social result of globalization in recent times has been the assertion of narrow national or other social identity in its least generous form.

In fact, this is a tragic irony: that the response of those across the world who are affected adversely by these economic processes has been the rediscovery of such local, particularist loyalties along with a greater fracturing of and conflict within previously accepted national units, rather than an alternative internationalist vision. Most of the current revivalist or fundamentalist tendencies articulate the insecurities, both economic and cultural, of people whose governments have succumbed to the lure of globalization. But because they seek to divide those who are adversely affected, and attack minorities and progressive social movements, these tendencies ultimately weaken the ability of people all over the world to withstand the inequalizing march of today's globalization.

A similar point has been potently made by the sociologist Benjamin Barber, in an analysis which explicates the dialectical relationship between the forces of economic and cultural globalization, or 'McWorld', and the tribalist reaction which he calls 'Jihad'.

> Jihad and McWorld operate with equal strength in opposite directions, the one driven by parochial hatreds, the other by universalizing markets, the one re-creating ancient subnational and ethnic borders from within, the other making national borders porous from without. Yet Jihad and McWorld have this in common: they both make war on the sovereign nation-state and thus undermine the nation-state's democratic institutions. Each eschews civil society and belittles democratic citizenship, neither seeks alternative democratic institutions. Their common thread is indifference to civil liberty. Jihad forges communities of blood rooted in exclusion and hatred, communities that slight democracy in favour of tyrannical paternalism or consensual tribalism. McWorld forges global markets rooted in consumption and profit, leaving to an untrustworthy, if not altogether fictitious, invisible hand issues of public interest and common good that once might have been nurtured by democratic citizenries and their watchful governments. Such governments, intimidated by market ideology, are actually pulling back at the very moment they ought to be aggressively intervening.'[4]

Another possible danger of these right-wing tendencies is that by donning an explicit and exclusive majoritarian garb in each country in which they operate, they seek to appropriate the mantle of 'national sovereignty', and in doing so they sour the concept itself. Yet, much as it may be misused by the dangerous forces of reaction and ridiculed by the mouthpieces of international capital, 'national sovereignty' remains an important concept. The politics of nation states, which must in this context be democratically accountable ones, is still one arena in which the collectivity of people can hope to fashion some resistance to the onslaught of international capital and create democratic space for more equal social and economic interaction.

This is particularly so given that in the present conjuncture, economic globalization has integrated almost everything except, most crucially, workers who increasingly have nowhere to go but where they already are. This suggests that it is necessary to be nationalist not so much because there is any intrinsic value in such perceptions of nationhood and the nation-state, but because the nation remains the only feasible terrain in which a struggle can be waged against imperialism, against large multinational capital and its allies, as also the basic space within which citizens can hope to achieve any democratic rights.

Of course, the perception that pits nation against nation in an economic war is fundamentally false particularly currently, since the major economic victories in the international arena are being won today not by countries vis-à-vis each other, but by large capital in its various manifestations against working people across different nations. This is as true of the functioning of the World Trade Organization as it is of the major movements of international finance capital. But this is precisely why some form of genuine economic nationalism, which limits the sway of capital within particular national boundaries and allows for patterns of development which are more favourable to most of the citizens, is required as a weapon in the fight against imperialism and the spreading powers of large multinational capital.

Thus, a unified nationalism is critical only because it lays the basis for a broader and more potent internationalism, based on greater economic equality, democratic engagement and tolerance of difference. In turn, only such internationalism—rather than the unequal and undemocratic world created by imperialism—can create the space for societies in which 'otherness' does not imply enmity, and cultural diversity is not threatened but celebrated.

The national context

The arguments mentioned above apply in a general sense to large parts of the world which are experiencing either a resurgence of revivalist sentiment of various sorts, or highly exacerbated civil strife based on perceived ethnic, cultural, religious or linguistic differences. But they have a particular resonance in India at the present time. The 1990s in India have seen more than the gathering strength of fundamentalist tendencies and violent expressions of aggression against groups defined as 'other'. They have also witnessed what is an even more disturbing trend: the emergence of majoritarian fundamentalism as an acceptable and accepted political trend, functioning even within the portals of standard bourgeois democracy, and achieving a degree of political and social legitimization which would have been unthinkable even two decades earlier. Thus, the tribalist tendencies which were earlier contained have not only been strengthened, but have emerged as part of mainstream perception and even expressions of what is called the dominant, or majority, community. Similarly, the gathering strength of other fundamentalist thinking based on different social/religious/ linguistic groupings, is evidence of the social proliferation of this particular tendency.

It can be argued that this process is indeed dialectically related to the forces of economic and cultural globalization. Much as in other parts of the developing world where the inequalizing aspects of global economic integration have often led to extreme social and cultural reaction, the greater social acceptability in India of Hindutva and similar forces has had a lot to do with the economic repercussions of a pattern of growth which leaves the vast majority of the population either untouched or even worse off, while generating spiralling incomes and an increasingly flamboyant lifestyle of a minority.

Consider, to begin with, some of the more obvious stylized

117

facts about economic welfare in the country over the past decade. There is no direct data on income distribution that covers a substantial part of the 1990s, but some idea of distributional patterns can be gleaned from macroeconomic indicators as well as other evidence on the regional spread of growth, aggregate consumption patterns, relative prices and poverty estimates.

The 1990s are widely seen as the period when growth of national income 'took off' compared to earlier decades. Especially after 1992, real Gross National Product (in constant prices) grew at an average annual rate of 6.8 per cent, well above the 5 per cent average of the 1980s, which itself was higher than the 3 per cent average of earlier decades. Because of the fall in the rate of population growth, per capita national income also accelerated, to an average annual growth rate of nearly 5 per cent in the period 1992-97. But remarkably, these higher rates of growth have not been reflected in equivalent increases in per capita consumption to be found in survey data such as that of the National Sample Survey (NSS). Since the NSS data is known to underestimate the upper ends of the consumption spectrum, more unequal income distribution could help to explain the discrepancy.

The share of agriculture in national income has fallen over the decade, from 33 per cent in 1990 to under 28 per cent in 1997, even though the sector continues to employ just under two-thirds of the labour force. But what may be more significant is the evidence of the Survey data that in the rural areas, the trend towards diversification of income and employment to more non-agricultural activities may have been halted or reversed. This in turn can be related to trends in poverty and employment, as described below.

The latest published official data we have for poverty (relating to 1993-94) based on National Sample Survey estimates, suggests that the secular decline in the incidence of poverty over all of India, which was evident from the mid-

1970s to the late 1980s, has been halted or possibly even reversed. The all-India data based on NSS surveys shows that there were substantial fluctuations but no long-term time-trend in poverty from the early 1950s until the mid-1970s, so that the incidence of poverty was between 50 and 60 per cent for the total population, with poverty being more extensive in rural India. But from the late 1970s, or more precisely from 1977-78, there is indication of a fairly sharp decline until 1986-87, and a more sedate decline until 1989-90, when the proportion of people below the poverty line fell to 34 per cent for the rural areas and 34 per cent for urban India.

However, the picture for the 1990s is striking, for the declining trend was reversed or arrested for rural India, although it was still evident to a reduced extent for urban areas. In fact, if the period after 1990 is considered in more detail, then there was a sharp increase in poverty until 1992 (the period immediately following the imposition of stabilization measures and various other structural reforms) and a tapering off of this increase in 1993-94. Thus the major conclusion for the past two decades is that the period between 1973-74 and 1989-90 was characterized by a sustained decline in poverty ratios in both rural and urban India (indeed, this trend of declining poverty in India can really be dated from that period) and also that this process is no longer clearly evident for the subsequent period of the 1990s.[5]

A recent study using the 'small samples' of the NSS actually indicates an increase in the incidence of poverty in both rural and urban areas over the period 1993-94 to 1997. The percentage of people living below the poverty line in rural areas is estimated to have increased from 37.3 to 38.5 per cent, while in urban areas the rise has been from 32.4 to 34.0 per cent. This implies that the number of people living in absolute poverty in India went up from 276 million in 1989-90 to 349 million by 1997.[6]

Explanations of poverty have hinged crucially on a few

119

variables: the structure of asset ownership, which forms the underlying backdrop, and the changing pattern of opportunities for productive employment along with shifts in the relative price of food and other necessities, which are important in explaining changes in poverty incidence. Both of the latter variables have changed in the 1990s—the period of 'globalization'—in ways which would operate to increase poverty.

The increase in food prices, absolutely as well as relative to the general price level and to money wages, has been a significant feature of the adjustment experience in India thus far. Between December 1990 and December 1998, the wholesale price index for all commodities rose by 86 per cent, but that for food articles rose by more than 116 per cent, that is more than doubled.[7] The problem of rising food prices was especially acute in (largely urban) areas where the Public Distribution System had been widespread and where recent cuts have been evident. So, prices of food and other basic items have gone up much faster than the overall price level, reflecting the combined impact of agricultural trade liberalization and cuts in government expenditure especially on subsidies.

One of the major failures of the adjustment strategy in India in the 1990s has been the inadequate generation of employment. The Indian experience thus far indicates that the rate of employment generation is below both the rate of growth of output and the increase in the labour force. In the eight year period 1990-97, total organized sector employment increased by a paltry 6 per cent overall, that is well below 1 per cent per annum. Employment in the organized manufacturing sector over the same period increased by only 9 per cent, while manufacturing output has increased by nearly 50 per cent.

The 1980s were characterized by a relatively slow expansion of employment, but also by rising real wages and a fairly substantial drop in both the incidence and the severity of poverty, particularly in rural India. It has been argued that this can be related at least partially to the rapid increase in various subsidies and transfers from government to households, the large increase in revenue (rather than capital) expenditure on agriculture by central and state governments, and a very large increase in rural development expenditure.[8] Thus, while there were some linkage effects with modern industry and commerce in the rural areas, these were geographically limited, and the pivotal role in the expansion of rural non-agricultural employment in particular, may have been played by government in this period.

However, since 1991, the official economic strategy has implied further reductions in the employment generation capacity of the organized sector as well as adversely affected rural non-agricultural employment. This strategy was no accident: it was very much part of both the standard IMF adjustment package as well as the mainstream perception of the diminished role of government in the market-oriented globalized world. This overall approach led to the following specific policies which have affected the pattern of employment: actual declines in government spending on rural development in the central budgets, as well as declines in the fertilizer subsidy; reduced central government transfers to state governments which have thereby been forced to cut back on their own spending; diminished real expenditure on rural employment and anti-poverty schemes; declines in public infrastructural and energy investments which affect the rural areas; reduced spread and rise in prices of the public distribution system for food; cuts in social expenditure such as on education, health and sanitation; financial liberalization measures which have effectively reduced the availability of rural credit.

As a result, there has been an absolute decline in rural non-agricultural employment since 1991. This has been accompanied by a large relative shift towards agricultural work, particularly by women, and since the rate of growth of agricultural output has slowed down after the reforms, and there have been increases in rural poverty, this appears to be evidence of a distress shift into agriculture given the lack of alternative income opportunities. So the post-reform increase in agricultural employment took place not in the context of greater rural prosperity but reflected greater adversity.

In urban areas, there has been a trend increase in casual employment and a trend decline in regular employment for both men and women. For men, the increase in casual employment has largely been at the cost of regular employment; and this trend appears to have continued into the post-reform period. For women, on the other hand, both casual and regular work appear to have increased after the reforms in the urban areas, but casual contracts have dominated. This is part of a wider process of feminization of work observed in all developing countries, which has also been associated with employers' greater preference for female employees largely because of the lower wages and inferior working conditions associated with such employment.

In rural areas, on the other hand, a trend of declining self-employment for both males and females appears to have been reversed with the reforms. This is due entirely to an increase in agricultural self-employment, reflecting the shift away from non-agriculture, and is also, in large part, caused by the distress induced increase in female unpaid family work noted earlier. Regular employment has continued to decline and casualization of wage employment has continued to increase. There has been a particularly sharp increase in female casual employment following the reforms, confirming the distress nature of rural employment developments.

Thus, employment in the formal sector has fallen in both rural and urban areas, and has not been compensated by the more insecure and typically lower paid employment opportunities in the non-formal sectors of the economy. This has created two related effects. Since the overwhelming majority of the workers in India are in the unorganized sector where wage incomes are not indexed to inflation, they are disproportionately affected by inflation and especially by the rise of food prices—and this proportion of population has increased over the 1990s. Thus, not only are the employment conditions faced by most of the labour force more volatile and insecure, the wages that emerge from such contracts are also less certain to command basic necessities for working class and peasant households. Second, the very insecurity of employment, especially in urban areas, has created pressures for secondary activities that could add to the household income and has also caused increased resentment of those with significantly higher standards of living.

At the same time, the process of economic liberalization along with the pattern of government spending has been associated with a multiplication of the real incomes of richer groups. Financial liberalization has involved an explosion in financial sector activities and incomes in this sector. Increasingly, professional incomes in finance approach the levels in developed countries, even while real wages in the rest of the economy stagnate and general employment becomes more precarious. Other white-collar services, and related incomes from activities such as construction, trade, advertising and so on which feed on the boom in consumption of higher income groups, have also increased dramatically. Trade liberalization has brought growing access to a much wider range of consumption goods and international brand names to the Indian upper and middle classes. The apparently insatiable hunger for imported goods is evident from the fact that non-oil imports have continued to increase hugely despite the ongoing recession in the domestic manufacturing industry.

Along with this, there has come a cultural revolution of the sort described above, which is also fed by the emergence of satellite television and huge increases in advertising budgets

123

of companies operating in the Indian market. This has greatly increased the role of the demonstration effect in the consumption patterns of Indian upper and middle income groups. And this cultural revolution has been associated with a much more open display of conspicuous consumption than was traditionally prevalent in Indian society. The implications of the spread of such communications and the effects of post-modern advertising trends in rural India in particular, have still not been adequately studied.

In the large metropolises and cities of the country, such a tendency towards open display of wealth and conspicuous consumption has been a feature that has been more and more evident over the past two decades. But observers have noted this tendency in rural India as well, in forms that were not previously so obvious. It is a reflection of the reduced interaction between the various rural classes, and a diminished concern on the part of rural elites towards the poorer sections, that used to mark the more paternalistic relations of the past. As social relations fragment and become more contractual, they also lose the few elements of cohesiveness that make location-specific communities functional.

It does not take a vast amount of sociological insight to realize that this combination of greater material insecurity in terms of both lower real incomes and more precarious employment opportunities for a very large section of the population, with the explosion of conspicuous consumption on the part of a relatively small but highly visible minority, can have very adverse social and political consequences. These consequences tend to be exacerbated by the cultural influences that come across as hegemonic, and which increasingly determine the aspirations of the youth in particular. Thus, as mentioned above, there is a premium not only on the joys of material consumption but also on individualism, the greater proliferation of the idea that success (which essentially is measured in terms of material advancement) reflects individual talent and achievement rather than any wider social processes, and that it can often be achieved only in competition with one's peers.

The alienation that comes from lack of such success—or even from success which is deemed to be inadequate given the ambition—can only too easily be directed towards any apparent or potential competitor in such a system, or even towards those who are not in competition but simply represent a group that can be attacked with relative ease. The current streak of venom that is being directed towards various minority groups can be seen as one expression of this trend. So the inability to confront those who are actually benefiting from the system, or even the lack of desire to do so given that they still have the power to distribute some amount of material largesse, means that they cannot be the objects of any aggressive vent for frustration. Rather, the outlet is found in terms of growing antagonism, increasingly finding violent expression, towards other categories of people who are nearer home, closer in terms of lifestyle and more susceptible to such attack.

It is worth noting that often these groups are already the most disadvantaged and materially weak sections of society. Thus, Muslims on average hold less property and other assets, have lower incomes and less education, and weaker access to more attractive jobs, than those calling themselves Hindus in most parts of the country. The recent attacks on Christians have been most marked in precisely those regions of the country where they are already among the poorest, the least developed and most marginalized elements of that particular society, whether by virtue of their tribal status or for other reasons.

What is being suggested here is that such expressions of antagonism towards what are called 'minorities' occur less because of very specific and particular causes than because, in a phase of general frustration and alienation with wider forces which seem too powerful to be taken on, these groups become

125

softer targets and vents for a more general rage. This is not to deny the role of particular historical and cultural relationships which are significant and can always be traced in any place and period of strife. The point is rather that some evidence of historical animosity or current grievance can always be found, and so this in itself may shed some light on the detail of a specific incident but does not really illuminate the more general process.

As it happens, there are always several layers of peaceful interaction and conflict that mark the relationship between communities. Indeed, the very definition or the self-perception of the community itself keeps changing depending upon specific social/economic/political/cultural configurations and the perception of who or what the 'other' is. Therefore, when there are episodes (or even continuing stories) of violence and aggression, the question that needs to be asked is why these flare up at this particular time, and why these seem to represent a more general tendency. Some of the explanation has been provided above, but of course it remains true that the economic factors can be only one part of what is a very complex social process.

The rise of Hindutva as a major social and political force urgently demands a more general explanation, rather than one couched in terms of the particular and the specific. But first it is necessary to make it clear that it is misleading to refer to it as a tendency of the majority of the population. The rhetoric is certainly majoritarian, and the aim is to present it as an assertion of nationalist or even civilizational identity, based on an imagined past and a manipulative approach to history. But in actuality it represents the interests of a very small minority—typically male upper class and upper caste— and even of a relatively small sub-section within that group. The ability of the ideology to influence so many people who are not likely to benefit from and may even emerge as victims of its spread, is the real question, but is not one that can be dealt with adequately here.

But there are other features of this brand of pseudo-nationalism which need to be highlighted, because we know that the destructive implications of its spread can be even worse than those that the society has already experienced. One important feature is the centralizing and monolithic character of the ideology, which seeks to suppress all forms of cultural variation and all deviations from its own rigid conception. Probably, in respect of society and culture, the unfortunate—and even dire—ramifications of such a position are only too well known, in terms of suppression of all sorts of freedom and artistic creativity, intolerance verging on aggression vis-à-vis any explicit attempts to be different, and so on. But there are also serious economic implications of this ideology.

In economic terms, this position is damaging not only because it is now clear that its claim to 'swadeshi' was fundamentally false, but because it does not accept the existence of domestic socioeconomic forces that have hitherto retarded economic development for most of the Indian people. In the Hindutva world view, the only internal enemies are those determined by social and cultural differences. There is no recognition of classes or even of domestic economic antagonisms in this perspective, and therefore no understanding of the constraining role on development which can be played by certain classes such as large landed interests and big capital.

This has several consequences in terms of economic policies and their effects on various segments of society. First of all, this position sees no need for a transformation of political and economic power configurations within the country. Because it preserves the status quo (except insofar as it seeks to further deprive the proclaimed 'minorities') it also adds to the effect of the broader economic policies which have been underway in the past decade. Thus, liberalization and globalization

127

processes continue to favour a small group of the already privileged, and either worsen or leave unaltered the economic conditions of the majority. Under the BJP-led dispensation, the interests of rural and urban working groups have continued to be systematically disregarded and denied, now with the added proviso that this is necessary in order to further supposedly 'national' interests, which actually means the already propertied groups.

In addition, the process of fiscal centralization, which has also become a significant part of the BJP's actual (rather than stated) agenda, is not only unfairly slanted across regions and inherently undemocratic, but also threatens much more social and political instability in the country by effectively promoting the strengthening of regional identities.

The more sophisticated of the ideologues of Hindutva have argued that their economic strategy is essentially a corporatist and consensual one which takes (Hindu) civilizational identity as its binding glue and uses confrontation with 'others' as a means of achieving national harmony. This is more than simply false. It would be deeply misconceived even if it were true. The problem is ultimately the same as with all corporatist economic strategies: that they are simply not sustainable unless some groups or classes are willing to continuously subordinate their interests to what is projected as the general good.

When such subordinate groups amount to the vast majority of the population—which is certainly the case given the class character of the Hindutva lobby and the Sangh parivar in general—corporatism is easily revealed to be yet another means for differential exploitation of workers. And economic 'nationalism' in this context really means allowing full rein to domestic capitalists in such exploitation.

Ultimately, the underlying problem with this type of economic pseudo-nationalism is that it fails to realize what the true basis of a desirable nationalism is in the current international context. This has already been outlined above. What remains to be noted here is that this type of pseudo-nationalism is very favourable to the imperialist interests not only because it serves to divide those whose interests are more in common, but because it deflects interest and energy into unproductive and debilitating conflicts which do not address the main enemy. Similarly, the other fundamentalist or tribalist responses that emerge also divert attention and energy from the more important divisive forces coming from international processes and domestic economic patterns.

Thus, the current Indian scene provides a good example of the effects of contemporary capitalist globalization, which tends to create processes which divide economies and societies even as it supposedly brings the world together. These divisions find many expressions, of which perceptions of difference based on various social/cultural criteria are some of the most important. The fragmentation that this entails, even when it spills over into violence, does little to improve either the situation or the perceptions of those who are affected by it. Rather, it encourages the perpetuation of a process of more inequality, division and separation between people.

Notes

1. Data updated from UNDP Human Development Report, New York, 1997.
2. Hans-Peter Martin and Harold Schumann, London, Zed Books, 1997, p. 14-15.
3. The role of the western imperialist powers in encouraging sectarian militancy in Kosovo was been carefully documented by Vinta Singh, 'NATO intervention in Yugoslavia: The Rest of Western Credibility', *Mainstream*, 22 May 1999.
4. Benjamin R. Barber, *Jihad vs McWorld: How Globalization and Tribalism Are Reshaping The World*, New York, 1996.
5. *Economic and Political Weekly*, Special Number 1996, Nos. 31, Nos. 35-37.

6. The study was conducted by Dr S.P. Gupta, Member, Planning Commission, Government of India, and presented in a paper 'Globalization, Economic Reforms and the role of Labour,' paper for ILO National Workshop on Economic Reforms and Labour: Lessons for India from the East Asian Experience, New Delhi, May 1999.
7. Data from the Economic Survey of the Government of India, and the National Accounts Statistics of the CSO.
8. ILO-ARTEP Working Paper, New Delhi, 1997.

The Gender Predicament Of The Hindu Right

Tanika Sarkar

I

A number of methodological and conceptual inadequacies foreclose a serious understanding of the Hindu Right in general, and of its women's wings and 'gender strategies in particular. It is difficult to understand why, even after the Hindu Right has dominated the centrestage of national politics for more than a decade, its critics are so very reluctant to even want to know it.[1]

Critiques of the Right avoid a close encounter with the object of their study through three distinct strategies of displacement and slippage. One is the method of displacement through conflation. The Hindu Right is described as a phenomenon of modern times, a modernity that is irretrievably mortgaged to post-Enlightenment forms of western knowledge. This large and somewhat vague generalization may be true enough. But from here, there is both an unwarranted leap and a dishonest displacement. The origin in modernity then becomes its sufficient criticism: that it, the Right, is at fault not because it is violent, authoritarian, majoritarian and anti-

democratic, but because it is modern, because it is tainted by
alien influence—a criticism that, incidentally, absorbs certain
important suppositions from its own target. Delicately but
surely, then, criticism of the Right is slid onto other
contemporary—though fundamentally non-comparable—
politics of modern times that, too, owe something to western
influences: nationalism, secularism, socialism, feminism.
Internal divergences among all these kinds of politics, and
their basic differences from the Hindu Right are implicitly,
without providing enough grounds, made redundant.
Eventually, what had promised to develop into a critique of
the Hindu Right's intolerance, emerges as a full-blown critique
of secular and Left politics or of nationalism of all varieties.
Because all are modern and West-inspired, all are essentially
many sides of the same coin. Of course, even this massive act
of conflation does not quite explain why—if all are the same—
the critique should revolve around nationalism, secularism
and the Left, eventually to the complete exclusion of any
serious criticism of the Right itself.

The second device for the avoidance of an engagement
with the Right proceeds through the method of reification.
The main function of the Right is—again, more or less
correctly—understood to be the inculcation of violence. At
this point, we leave the specific purpose of the violence that
is unleashed by the Right and its political-ideological
characteristics, the history of the conjunctures which allowed
this violence to unfold in very precise circumstances and ways.
Instead, we have as our subject a transcendental, meta-historical
figure called violence with definite characterological
manifestations, which stalks across all kinds of times and
spaces with innate, uniform drives and tendencies of its own.
It is then conjoined by its effect or offspring—Pain—which,
too, has universal and singular traits. We forget about little
things like communalism, fascism, or about even smaller
matters like Indian politics—be it of 1946-47, 1984, 1992 or
1998—or about distinctive political groups, interests, classes,

castes. Violence becomes the subject of enunciation, the proper noun, which activates the verbs. Indian men and women become mere sites, props in a theatre in which Violence or Pain speaks and moves.

The third way of skirting round the issue of the Right—and, politically, the most costly one, perhaps—is the strategy of Left discourses. There is, first of all, an impressionistic generalization about its class-base—that it is an urban trader-business-service sector, largely of upper castes. But having asserted that, there is an instant description of its political character as fascistic or semi-fascistic. Again, true enough, possibly, but the connecting links are not established through a close, detailed historical analysis of its formation, political work, ideological apparatus, organizational methods or propaganda tactics.

Given the dimness of the figure of the Right, it is understandable that a feminist understanding of its gender ideology or the politics of its women does not seem easily possible. For here, even journalistic inputs are more or less lacking, and information is hazy. At the most, attempts are made to establish that despite its talk about the Uniform Civil Code, or its display of prominent women politicians, or its critique of the problems of Muslim women, the Right is, at heart, a patriarchal force. And this patriarchalism is from time to time described, somewhat inefficiently, as fundamentalism—a label that may well be true, but which needs to be established through more serious research. Again, the problem lies not so much with the answers as with the fact that questions are not being asked.

II

I would like at this point to briefly and schematically draw out some general conclusions from nineteenth centry debates on the Hindu woman's conjugal life and from the discourses of political nationalism. It is important to recall the trajectory of those discourses because they provided a language and a range of problems and tensions that the Right has to negotiate with even to this day.

Pundits of modern Indian history have kindly and patronizingly allocated the entire sphere of women's history to a 'lower' rung of women and feminist historians since they consider it a domain of no great importance in itself. But they have done so at some peril even to their own conception of the important issues of our history. For, a history of Indian women in modern times is also a specifically Indian history of rights—at the level of concept, of political movements and political language. It is also a history of resistance to the discourse of equal rights. In colonial times, there were some efforts to rectify some extreme aspects of brahmanical patriarchy which had percolated down to the normative worlds of all upwardly-mobile segments of Hindu castes. The mode of intervention was legislative change—most notably in the cases of banning of widow immolation, the legalization of widow remarriage and the escalation of the age of consent. Feminists have tirelessly pointed out that there was not much immediate or practical import on actual female lives. At the same time, lawmaking as a process had two momentous and related consequences. For the first time, Hindu marriage was debated and discussed in the public sphere where a few women participated as critical and privileged commentators. Also, for the first time, lawmaking had become a public activity, a transparent process, even when the actual law was framed by a closed colonial state.

As a result of the public debates where multiple alternatives were arguing with one another, not only were many dominant paradigms of thinking about marriage, family and intimate human relationships articulated, but they were also required to compete with one another in terms of self justifications and mutual critiques. If earlier marriage codes and customs—however diverse and plural—were non-negotiable presumptions that were given as fixed, and demarcated as the natural order of things, now all alternatives needed to defend themselves in public, in the presence of women, to persuade and convince. Because they needed to convince, all shades of opinion—liberal, orthodox, revivalist—began to go beyond the statutory references to scripture and custom and to claim that their particular alternative safeguarded the woman's best interests. More, that it enjoyed the woman's will, consent and pleasure. Of course, most such claims were manipulative, dishonest, products of instrumental reasoning. It is still important to point out that in the process of such arguments, the woman's will or consent gained acceptance as a new ground for normative constructions.

Liberal reformers relied on laws. To women this gave—at least nationally—a legal personhood that could sit at odds with the commands and prescriptions of her traditional guardians and masters—husband, family, caste and kin-group, community. It was a step towards a possibility of individuation away from the rule of custom and scripture, if they threatened her death—her physical death, in case of sati and infant conjugality, and her sexual death in terms of celibate widowhood. This individuated space was the first ground on which something like a notion of absolute individual right to life began to emerge. In contrast, revivalist reformers like the Arya Samajists bypassed the legal process altogether. The modifications in the conjugal system that they advocated came not so much from an individuated selfhood that could lead to a notion of immunities or rights, but as a gift from the reformed husband, family, from the new community of the Aryas. They, therefore, knitted the woman more securely into the old structure of commands.

Neither liberal reformers nor revivalists nor the colonial state articulated the notion of a female selfhood based on an

135

absolute possession of rights. Yet, their public arguments created a space for at least a qualified acceptance for the notion of the woman's assent to her prescribed condition. The new ground was reinforced through the emergence of the discourse of political nationalism and its anti-colonial agenda. This developed and refined the concept of self-determination by people as the site for nation formation. Even before Gandhian nationalism and Left anti-imperialism had, in their different ways, recognized labouring classes as the privileged subjects of anti-colonial nationalism, nineteenth century nationalists had increasingly been talking about the innate right and capability of a people to decide on the basic nature of governance. Political nationalism acknowledged self-determination as a moral imperative, if only in the sphere of nation-making.

Hindu revivalism or cultural nationalism, however, provided a very different moral imperative. Instead of self-determination as a right of the female individual or the people, it referred to the uniqueness of the culture of the Hindu *volk*. It also referred to the powers over individuals that it required in order to preserve itself from extinction when faced with a different and triumphant cultural system. Here the Hindu woman was allotted a unique responsibility as the site of past freedom and future nationhood, since the Hindu man had already supposedly compromised his cultural authenticity. On her fixed, unchanging obedience to community prescriptions would depend the life of her tradition and religion. She was, therefore, the source of authenticity, nation-making, freedom. But this huge political role depended on an abdication of all agency and self-determination in actual practice. The discourses of liberal reformism and political nationalism on the one hand, and that of Hindu revivalism and cultural nationalism on the other, can be differentiated from each other on this ground: are people a site of autonomy and self-determination, or of authenticity and culture preservation? Is the woman a

136

rights-bearing individual, or a culture-bearing one?

The Hindu Right has inherited this structure of possibilities and problems and it has had to steer a very delicate and difficult course. When it emerged in the 1920s, political nationalism, Left anti-imperialism, womens' movements and low caste protest movements had, despite their mutual differences and conflicts, all fed into a discourse of rights and self determination which had already emerged as a deeply-ingrained value in the political sphere. So hegemonic was this as a political value that its overt and explicit refutation would be suicidal for any political interest striving for hegemony and power. The Right's political articulations have had, therefore, to verbally confirm the validity of a democratic, constitutional mode of governance that is based on notions of universal citizenship rights on the one hand, and on affirmative supports to historically disadvantaged groups on the other.

On the other hand, a formal commitment to this order does not constrain the Right's authoritarian, anti-emancipatory agenda unduly. For, it can simultaneously rely on and bring to play another resource that has also come down from the nineteenth century: the intentions and the discourses of Hindu revivalism and cultural nationalism. Through its arguments around the Hindu woman's ideal mode of being, nineteenth century cultural nationalism had created a larger theoretical justification not only for the brahmanical form of conjugality, but, by implication, of the entire complex of the brahmanical hierarchical system. It was now defended on the ground of an embattled Hindu cultural and religious authenticity. Revivalistic cultural nationalism tried to reinforce an adherence to this comprehensive system of absolute inegalitarianism by branding all projects that had any emancipatory potential—however slight—as borrowed, alien, a surrender to colonization of culture and minds of Hindus. The large, comprehensive implications of the nineteenth century debates on Hindu conjugality, and their historical implications for caste, class and the poor and the dissident, are extremely significant, for the assumptions that were developed about the condition of the woman could serve as a metaphor and a protean argument for a freeze on any discourse of equal rights.

The Hindu Right today has been able to manoeuvre very skilfully with this inherited tension and debate: openly it rarely challenges the discourse of rights as such, though it has tried many times to suppress different kinds of rights that do not belong to upper-caste rich Hindu males of its own political persuasion. But it has successfully cast the very intention of emancipatory, libertarian politics of equal rights into doubt by branding it as an alien product that will doom the future of Hindu cultural authenticity.

The Hindu Right today stands at a transitional moment in its history when it still tries to hold on to the possibilities generated by both kinds of discourses that are fundamentally incompatible—equal rights and cultural authenticity. It attempts a resolution by stitching up the two. It talks incessantly of Hindu rights, the rights of the majority community and the rights of a threatened culture and nation. Hindus are signs of both weakness and strength—as the majority community, and as threatened culture. In either capacity, they are to be granted superior rights that preclude notions of equality.

The tension forms a language that to secular ears sometimes sounds like either doublespeak or incoherence. In the area of women's conditions, a critique of Muslim polygamy or sati, the foregrounding of women politicians of the BJP, are aligned to paeans of praise to traditions of brahmanical Hinduism, and to occasional fundamentalist pronouncements even by their women leaders which applaud sati, criticize women's employment, divorce and widow remarriage and flay rebellious sexual preferences like lesbianism.[2] Amrita Basu considers that it is futile to look for any logical structuring behind the incompatible issues; they are dictated by sheer political expediency, decided according to vote banks and constituencies.³ While this may hold true for the BJP, for the Sangh parivar as a whole, I think it is possible to uncover an underlying logic that is extremely complicated and tortuous but that, nonetheless, binds the contradictory stances together.

III

The Rashtriya Swayamsevak Sangh, founded in 1925, has steadfastly remained an all-male organization down to this day. Its founder Hedgewar had initially refused to consider the opening of a women's wing. However, in 1936, eleven years after its own beginning, the RSS responded to the pleas of Lakshmibai Kelkar, mother of an important Sangh member. The Rashtrasevika Samiti was founded in 1936 with daily shakhas that provided physical, martial arts as well as ideological or *boudhik* training. It remained, however, a small and low-keyed affair. Though the second oldest women's organization affiliated to a political body, it was overtaken and completely overshadowed by nationalist and Left women's movements. It participated in no mass struggles—anti-colonial or for women's rights—and it was not foregrounded by the RSS in any of its own activities. The second *sarsanghchalak* and supreme ideological guru of the RSS, M.S. Golwalkar, saw no reason to specify a distinctive or important role for it within the Sangh complex. His strictures to the women of Sangh families taught them how to run their homes and to bring up their children on the correct Sangh values. The Samiti was not required to play a significant part in RSS self-fashioning.⁴

Around 1989-90, in a sudden and dramatic spurt of activities, the Sangh parivar threw up a large number of women's organizations and women leaders into dazzling prominence—the BJP Mahila Morcha, the VHP Matri Mandal and Durga Vahini with their different regional versions. Thousands of karsevikas participated in the attacks on the

Babri Masjid and in its demolition and their role was highlighted in the Sangh media products—the Jain Studio videofilms, the VHP fortnightly magazine *Hindu Chetna*, Hindi video newsmagazines like *Kalachakra*. On 6 January 1993, a month after the demolition of the Babri Masjid, a women's celebratory demonstration was held at Ayodhya where Sadhvi Rithambhara was a guest of honour.[5] Women were active and prominent in the bloody riots that swept across India in the course of the Ramjanmabhoomi movement—in Bhagalpur, at Ahmedabad, in Bombay.[6] The role of Rithambhara's audiocassetted speech and Uma Bharati's propaganda tours in stoking ferocious anger and aggression against Muslims was memorable.[7]

I did extensive fieldwork among Delhi-based women of the Hindu Right between 1990 and 1993, at a time when the Sangh parivar was simultaneously engaged in a mass movement of violence against Muslims and in an electoral bid to capture power at the Centre. The Sangh began to flaunt its women, for the first time in its history, in public places and roles. It was a special moment, very upbeat and self-confident, a moment of spectacular growth and spread, a phase of mass mobilization and movement—all of which were new and heady departures for the Sangh and its women. At the Samiti office, officebearers told me of an internal struggle that had preceded the Samiti's decision to allow and train women as karsevikas. They said that it had been the young members who forced the hands of the Samiti. The Samiti was in an excited and hopeful mood, claiming credit for the growth of women's wings and activism.[8]

I observed at that time that the Samiti had come a long way from the parametres laid down by Golwalkar about pure domesticity. The women of the Sangh come from conservative, domesticated urban, middle class and upper caste backgrounds. They were now beginning to go in for some education, and even into jobs and political work for the first time. The Samiti trained such women for their newly-gained public roles and identities. Although the primary focus remained on women within the home, for a new generation of more active women, it could impart self-confidence and competences. I had also observed that these new possibilities had opened up some fractures within the established pattern of work and ideas. The Samiti's journal *Jagriti* reflected deep ambivalences about the women's movements, with older Sangh leaders warning against their disruptive influence, but ordinary contributors occasionally identifying themselves with them. There were articles about the woman's empowerment needs against male domination, discrimination and violence. There were observations that seemed to criticize all Indian traditions as implicated in that. Young Samiti activists like Vidushi criticized sati more comprehensively and stridently than would her elders. She also underlined the Samiti's autonomy from the Sangh more strongly than did senior officeholders like Rekha Raje.[9] Young girls from RSS families at Khurjha complained that their political activism was cruelly thwarted by early marriage and the burden of housework from which their families would not exempt them.[10]

The tension, however, was structured by and contained within a generally conservative domesticity—a modernized and somewhat loose and flexible version of brahmanical patriarchy. That allowed and encouraged education, employment and a more informed and activist politicization only on the basis of communal violence and commitment to an extremely inegalitarian social perspective. The women were upper caste and middle class. They were stitched securely into the class-caste interest and politics of their milieu. They rarely raised issues of gender justice very openly or fully, and never participated in any struggles against gender oppression. At the same time, certain incipient dissonances were unleashed even by their politics of communal violence and through the transformations in new urban middle-class households in this generation.

141

I found the fieldwork a profoundly disturbing and revealing experience. As feminists, we had always celebrated the release of women from pure domesticity, their politicization had always been assumed to be an emancipatory possibility, and the relationship between communal violence and women had been seen as one of male-inflicted violence and female victimhood. A communalized female subjecthood seemed a new and unsettling phenomenon.

The last year of the century finds the Sangh parivar in significantly changed circumstances. The mass phase of this fascistic formation is closing down, movements being replaced with rhetoric and even their few feeble populist gestures dying out fast. Expansion, especially among lesser social strata which are not the traditional Sangh strongholds, is now replaced with consolidation of existing gains. State power, or its very close proximity in a loose coalition with many political groups, has necessitated a sharper differentiation between the electoral front of the BJP and other Sangh affiliates like the Samiti, the VHP or the Swadeshi Jagaran Manch. Much accommodation has been made with globalization in State policies and its cultural impact has led to acute discomforts among the old guard. In short, an unprecedented preoccupation with the grasping of State power and with its maintenance has led to prospects of the dilution of the old Sangh character, with a need to juggle with its different affiliates at different times with amazing dexterity. While doors had to be opened, perforce, to new allies, constituencies and policies hitherto unthinkable for the Sangh, there has been an acute need, also, to revive and preserve old values and to harden old convictions in certain areas within the parivar. It is my impression that the women's wing has been entrusted with the conservation of old and inner values.

Going back to the women of the Samiti in April 1999 opened up new sources of disturbance for me. It, however, also brought a few crumbs of comfort. If we feminists had found the communalized public identity of Sangh women disturbing, the Sangh men seemed to have found it even more so, for different reasons. I went back at a moment of deliberate withdrawal of women's activism and a folding back of the public potential. The women are, with some exceptions that I shall discuss later, being pulled back into homes. Golwalkar's restricted and restrictive strictures on domesticity and the housebound woman have been retrieved and refurbished. The Samiti has been socialized into a less expansive future. I had hesitated to use the word 'fundamentalism' in the early 1990s, either about the Sangh's gender ideology, or about its women's organizations. I am convinced that the fundamentalist turn is now accomplished. I feel, moreover, that it was not my misrecognition that had earlier missed the point. It was something that has unfolded later, partly because of the dissonances and paradoxes that I had observed at that time. But, above all, it happened because of a changed historical situation and its new logic. I shall come back to this later.

Let me, first of all, establish my point about the retreat. The BJP had been in power in Delhi, till fairly recently, for five continuous years. It had ruled for more than a year at the Centre. Yet, the Delhi Samiti membership seems to have been halved. It had stood at 2000 in 1991, according to Samiti reckoning. Now the same office-bearers put it at 1000, or a little more than that. The *shakhas* have gone down from sixty in the past year to a maximum of fifty-two at present. Earlier I had been given to understand that *shakhas* met twice a day, but now there seems to be only two that do so. Most are bi-weekly affairs.[11] The areas of concentration seem to remain the same—those settled by refugees from west Punjab initially, which are now doing very well, or in old, affluent trading, service-sector areas: Kamala Nagar, Lajpat Nagar, Rohini, Vikaspuri, Punjabi Bagh, Paschim Vihar, Karolbagh, Rajindar Nagar, Moti Nagar. The social catchment areas are the same as with the Sangh, though far less numerous: traders, middle-ranking service people, mostly of refugee origins, i.e. people with bitter memories of Partition and riots that the Samitis do much to keep alive. Poonam Gupta, the *pracharika*, confessed that young girls are not all that active, though older married 'ladies' seem more enthusiastic—so that, most popular Samiti timings are 11 a.m. *shakhas*, when middle-class housewives gather together. Trading and middle-class service sector families tend to be almost entirely upper caste and officebearers did not refute my supposition that most of their members are also from these circles.

Socially and geographically, there has been stagnation and even decline in Delhi. On an all-India scale, the total membership has remained constant at two lakhs over the past decade, even though the Sangh parivar has seen a rapid growth in its power. Again, the 5000 urban sites that the Samiti covers, have remained fairly constant over the decade, with some recent growth in the South and Punjab. It is fashionable among guilt-ridden secular feminists to declare that the Right has seized the initiative in the women's movement from the hands of secular forces. Apart from the fact that the Samiti is part of no movement, and, indeed, abjures all plans of starting one, the impression of growth is based on total ignorance of facts and figures. In fact, women's movements and organizations are one area where Left and radical forces enjoy an overwhelming edge over the Right. The All-India Democratic Women's Association alone has a membership of more than 50 lakhs and it has grown very rapidly in the last decade. The bulk of the force is recruited from rural women.[12] The Samiti, on the other hand, admits that the rural breakthrough is still awaited.[13] Add to the AIDWA a very large number of organizations all across the country that are engaged in radical movements and programmes, and we get numbers that are impressive by any count, certainly breathtaking by Sangh-Samiti standards. We need to remember that the growth in Leftist women's organizations occurred in the teeth of adverse circumstances.

While the last decade has been a fortunate one for the Sangh, Left forces have not done well except in this sector. In Delhi, which has for very long been a Sangh stronghold, the membership stands at about a thousand. The Left, always very insignificant in the city, numbers about 20,000 in the CPM-affiliated women's organization, and many more outside it in autonomous groups.

There are, however, two important new growth areas in Delhi. In some trans-Yamuna slums in East Delhi, and in the Jawaharlal Nehru University, the Samiti runs fairly regular *shakhas* among daughters of domestic servants, though the JNU wing is also patronized by some students.[14] It is significant that the areas are strictly segregated, so the middle-class and the lower class segments do not mix.

In the early 1990s, the Samiti was engaged in a variety of programmes. It ran a fairly substantial monthly magazine *Jagriti*, provided orientation courses for wives of RSS men who had come from non-RSS families,[15] conducted correspondence courses for newly married Samiti members who had joined non-RSS families and who found it difficult to attend *shakhas*.[16] All these programmes have been discontinued. The only new addition has been to open discussion groups for old women[17]— presumably because the reinforced patriarchal declarations of the Samiti would not be resisted by them. Also, they would be less aligned to the 'westernized cultural perversions' that Samiti elders are most concerned about and that they see as a major problem among young girls. Would the declining affiliation among girls and the new interest in older and elderly women indicate an interesting retreat among the new generation, a partial failure among the new middle classes whose daughters might benefit from physical and even communal training, but who would still go the 'western' way, leaving the Samiti paradigm behind in some vital respects, thus further fuelling the Samiti's current obsession with modern libertarianism? This reminds me of some research that I did on RSS-run schools in Delhi 1994. The schoolchildren were loyal enough to the school, except when it came to cultural activities. They were unhappy about the ban on western pop music and they were bitterly sarcastic about the fact that at school picnics, they had to sing *bhajan* after *bhajan*. This might sound like a familiar conflict between generations, but we need to remind ourselves that the RSS self-definition is that it is a 'cultural organization'. From its inception, it has remained committed to taking over the entire political and cultural universe of its young volunteers. Its central agenda has always been the training of the future citizens of Hindu Rashtra: young, upper caste, affluent, educated men and women. The possible partial failure in this respect would be a major retreat for them.

Now the *Jagriti* has been discontinued, replaced with an annual news sheet, Sevika. The difference in nomenclature is interesting, for *Jagriti* or Awakening had a dynamic, forceful ring to it that tried to merge into the mainstream women's movement and its language. The cover depicted a young girl resolutely stepping out of darkness into a circle of light.[18] Again, the visual self-representation would not jar on the sensibility of the women's movement. The articles talked mostly about women's problems in modern cities, and provided some instructions about how to negotiate them with strength and dignity. They also discussed citizenship rights and how these could be realized. There was a strong note of protest against discrimination, an untheorized yet implicit recognition of patriarchal oppression. Even though *shakhas* did daily brainwashing about the plight of Hindu women at the hands of Muslims, the journal was concerned, by and large, with women's problems—if not so much at home, then certainly in public places. The new newssheet firmly put the Samiti woman in her appointed place—that of service. It was concerned about distinguishing itself from aspirations of the women's movement, not about appropriating and subverting some of them.

In the early 1990s, the Samiti saw itself as performing the same functions vis-à-vis the women's fronts of the Sangh which the Sangh performs with respect to its own subordinate affiliates. It claimed that all these subsidiary women's fronts were trained by them, and that their leaders were simultaneously Samiti members. Now they repudiate all ambition of repeating the Sangh's role within the cluster of women's fronts within the Sangh parivar. They do mention that BJP MPs Sumitra Mahajan and Vijayraje Scindia as well as Krishna Sharma from the VHP Mahila Mandal are Samiti members, but they do not claim that this indicates a substantial pedagogical function for the Samiti.[19] If anything, they try to gesture at a growing separation among the various affiliates of the Sangh, though the Sangh does contain, train and nurture all of them.[20] Especially, there is an attempt to differentiate between the Samiti and the BJP women politicians.

The Samiti, in the early nineties, had taken the decision that women should join the karseva movements and the attacks on the Babri mosque. They had proudly pointed out the Samiti's icon of the eight-armed Durga, carrying weapons. They had recited the Samiti mantra which exhorted them to lay down their lives in the service of the nation—and said that it was a literal call to war for the sevikas. They had explained that this was to be a 'civil war' against enemies within. This urge for violence, destruction, revenge, for trampling over Muslims and Christians, is, if anything, even more strident today. Both Poonam Gupta and Asha Sharma, Samiti officebearers, indignantly refuted my timid suggestions that Rithambhara's audiocassette and her call for a slaughter of Muslims might be a 'bit' problematic; they both said, in identical words, that these things needed to be said, and that Rithambhara 'was the only one who could have said them'. Poonam Gupta referred to Rithambhara's current work with an orphanage and her low-keyed existence in the middle-class Agrasen Apartments at Patparganj with some regret. At the same time, an equal agency in violent politics does not seem to be on the agenda. The heady hopes of going into war are no longer articulated. The Samiti is content, as we shall see later, to remain the transmission belt for the RSS, conveying stories about Muslim and Christian 'atrocities' among Hindu women. There is a retreat to older female functions and roles where women gossip about things that they have not seen themselves but have heard from their men.

Retreat from active violence or public politics does not mean an emphasis on women-centred work. Samiti officebearers often refer to the 'social work' that their women do so well from their homes, but when they are pressed to specify, they fall back upon 'writing letters to newspapers about oppression of Hindus and about sex and violence in western movies and TV shows'.[21] The Samiti celebrated its sixtieth year in 1996 with a national seminar on this theme. They also conduct workshops on the Vande Mataram hymn of Bankimchandra which the RSS considers to be the national anthem. The seminars and the letters to the editors—largely restricted to stories about Hindu suffering and cultural degradation—seem to be the only other things that they do, apart from running *shakhas*. Despite five years in Delhi government and access to funds, they have not set up shelters and counselling or legal help centres for battered women, or significant schemes for employment-generation or slum welfare. Elsewhere, too, a picture of minor, sporadic activity emerges. The Samiti runs a girls' hostel at Nagpur, and a new one has been opened at Jalandhar in Punjab. Interestingly, perhaps as a rejoinder to Graham Staines's work, the Samiti officebearers proudly referred to a hostel at Bilaspur in Madhya Pradesh where girls from homes afflicted with leprosy are enrolled. However, they hastened to assure me, the girls themselves are 'healthy' and they remain segregated from their infected surroundings, as do the sevikas who cater to them. A more telling contrast to Staines cannot be imagined.[22] They have not started any schemes for training women members of Panchayati institutions, nor do they have any ideas about how women function within them. Again, the contrast with the Left and radical women's organizations comes readily to mind. Despite great opposition and obstruction from patriarchal and State agencies, Left and radical women's organizations provide precisely these services and empowering resources to women.

At the same time, *shakhas* remain central to their enterprise. They see them as mobilizing points for entire localities, since through intimate relations with the women, they gain entry into their homes. Since each *shakha* trains twenty to twenty-five women at the most, relations are warm and close, spiced with 'enjoyable' activities like storytelling and games.[23] Parents who do not subscribe to Sangh ideology would still like to send their daughters to *shakhas* since they teach deference and obedience, inculcate conservative values like arranged marriages, good housekeeping, modesty in dress and behaviour and diligent service to men and elders. Girls themselves like to go because of the physical training programmes which are invaluable ways of gaining control over their own bodies when they have control over so little else. The sense of physical well-being, strength and empowerment remain valued resources, even when no other kinds of empowerment are offered. Also, the ideological instructions about services to a militaristic, aggressive Hindu nation, of vengeance against its enemies, about heroic qualities of legendary men and women who resisted 'enemies' of the nation, fulfil aspirations for a life above pure self-interest, release frustrations built up as a result of having been marginalized members of orthodox families. Moreover, they are not told anything that offends mainstream patriarchal, Hindu nationalistic values and myths very deeply. Kanchan, an old woman coming from a non-RSS home, affirmed: 'All that they say is part of our environment (*vatavaran*).'[24] Although they do admit that young girls are not the most enthusiastic members, they do not prohibit all the new pleasures in the name of fighting western culture. Girls are encouraged to look good the modern way. They can visit beauty parlours and spend money on buying up beauty products—provided most of these are home-manufactured. Though mini-skirts and shorts are out since they expose the body, jeans are all right if they suit their figures. If they do not have the right figure, then they must cultivate one.[25] These are important concessions. The new consumerist self-absorptions of the middle-class woman, fanned by the ad-culture and the flood of beauty-aids, cosmetics and household gadgets, are encouraged, since they provide the economic strength of much of the country's manufacturing-trading classes. And this class is also the major basis for the political constituency of the Sangh parivar.

What cannot be tolerated, however, and what is powerfully and continuously denounced as the fruit of the western poison tree is the notion of equal gender rights. Poonam Gupta said that there has been 'far too much talk about the rights of Indian women', it has led to domestic competition, broken families, unhappy children.[26] It was the poison injected by the colonial State and its educational policies, said Asha Sharma. The colonial, foreign education is the biggest single problem of today's India, especially since it taught women all the wrong things. A proper Hindu educational system would restore to her the ancient knowledge about how to be pure wives, good mothers. When I asked her how she would distinguish herself from other women's organizations as a Samiti activist, she said immediately: 'They teach women about their rights, they tell them to fight their men about these rights. We teach them how to *sacrifice* themselves to keep the family together. Rights may be there, but it is wrong to fight for them. Women lose more eventually that way. Don't you remember your mother? Did she need to go to the law court to be happy? My mother was worshipped like a queen in the family. A good, pure Hindu woman can achieve such respect, such happiness by being a mother. Why do they want to throw it away by fighting for rights?' When I asked her how women will cope with dowry demands, domestic violence, desertion and discrimination, she said: 'We teach them how to do it, how to possess honour, dignity and authority in the family. They do so by being good mothers. They do not need anything more. How can they be good wives, good mothers if they think all the time of how to be the equal of men, of doing better than them, of competing with them and fighting with them over rights?'[27] Poonam Gupta used a colourful analogy to make the same point. 'Because seats are reserved for women on buses, they get only the reserved seats to use, but no more than that. If seats were not reserved for them, all the men on buses would give up their seats to each woman who did not have one. Talking of laws on equality deprives women in this way.'[28]

Their critiques of the concept of equal rights and their legal guarantee is based on an absolute silence on gender problems. The old *Jagriti* was equally silent about problems within the family, but it had a lot to say about discrimination in public spaces, in state agencies, in work places. The sevikas now refuse to discuss even that. When I asked *pracharika* Poonam Gupta about what she would consider to be the biggest problem for Indian women, she could not think of a single thing to say for a long time. Eventually, she came up with rape. Similarly, when I asked Asha Sharma about the same thing, she mentioned the British education policy which closed women's eyes to questions of 'nationality, patriotism, culture and motherhood' by teaching them about 'struggles, law, fighting men'. She shrugged off my queries about dowry and domestic violence impatiently as things that do not merit a discussion. At length, she said that rape was a problem of great proportions.

Of course rape has been a central concern for women's movements. The new phase of Left-secular-feminist women's polities had developed around rape as a symbol of the most violent expression of patriarchal values, of the complicity between the State and the violent man. From a very different standpoint, the founder of the Samiti, Lakshmibai Kelkar, had urged *shakhas* for women when she saw a wife being assaulted in the presence of her husband and concluded that since Hindu men cannot defend their wives, the wives must learn to protect themselves. The present reasoning of the Samiti is different from both understandings. Rapes occur, they say, since women have forfeited their older modes of honour and motherhood status by being addicted to struggles and enmity with men.

Moreover, the western films and cable-TV programmes have created a vulgar preoccupation with sex and desire that was unknown to Hindu society of the past. The resolution, unlike that of their founder, is not physical empowerment of threatened women. It is the retrieval of past honour by the recuperation of the motherhood ideal and by the banning of media products.[29]

Rights and equality were under attack from a different direction. When I asked her about the *Fire* controversy, Asha Sharma expressed her revulsion against what she called 'interrelationships among women'—she could not make herself say the word lesbianism. She was emphatic that such '*vikriti*'—a product of western culture—should be banned, as well as its sympathetic portrayal. When I asked if some other categories of women should not lose their rights, she was perfectly willing to extend the boundaries: Hindu women do not know how to be unfaithful, but if some degenerate elements do indulge in impure activities, they cannot have any rights at all.[30] So rights are to be whittled away at both ends. Certain kinds of rights—to 'perversion'—should not exist at all. Certain kinds of persons who do not conform to Hindu standards should not possess any rights either. On top of that, the very notion of rights is inducement to rape, to domestic unhappiness. It is the sole cause of male oppression of women. Moreover, women have a duty to forgo such dangerous ideas, since they are western, alien, colonial. It they succumb to that seduction, they ruin their faith, their culture. It is, therefore, a form of unchastity, a kind of adultery in itself, an unfaithfulness to their higher lords and masters.

Rights are pitted against the pure wife, the good mother, the Hindu woman—a very big burden of sins. Let me cite a few instances of the vocabulary of opposition and denunciation. Ashoke Singhal, quoted reverently in the Samiti's commemorative number of 1996, *Vishwambhara*: 'Vedic sages gave all responsibility to brahman women for the welfare of the family . . . Today our women are competing with men about same rights. This shows the downfall of women . . . Nudity is more valued than purity . . . under western influence, they feed their own babies from bottles, not from their breasts . . . they value their youth more than they value their wombs, they will kill their own foetus to protect their looks . . . It is vital that they return to their Hindu roots . . .'[31] If this seems like the lunatic fringe, let us turn to an article by Sumitra Mahajan, BJP MP: at the Beijing Conference of Women in 1995, she found out to her horror and grief that the Indian delegates no longer recognized that Hindu women need to be different from their western counterparts. They even organized demonstrations—'without shame or modesty'—to protest against the behaviour of their own men. '*Saman adhikar ke liye mahilayen lalayit hai* (women are lusting after equal rights) . . . They are greedy for *adhikar aur apabhog* (rights and pleasure) . . . they were content with two small meals a day, but now they are so greedy that they will serve beer to men at bars in Mumbai late at night so that they can make more and more money.'[32] The leader of the Sangh's trade union front of Bharatiya Mazdoor Sangh, Dattopant Thengde asserts: '*Nari vikas ka adhar adhikar aur andolan nahi* (the basis of the uplift of women is not rights or movements).' Predictably, he

153

counterpoises the wife and the mother, thus making the woman in movements for rights necessarily a non-wife and a non-mother.[33] In fact, motherhood and wifehood are also made incompatible with employment and public identities. It is assumed that women seek jobs for consumerist desires. Asha Sharma forbade jobs except in cases of dire economic compulsion.[34]

Let me cite the Samiti Prayer at some length on this;

Benevolent, auspicious Hindu Land
I dedicate my life to you . . .
Your ideas about only chastity
Embrace your beloved daughters . . .
Bless our meek, pious, devout women
Dedicated to their religion and tradition
We are the blessed mothers
Of this powerful nation . . .

Hindu women are made in the image of Motherland herself. An unfaithful surrender to alien values like equality and rights will, therefore, ruin not only themselves, but the Hindu Rashtra too.[35]

To counter dangerous ideas, Asha Sharma explained that she teaches the ideal of obedience. Girls must submit to parents, wives to husbands; otherwise, homes would break up and children left bereft of solace and shelter. The theme of the suffering child is used as the most powerful anodyne. Western ideas like widow remarriage are sought to be brought under control. Widows with children must not remarry, for then the children would lose both parents. Broken homes were caused by self-indulgent women who seek to satisfy desires, seek pleasure. Pleasure, desire and rights are aligned together as the Other of motherhood and tradition. To teach them young, a detailed code of 'decent' behaviour and dress is elaborated to *shakha* members. If they conform, they will be protected from rape and gain happy homes.[36]

The major political function of the Samiti remains the dissemination of communalism. Women are taught to 'analyse' current affairs and newspapers at *shakhas*. They are told about Hindu Rashtra, about Christian-colonial and Muslim 'misdeeds' of the past, about Christian aggression and violent attacks on Hindu women, men and temples in all parts of the country in the past year. They are told horror stories about attacks on Hindu women in communal riots. They are told that no Hindu has ever attacked a Muslim or a Christian so far—not a single Muslim or Christian has been killed by a Hindu. But Christians annoy Hindus by inciting dalits.[37] Dalits are like ignorant children, said Poonam Mahajan with a contemptuous laugh. 'You just smile at them, say a few sweet things, and they have lost their hearts to you.' The tone strongly suggested a mongrel wagging his tail at a morsel thrown at him.[38] The communal perspective slides into social hierarchy smoothly. They reiterate all the time: 'We do not approve of reservations, whether for women or for some castes. It does not help anyone, merit must be observed.'[39]

Sevikas, therefore, are home-based, insulated from contamination from lesser social circles. There is only one major exception to this. Some of them—mostly the unmarried *pracharikas*—work with the Sangh's slum-rehabilation programmes under the Seva Bharati scheme. Some others train the teachers who work in the RSS schools under Vidhya Bharati. Both are huge growth areas of the sangh—the Vidhya Bharati competing with the government chain of Model schools, and Seva Bharati running 107 centres in Delhi alone. Most teachers in the Vidhya Bharati scheme are women, and Seva Bharati's work of rehabilitation would seem to require 'womanly' nurturing services. Yet, Samiti participation is highly restricted. The Samiti, at best, is an auxiliary to certain fronts under the Sangh.

IV

The Sangh parivar seems launched on a curious course of acion. It proudly forefronts elected women members in the higher legislative and executive bodies. In this respect, its record is far better than that of the Left. On the other hand, the women who are thus exalted do not come from women's organizations, nor do they have prominent bases among the women of their own political clusters. They also are quite indifferent to women's issues, problems, demands. What is the implication of this split between the women's organizations and women is electoral politics? Incidentally, the same pattern is repeated among the women of the Shiv Sena in Mumbai. Prominent, longstanding women corporators and MLAs have no contact with or knowledge of the Mahila Aghadi. Sudha Chari, founder of the Aghadi and a very senior Shiy Sena member, has no power or visibility within the Party, nor was she ever given candidacy for any kind of electoral seat.[40]

The need to field women candidates is obvious, given a steadily-growing women's constituency, reinforced by extremely vocal and active women's movements. Also, reservation of seats for women in local and state-level elected bodies makes it indispensable. The interesting thing is the careful insulation of such candidates from women's issues and organizations even within the Sangh parivar.

I would argue that the need to push women into electoral politics is counterpointed deliberately by efforts to ensure that this does not add an edge to gender concerns or to empowerment of women within the Sangh parivar. Women enter electoral politics and earn for the party some kudos for its 'progressive' attitudes, without a concomitant compulsion for the Sangh to sensitize itself to women's needs and encourage the female constituents of the parivar on an organizational level. Moreover, women MPs and MLAs of BJP cannot enter the sanctum sanctorum of decision-making—the

Sangh itself, which remains exclusively male. The implications
of their prominence in public politics are thus clipped at both
ends. Women's organizations, on the other hand, cannot
borrow the lustre of their elected sisters who are individuals,
unconnected with organized women as a front within the
parivar. I found it interesting that Samiti office-bearers and
pracharikas were quite contemptuous about the issue of women's
reservation in Parliament, arguing that it denoted a tragic
dilution of the principle of merit.

If the Samiti is a small, bounded, non-expansive affair, like
the good, modest, non-competitive Hindu woman, then what
is the significance of their beliefs, and in the pattern of
changes, new accents and stresses within them? I believe that
the Samiti has a great relevance. Its women are the repository,
the custodians of the essential Sangh values, of its authentic
ideology, that the other fronts have somewhat diluted and
imperiled in the current war games over electoral power.
Since those preoccupations will grow and reach a peak, the
conservation of older values becomes all the more crucial.
Hence the Samiti is important as both a guarantee as well as
a mirror of the 'real' Sangh.

Secondly, if the battle over electoral power is won, as
seems quite likely, then the Samiti is the nucleus of the new
Hindu domesticity. Its women will be the living pattern for the
Hindu Rashtra of the future. Therefore, precisely at a moment
of expected triumph did it need to contract its activities and
affirm its purity, morality and conservatism at the cost of its
public activism.

We will be quite misled to believe that it is an entirely
imposed change enforced by the male Sangh. Women have
genuinely invested in this commitment. They see a bright
future for themselves as the soul of the Hindu Rashtra, as the
defender of tradition against the West, as partners in an
internal colonization over the Muslim and the Christian.

Finally, the convictions that the Samiti expressed go beyond gender—or, rather, gender is the pattern, the inspiration, the exemplar for relations between castes and classes. Since it can mystify its operations of power with intimacy, it is the most effective argument for all hierarchies. The battle against equality and rights that the Samiti had undertaken in the name of Hindu traditions is also a larger, unnamed struggle that the Sangh is engaged in to reorient power relations in the Hindu Rashtra of its dreams.

Notes

1. There are, obviously, certain notable exceptions, and some detailed research. See, for example, Christophe Jaffrelot, *The Hindu Nationalist Movement and Indian Politics: 1925 to the 1990s*, New Delhi, 1996.
2. See, for instance, S. Anitha, Manisha, Vasudha, Kavitha, 'Interviews with Women' in Tanika Sarkar and Urvashi Butalia (ed.), *Women and the Hindu Right: A Collection of Essays*, Delhi, 1995.
3. Amrita Basu, 'Feminism Inverted: The Gendered Imagery and Real Women of Hindu Nationalism,' Ibid.
4. See Tanika Sarkar, 'The Woman as Communal Subject: Rashtrasevika Samiti and Ramjanmabhoomi Movement,' *Economic and Political Weekly*, 31 August 1991. Also M.S. Golwalkar, 'A Call to Motherhood' in *Bunch of Thoughts*, Vikrama Prakashan, Bangalore, 1980.
5. Interview with Asha Sharma, Delhi, April, 1990.
6. See Teesta Setalvad, 'The Woman Shiv Sainik and Her Sister Swayamsevika' in *Women and the Hindu Right*, op. cit.
7. In the early 1990s, I talked to VHP office-holders at the office at Ramakrishnapuram, Delhi. They gratefully recalled her signal services to the cause.
8. Sarkar, 'The Woman as Communal Subject,' op. cit.
9. Ibid.
10. Interviews with women of the Sanghchalak's family, December, 1991. See Basu et al, *Khaki Shorts and Saffron Flags: A Critique Of the Hindu Right*, Delhi, 1993.
11. Interviews with Asha Sharma.

12. Interview with AIDWA leader Kanak Mukherjee, Calcutta, February, 1999.
13. Interview with Asha Sharma and Kanchan Lalporewala, Delhi, April, 1999.
14. Interview with Asha Sharma.
15. Interview with Rekha Raje, Delhi, December 1990.
16. Interviews at Khudah, op. cit.
17. Kanchan, an eighty-year-old woman from Rajasthan, was visiting her daughter in Delhi when the neighbours drew her into such familiar and approved talk. Though without any previous exposure to the Sangh, and coming, if anything, with Congress leanings, she promptly recognized the validity of the discussions, and became a Samiti wholetimer. Currently, she is the 'guardian' of *paracharika* Poonam Gupta, whom she chaperones during her stays at the Delhi head-office at Patel Nagar.
18. See discussion of the magazine in my 'The Woman as Communal Subject', op. cit.
19. Interview with Asha Sharma, op. cit.
20. Interview with Poonam Gupta, op. cit.
21. Interview with Asha Sharma, op. cit.
22. Interviews with Asha Sharma and Poonam Gupta.
23. Interview with Poonam Gupta, op. cit.
24. Interview with Kanchan Lalporewala, op. cit.
25. Interview with Asha Sharma, op. cit.
26. Interview with Poonam Gupta, op. cit.
27. Interview with Asha Sharma, op. cit.
28. Interview with Poonam Gupta.
29. Asha Sharma, interview, op. cit.
30. Ibid.
31. Ashoke Singhal in *Vishwambhara*, Delhi, 1996.
32. Ibid.
33. Ibid.
34. Interview, op. cit.
35. See *Vishwambhara*, op. cit.
36. Interview with Asha Sharma, op. cit.
37. Asha Sharma, interview, op. cit.
38. Interview with Poonam Gupta, op. cit.
39. Interview with Asha Sharma and Poonam Gupta, op. cit.
40. Interview with six Shiv Sena corporators and with Sudha Chari in Bombay, March 1999. I am grateful to Ramlat who conducte~. them under my instructions.

The Ink Link: Media, Communalism and the Evasion of Politics

Siddharth Varadarajan

O ver the past two decades, as the frequency of communal violence has increased and the conflation of religion and politics has become more common, it is only natural that the role of the media should come under greater scrutiny. These have been years of savage killings in which various political parties and organs of the state have been involved. Political campaigns have been conducted in which, at different times, religious minorities like the Sikhs, Muslims and Christians have been vilified and targeted. Places of worship have been attacked and demolished and the right of citizens to freely choose and practice their religion has been made the subject of officially-sponsored debate.[1] That the country's political class is largely responsible for this sorry state of affairs is not under dispute. But is it possible that the mass media too stands implicated in the manifest communalization of society and politics that has taken place since the 1980s? Or, even worse, in the orchestration of violence? Certainly, in the eyes of a distraught survivor of one of the worst instances of communal carnage in living memory, the November 1984 massacre of Sikhs, there is no doubt about the guilt of the media:

> I knew that something was going to go wrong . . . Simply
> because for the first time in my life I saw very strange
> expressions in people's eyes . . . No one has said anything to
> me. But the manner in which the propaganda through the
> media is being carried out . . . their role is clear from it . . .
> (People's) minds are being affected by what they see in the
> newspapers, what they see on the TV . . .[2]

If we were to accept this imprecise but viscerally felt assessment
as a fair one—and there are good reasons for us to do so—the
question of media complicity in communalism would appear
to be very important indeed. What imparts additional urgency
is the transformation the mass media in India has undergone
since the onset of liberalization. The number of players in the
communications industry has increased dramatically, while
new technologies have led to a profusion of media forms:
video and audio cassettes, FM radio, satellite television,
magazines catering to a variety of special interests, and the
Internet. Alongside these are other communicative media like
films and even comics, which construct influential narratives
about the present—and the past—and exert a distinct pull on
popular consciousness.

Though never before have so many Indians been brought
under the purview of the media, the relative numbers still
appear small by international standards. By one estimate, only
eight out of every 100 Indians own a radio and six a television.
The number of newspapers bought per 1000 persons in India
is just thirty-five, compared to 117 in Malaysia and 400-500 in
Sweden, Japan and Britain.[3] And yet, if one goes beyond a first
approximation, newspaper density in India is more than
respectable. As Robin Jeffrey has argued, the levels of
penetration reached by Indian newspapers today is roughly
comparable to the situation in England and the US in the
middle of the nineteenth century, when rising literacy
combined with political consciousness to produce mass
movements such as that of the Chartists and the pre-Civil War

161

mobilization against slavery. In fact, if we take into account the fact that 20 per cent of the population in India today is too young to read, and that each copy of a newspaper reaches, on average, up to a dozen people, then as much as half the total adult population is, conceivably, within reach of a daily newspaper. Thanks mainly to the expansion of the vernacular press, 'most people who vote are thus for the first time in India in a position to be newspaper readers'.[4] Similarly, the true figures for television viewership must be much higher than what the ownership figures suggest. Cable television has penetrated every corner of the country—according to the Press Council of India, 40 per cent of TV-owning households subscribe to cable broadcasts—and it is not uncommon for the average middle class home to receive between twenty to thirty channels. Access to audio cassettes is even higher, a fact which is not without significance for the subject at hand, given the use political propagandists like Uma Bharati and Sadhvi Rithambra have made of this medium. Internet access, however, is still restricted; the extremely low density of PC ownership and the parlous state of telecommunications in India mean growth of this medium will be slow at least for some time to come. Though the Internet has brought about important changes—mostly positive—in the Indian communications scenario, it is also a double-edged sword because of the information overload it brings and the ease with which it can be used to spread disinformation, either by powerful economic and political interests or by fringe elements. In Germany, for example, the Office for the Protection of the Constitution has expressed its concerns about the use neo-Nazi extremists are making of the Internet[5]; of course, this is not to say that the use governments in the West or elsewhere make of the Internet is altogether benign.

In assessing the impact on Indian society of the changes in media breadth and depth, it is important that the abundance of media not be equated with diversity of content. By itself, the communications explosion in India is unlikely to bring about a more inclusive, participatory and democratic media; indeed, the experience of the US and other advanced industrialized countries does not provide grounds for optimism. Besides, as Peter Manuel has argued, relatively demotic media like cassettes are perhaps more prone to abuse (for example by political groups wishing to incite hatred on religious grounds) and more dangerous in terms of reach than other forms of mass communication, especially in a country where so many are unlettered.[6] To the extent to which decentralization of the means of opinion formation provides space for debate and dissent, the Indian media is open to a variety of perspectives, often even more so than the media in the US. Yet, even these usually conform to the terms of reference of 'mainstream' discourse, which in turn are fashioned by the interests of the corporate houses which either own the media or use it for advertising, or by the state, in its multiple capacities as owner (i.e. Doordarshan, All-India Radio), advertiser (i.e. DAVP etc.), allocator of newsprint, and, crucially, defender of the 'unity and integrity' and 'national security' of India.

Mass Media and Depoliticization

Any analysis of the mass media's role in the communalization of society must differentiate between two distinct but mutually dependent phenomena: (a) the act of incitement of violence and the rationalization of the same after the event; and (b) the act of disarming the citizen-reader/citizen-viewer—by conflating religion and nation and negating citizenship, by constantly lowering the level of political discussion, by inundating readers and viewers with diversionary or trivial issues, and by the very forms and techniques of news dissemination. In fact, it is only when 'civil society' has been vitiated and anaesthetized in this manner that violence can be orchestrated, rationalized and made palatable; that involvement in acts of violence need not be politically or legally compromising, either for politicians or state functionaries.

In a celebrated essay written in the 1930s, Walter Benjamin described the modern newspaper as a 'theatre of literary confusion' in which genres and subjects that fertilized one another in earlier periods have come to be irrevocably compartmentalized. 'Thus science and belles-lettres, criticism and production, education and politics, fall apart in disorder.'[7] Even though he argued that this suits the political agenda of newspaper owners, Benjamin considered the reader to also be a collaborator: 'The fact that nothing binds the reader more tightly to his paper than (an) impatient longing for daily nourishment has long been exploited by the publishers, who are constantly opening new columns to his questions, opinions, protests.' In other words, to restate Fredric Jameson's well-known formulation on mass culture in a different context,[8] newspapers, or the mass media in general, are neither wholly manipulative nor wholly authentic. Rather, they work by providing an outlet for the ventilation of grievances within a structure which automatically defuses them. Thanks to this indiscriminate and arbitrary assimilation of facts, opinions and controversies, crucial issues get obfuscated and social relations which are tangible and concrete get fetishized. Worst of all, ordinary citizens get depoliticized, condemned to remain in the ghetto of civil society from where they may only petition and lobby while the state remains the preserve of the economically powerful.

Even if one disagrees with Habermas's roseate assessment of the eighteenth century European public sphere as a collective rational arena, an *agora* in which everyone participated as equals, there is no doubt that he is correct in arguing that today, political discourse in the public sphere dominated by the mass media is inevitably dominated by corporatism, advertising and the state. Instead of rational public discussion we have power politics in which 'major organizations negotiate with one another and the state, thereby excluding the public'.[9] Paradoxically, the very expansion of the mass media becomes a source of disempowerment for the public. For as the media becomes more complex and expensive to operate, it also becomes more centralized, and the process of selecting what to report or analyse becomes a new source of power. The way in which every minor utterance of big political parties like the Bharatiya Janata Party and the Congress becomes headline news confirms the fact that much of what passes for political coverage on TV and in the newspapers essentially originates as 'issues that are professionally produced as media input and then fed in via press conferences, news agencies, public-relations campaigns, and the like'.[10] Thus, the parties themselves set the agenda—which are more often than not diversionary (e.g. the Ram temple) as well as the terms of debate (i.e. for or against)—and the media goes along as accomplice, either willingly or out of ignorance and lack of professionalism. In contrast, political activities or initiatives that do not originate from within large organizations, and especially those that deviate too far from the range of 'mainstream' opinion, tend not to influence media content and views. That is why one secularist critic is slightly off the mark when he equates the communalization of the media with the increased (and benign) coverage given to the BJP and its leadership.[11] True, corporate preferences and the biases of editors and journalists have tended to favour the BJP in recent years. Yet, it was a similar constellation of interests which favoured the Congress earlier and helped to communalize the media during the Punjab crisis (see below). Tomorrow, then, these same interests might well move on to another party, issue or diversion. While it is legitimate to criticize the prominence given to a party or politician in the mass media—especially if such coverage has the effect of 'normalizing' criminal or sectarian activity—it is clear that what one must strive for is a break with prevailing media epistemology.

And yet the hegemonic nature of the mass media is not a question of content alone: the evasion of politics engendered by it is facilitated by the very form of communication: 'Reporting facts as human interest stories, arranging material episodically, and breaking down complex relations into smaller fragments—all of this comes together to form a syndrome that works to depoliticize public communications'.[12] For Schiller too, the form of communication tends to subvert public consciousness: 'Fragmentation . . . is the dominant—indeed the exclusive—format for information and news distribution . . . Radio and television news is characterized by the machine-gun recitation of numerous unrelated items. Newspapers are multipaged assemblages of materials set down almost randomly.'[13] In the US, the newspaper *USA Today* has taken matters the furthest, doing away with the inefficient and advertiser-unfriendly 'turn', where articles beginning on one page would end on another. Instead, it slashes news stories to ensure they finish on the same page. Of course, the end product of this junk food journalism, which one author has labelled 'News McNuggets', is 'news' with only the 'bare facts' and an extremely sparse narrative structure; obviously, there is no room for nuance or complexity.[14] Under these constraints, the easiest way to make a subject intelligible is for both writer and reader to take refuge in stereotypes and clichés. When such an approach is followed in writing reports about communal violence, the dangers can well be imagined, as we shall examine below.

If the mass media's tendency to fragment news serves to depoliticize the body politic, its preoccupation with immediacy is also highly problematic. By itself immediacy is desirable, just as one's arguments against fragmentation should not be taken to mean advocacy of turgid prose and tome-length reports. Under the present conditions, however, the immediacy of information also tends to mean its evanescence. It reduces history to a series of spontaneous, miscellaneous and sanitized news items; it deprives the public of its memory. The chronologies of the Kosovo crisis at the CNN website, for example, do not go beyond the past few years; everything is so arranged as to justify the bombing of Yugoslavia by NATO. Recent western reporting about Cambodia ignores the support Pol Pot and the Khmer Rouge received from the West from 1979 till the end of the Cold War. The tendency of TV networks to focus obsessively on a story before forgetting it altogether led the American poet June Jordan to write 'Nightline: September 20, 1982', with tongue firmly in cheek:

> I know it's an unfortunate way to say it, but do you think you can put this massacre on the back burner now?[15]

When combined with fragmentation, the immediacy of news generates individual passivity and a public sphere that is generally inert—except when the mass media itself is used by power politics to mobilize it. In the context of communalism in India, the layers of combustible myths which accumulate around most riots as time passes make this kind of memoryless media all the more manipulatory and dangerous.

Media and Public Sphere in India

If Benedict Anderson is right in arguing that it was 'print-capitalism' which helped to consolidate national consciousness and the emergence of the nation as the pre-eminent—and certainly most dominant—'imagined community' in Europe,[16] it is pertinent to ask how the development of print-capitalism in nineteenth century India might have contributed to the physiognomy and trajectory of Indian nationalism. For Anderson, print-capitalism was synonymous with the development of standardized print languages and laid the basis for national consciousness in three distinct ways. First, it created 'unified fields of exchange and communication' above

167

the spoken vernaculars, fashioning, for example, out of the huge variety of Frenches or Englishes, a standard form of French and English. Second, it gave a new fixity to language, a sense of timelessness, which built an 'image of antiquity so central to the subjective idea of the nation'. Finally, print-capitalism created 'languages-of-power', in which the dialects spoken by sub-nationalities lost caste by being unable to insist on their own print-form. But print-capitalism did more than consolidate the nation linguistically; by greatly expanding the public sphere in which ideas and issues circulated, it also helped to give political coherence to the idea of nationhood as well as legitimacy to the state. This process should not be confused with democracy, though the expansion of the public sphere brought about by the mass circulated printed word did go hand in hand with advances in democracy, such as universal adult franchise, workers' rights, and so on.

In India, the newspaper came as a by-product of colonialism; the country's first newspaper was the weekly *Bengal Gazette*, which began publication on 19 January 1780, announcing itself as 'a weekly political and commercial paper open to all parties but influenced by none'.[17] Subsequently, the English started other newspapers like *Friend of India*, the *India Gazette*, and the *Bengal Hurkaru*, but once press censorship was abolished in 1818, a 'national' press, especially in vernacular languages, quickly emerged. Raja Rammohan Roy may not have been the founder of Indian journalism but he was 'unequivocally its chief architect'.[18] He started the Bengali language *Sambad Kaumudi* and the Persian *Mirat-ul-Akhbar* for social, religious and political issues, and the *Brahmana Sevadhi* to defend Hinduism against the polemics of English missionaries. The *Mirat-ul-Akhbar's* statement of purpose makes it clear that what Rammohan Roy had in mind was the creation of a public sphere in which colonialism's exactions could be contested:

In taking upon myself to edit this Paper, my only object is, that I may lay before the Public such articles of Intelligence as may increase their experience, and tend to their social improvement; and to the extent of my abilities, I may communicate to the Rulers a knowledge of the real situation of their subjects, and make the subjects acquainted with the established laws and customs of their Rulers: that the Rulers may the more readily find an opportunity of granting relief to the people: and the people may be put in possession of the means of obtaining protection and redress from their Rulers.[19]

At the same time, Roy took up other tasks—such as countering the criticisms of Christian missionaries and promoting the reform of Hinduism—which also meant that his newspapers frequently spoke exclusively to the 'imagined community' of Hindus. In other parts of India too, the vernacular press often focussed on such issues; debates with missionaries on the inadequacies of Christian theology and in defence of Hindu beliefs were the bread and butter of mid-nineteenth century Marathi newspapers like *Dhumaketu* and *Vartaman Dipika*, for example.[20] In the main, such debates were conducted with great civility and even wit. It would be a grave mistake to telescope the crude accusations made by some politicians against Christian missionaries today (most of whom are Indians) back into the previous century and come to the conclusion that those religio-polemical and nationalist impulses were 'communal'. Muslim and Hindu theologians would often borrow each other's arguments against Christianity, which for them was synonymous with colonial rule. As Barbara Daly Metcalf has argued, the spectacle of public debate with missionaries 'brought Indians of all backgrounds together ... (as there was) a general enthusiasm, not specific to community, to see Europeans held up to ridicule'.[21] At the same time, one of the undeniable results of these disputations between Indian theologians and foreign preachers was the crystallization of religious identity on the part of Hindus and Muslims, or, at any rate, on the part of the elites and literates within these two 'communities'. Yet even this construction of two mutually exclusive and monolithic religious communities might not have been so significant in historical terms had it not been accompanied by the colonialist imperatives of British rule. For that turned what would otherwise have remained a social and cultural difference into a political—and, therefore, infinitely more dangerous—schism.

1857 and After

In western Europe, as we have noted above, print-capitalism and the development of newspapers were instrumental in the evolution of both public sphere and nation. This public sphere may have been partitioned by class and gender but it was still very much a 'national' sphere of citizens rather than a series of interlocking religious or ethnic spheres. In India, on the other hand, the emergence of print-capitalism and the media did not produce the same results; no such public sphere emerged. The reason, of course, was colonialism, which disrupted whatever indigenous process of nation building was under way. Though the undermining of Indian political theory and philosophy began from the very first day of colonial rule, it was only after the defeat of the First War of Independence in 1857 that a profound ontological break was sought to be imposed on Indian consciousness. Indians were forced to accept a community-centric political culture that was inimical to the very concept of citizenship and Indianness. In this, the emerging media was to play an important role. Print-capitalism in India was not to be the unifier of the nation, the vehicle through which national claims would be asserted. Rather, it would primarily help mediate the claims of various religious communities. To understand this role that most of the media would come to play until the 1920s, it is useful to examine how the Indian press performed during a moment of contrariness, the 1857 revolt.

1857 was an outstanding year for Indian journalism. The nationalist press—especially in Delhi, Agra, Lucknow and elsewhere—played a leading role in mobilizing public opinion against the British and seeking to unite Indians of all faiths. For probably the first time in the history of the country, newspapers spoke to the Indian, who, though adhering to this or that religion, would find salvation only in the expulsion of the British. In some of the newspapers of 1857, and in the inchoate, amorphous political philosophy of the rebels, 'citizens' made their first appearance on the soil of India. Theirs was a nervous appearance, a fleeting moment of arrival which left virtually no trace as soon as the rebels were defeated and Delhi was recaptured. In their place, as the British watched over, came 'Hindus' and 'Muslims', crawling out from under the rubble of the destroyed capital. In a sense, they have been with us ever since.

While it lasted, the Persian, Urdu and Hindi press of north India wrote extensively about the rebellion. The most important of the Delhi newspapers were the *Saiyedul Akhbar, Zubdatul Akhbar, Dehli Urdu Akhbar, Sadiqul Akhbar, Mazharul Haqq* and *Buddhi Prakash.* During the war, they 'relayed news of the success of the armies . . . broadcast the various proclamations and news of the promised help from Iran, Kabul and Russia . . . gave people hope and courage and exaggerated the weakness of the enemy'.[22] Prominence was given to revolutionary manifestos like the 'Risala-i-jehad' and 'Fatwa-i-jehad'. The *Sirajul Akhbar* was a court gazette whose news was reprinted widely by the other newspapers. At the subsequent trial of Bahadur Shah Zafar, the British prosecution entered several 'inflammatory' reports from it as evidence against him. Equally notable was the *Dehli Urdu Akhbar,* founded in 1836 by Maulvi Muhammad Baqir, a Shia cleric who is among the most important pioneers of the free press in India.

171

Before 1857, he criticized the British and once the war broke out, 'he left no stone unturned to rouse the people against them . . . He appealed to everyone irrespective of religion to join the war, which he considered a unique opportunity to expel the English from the country.'[23] The Maulvi was also perhaps the first Indian editor who advocated the unity of the people and sought to transcend religion in his newspaper to be killed in harness. He was shot dead by Hodson after the fall of Delhi.

The newspapers of 1857 were not 'secular' as we would understand the word today but they certainly recognized the importance of a state that would leave religion to its citizens and instead concentrate on administration. Their political line closely mirrored Bahadur Shah Zafar's historic *firman* of August 25 1857, which the pro-British *Friend of India* called 'the most invaluable contribution to the history of the rebellion'.[24] In this proclamation, even though Indians were still exhorted to come in to the battleground inspired by their various religions ('Muslims by raising the standard of Mohammad, Hindus by raising the standard of Mahavira'), the promise was that if victorious they would emerge as citizens with distinct claims on the state which stemmed not from their religion but from their economic role in society. Thus *zamindars* were promised lighter taxes, merchants the free carriage of merchandise at state expense and men of service and sepoys better pay and prospects. The artisans, 'who have been thrown out of employ by the English policy and been reduced to beggary will, under the Badshahi government, exclusively be employed in the services of the Badshah, the rajas and the rich'; finally, 'scholars of both creeds' were also promised help and support.[25]

Of course, neither the British nor those Indians who had drawn close to them saw the revolt in quite the same way as the patriots. Recognition of the fact that two communities which were supposed to be hostile to one another had made common cause was tinged with the belief that the 'Mahomedans' had incited the 'Hindoos'. For example, one reader of the *Times* (London) wrote a letter to the editor under the mischievous pseudonym 'Akhbar', the Urdu word for newspaper:

> (I am convinced) that the present revolt is chiefly the work of the Mohammedans, who have . . . successfully aroused the sensitive Hindoo to a belief that his religion was endangered . . . No thinking or observant person who has any knowledge whatever of the Hindoo and Mahomedan can for a moment believe that it is the Hindoo who has urged on or influenced the Mussulman; yet we find the two coalescing and acting well together in their revolt against the English authority, with results, however momentary, yet all in favour of the Mahomedan.[26]

'Akhbar' may have been an Indian resident in London (the *Times* only records he is from Bayswater), or perhaps an old 'India hand'. One will never know and it is not very important. His analysis was not unique and was generally similar to the kind of comments appearing in the pro-British press of Bengal like the *Englishman* and others. The communalist element was always the most prominent, second only to fervid expressions of loyalty to the Raj. Thus, Ishwar Chand Gupta, editor of the Calcutta newspaper, *Sambad Prabhakar*, denounced the 1857 war of independence as a Muslim conspiracy whose success would mean the re-establishment of Muslim rule: 'This (English) rule is as blissful as the rule of Rama . . . we are all getting our fulfilment in all aspects of our life as children by a mother under the aegis of the ruler of the world, the Queen of England'.[27]

The *Sambad Prabhakar* editor's prose may have been especially florid—other contemporary newspapers might not have seen Lord Rama in Queen Victoria—but the idea that Hindus and Muslims had different and competing aims was widely shared. Such notions received a boost from the post-1857 British policy of using religion as the primary basis for representation to and accommodation in the colonial state. This meant the division of the national elite along community lines since the only prospect for legitimacy in the eyes of the Raj was to claim to speak on behalf of 'Hindus' or 'Muslims'. Most Indian newspapers in the latter part of the nineteenth century had internalized the colonial political culture to such an extent that even when colonialism was challenged or excoriated, it was often from a 'Hindu' or 'Muslim' point of view. Even language became a bone of contention. The Urdu-Hindi divide began shortly after the advent of British rule and was reflected in some newspapers using Devanagari and others the Persian script. Over the years, the linguistic chasm also widened, with Hindi getting progressively more Sanskritized and Urdu Persianized and, later, Arabized. While the merits of this bifurcation will continue to be debated for a long time, it is obvious that the emergence of two languages contributed its bit to the politically-induced division between Hindus and Muslims in north India. In Punjab, the rise of the Arya Samaj movement, once again accompanied by the use of newspapers and other written media like pamphlets, did a lot to cement communal identities, both along the Hindu–Muslim axis as well as the Hindu–Sikh one.[28]

Sudhir Chandra has analysed the ambivalence in late nineteenth century Hindi literature and literary journalism of Hindu elite attitudes towards the Muslims.[29] Writers like Bhartendu Harischandra, Pratap Narain Misra and Radhacharan Goswami straddled the boundary between literature and journalism; they were litterateurs in the modern sense of the term but they were also journalists who brought out their own papers and wrote extensively on public affairs. Bhartendu brought out *Haris Chandra's Magazine*, Pratap Narain Misra wrote regularly in the monthly *Brahman*, while Goswami brought out another monthly, *Bharatendu*. These publications,

174

and the literary, journalistic output of the three writers, were extremely influential in the formation of public opinion in northern India. Unfortunately, their conception of nationalism was imbricated with a communal remembrance of the past. As Sudhir Chandra writes, 'communal consciousness runs as a kind of recurring theme in (their) works . . . and merges ineluctably into national consciousness'. What made Harischandra's case especially interesting was that even when he explicitly set out to advocate Hindu–Muslim unity—as in an 1874 critique of a school history textbook which was rather too lurid about the oppression of Hindus by Muslim rulers in the past—he 'betrayed an ambivalence towards the Muslims'. Goswami, writing in *Bharatendu*, more freely indulged his prejudice. In 1883 he wrote: 'Whether today or 800 years ago, the Hindus never fought the Musalmans without being provoked. It was Musalmans like Mahmud Ghaznavi, Mohammad Ghori, Aurangzeb, Nadir Shah and others who harassed the Hindus perpetually in earlier times. And to this day their grandchildren and great-grandchildren are maintaining their hereditary enmity.'

Two years later, he struck an even more tendentious tone: 'The aggressive and strife-loving nature of the Muslim community is hidden from no one. Mischief-making courses through their veins. Quarrelling, rioting, doing ill unto others, oppressing the oppressed.' Then shifting voice and addressing himself directly to the Muslims, he writes: 'You were baptized with blood, and we with milk. The essence of your religion is discord, and that of ours peace. We do not therefore provoke anyone. But when you nettle us needlessly, our policy too is to meet evil with evil.'[30] Central to Harischandra, Misra and Goswami's idea of nation was the equation of 'Hindu' with 'India'. Misra, in fact, went one step further when he coined the slogan 'Hindu, Hindi, Hindustan' in 1882. In due course, the idea that all Indians were Hindus (Harischandra's formulation) or that Hindus were the real Indians (Misra's argument) was to become a staple of communalist discourse, both Hindu and Muslim. But in the meantime, thanks to Hindi literary and journalistic writings such as we have seen above, as well as movements like those for cow protection, the idea that Hindus and Muslims were two mutually exclusive communities seems firmly to have been planted in the consciousness of elite sections by the turn of the nineteenth century.

Naturally, this communal ethos extended to the national movement. Leaders like Sir Syed Ahmed Khan and those who founded the Muslim League obviously reflected this trend; but even a party like the Indian National Congress, which saw itself as the representative of all Indians, had leaders who traded on their community affiliation and saw nothing wrong in working for the uplift and advancement of their community even as they took part in the struggle for independence.[31] As a logical corollary, Muslims were often seen as the political Other. In a famous speech on the Seditious Meetings Bill in 1907, for example, Gopal Krishna Gokhale—incidentally a political personality not known for being communal—could make a distinction between the 'Mahommedans' and the 'people of Bengal' without batting an eyelid.[32] Tilak also used his newspapers, *Kesari* and *Mahratta* to glorify Shivaji. '(Their) reading of the past . . . attracted a large constituency among the Hindus of Maharashtra, although many Muslims were offended.'[33] Taking advantage of expanding literacy, many 'community-oriented' political leaders involved themselves in the media. Mohammed Ali, for example, used his newspaper *Camrade* to advocate a pan-Islamic identity. The founder of Banaras Hindu University, Madan Mohan Malaviya, launched major newspapers like *Leader* and *Abhudaya*. 'Hindu populism', as Sandria Freitag has termed this phenomenon in north India, benefited greatly from the expansion of the Hindi press. 'In its efforts to forge connections with a large portion of the populace, such populism bore a close relationship to the development in western Europe of a public sphere and its reliance on print-capitalism. Yet the developments in north India remained distinctive, for the society so affected consisted not of the general public, all members of which had equal access to the public sphere, but solely of those who identified themselves as "Hindus".[34] As to why this happened, we have already emphasized that the kind of polity which developed under colonial rule was intended to produce precisely such an outcome. As Metcalf puts it, 'the importance of a form of government structured on representation in which leaders to be effective had to claim to speak for the interests of communities, cannot be underestimated; representation and communalism were indissolubly linked.' She also argues that with public and civic institutions under British control, Indians had no option but to 'retreat to domestic and religious space as sites where cultural values could be reworked and renewed'.[35]

Thanks to both of these processes, much of the Indian media suffered from the tendency of mediating nationhood by religious community. Milton Israel has argued that though 'urban-based English-language papers tended to be more restrained than the vernacular press in this regard, they set examples and suggested themes that often became violent in translation'.[36] Even if they were not partisan to this or that religion, most newspapers, as indeed the mainstream national movement, saw Indians as an agglomeration of communities. According to Gyan Pandey, the national movement in its initial stages had conceived of 'India, and the emerging Indian nation . . . as a collection of communities: Hindu + Muslim + Christian + Parsi + Sikh, and so on', but 'sometime in the 1920s', the vision of an India made up of 'citizens' took hold.[37] Considering that even today most major parties do not subscribe to this vision (except rhetorically), this cut-off date might not be such a robust one. Pandey himself recognizes the hold of the communal conception of an Indian in the political work of Malaviya, Lala Lajpat Rai and Ganesh Shankar

Vidyarthi, all important Congress leaders and newspapermen to boot. Vidyarthi—who edited the Hindi *Pratap* in Kanpur until he was murdered in March 1931 (while trying to save people during communal riots)—provides an interesting study in contrasts. By any definition an outstanding journalist and publicist, Vidyarthi wrote passionately against the mixing of religion and politics:

> We pray to God that our leaders may learn to rely not on the weak crutches of religious organizations and diffident, moderate political tactics but on the true strength of the country, which is to be found in her millions of ordinary people . . . The days of religion and religious organizations are numbered, the trend of world history and the future of India are against them. Whosoever wishes to be a 'Hindu' or a 'Musalman' is welcome to be a 'Hindu' or 'Musalman' inside the home. The rising nationalist forces will put up with these pastimes (*khilvad*) only so long as they present no obstacle to the . . . advancement of the country and nation.[38]

Yet the same Vidyarthi, as Pandey points out, wrote an article two years later criticizing the British for banning Hindus from playing music outside mosques in Bengal, and even congratulated the Hindu youth who broke this law. If even in a staunch anti-communalist like Vidyarthi there can be some slippage from secular notions of national identity, this is only because a clean rupture with the 'India as collection of communities' idea never took place, either at the political level or at the level of the public sphere and the media. The more nationalist and secular of newspapers advocated a citizenship based on harmony and tolerance between communities, which was also the political line favoured by the mainstream within the Congress.[39] But even they stopped short of providing a definition of citizenship based on secular, modern and democratic notions of inalienable rights, according to which Indians would be known not by their religion, caste, sex or language but only by their duties and rights, guaranteed by law and by a political process which would help them to exercise control over their political representatives.

Instead of this, all Indians got for the solution to the problem of communalism and communal violence was secularism as state ideology without the effective power to ensure secularism as state practice. To make matters worse, secularism was simply defined as tolerance and equality of all religions. Paul Brass is surely right when he says that the state which demands that citizens tolerate each other's religions is itself violating the principle that state and religion should have nothing to do with one another.[40] Similarly, it is not the state's business to say that all religions are equal. However, the point really is that 'tolerance' was a weak basis on which to negate the communalism which had become so integral a part of the body politic, so intrinsic to the system of rule. Especially since it was predicated not on the tolerance of communities for one another but on the *tolerance of tolerance* by those who control the state. What would happen when those who controlled the state simply chose not to be tolerant by either orchestrating—or turning a blind eye to—violence against a minority group? In the first light of freedom, the answer to such questions, if ever they were posed, would have seemed obvious enough: democracy would provide the safeguard. Fifty years later, we know that the political institutions and processes adopted by independent India simply do not empower ordinary citizens. There have been several instances where the secularism of the Indian state has broken down, when 'tolerance' has evaporated, but the media has tended not to ask the difficult questions. It has evaded, prevaricated and fudged the issue, clinging all the while to the same petrified nineteenth century notion of India as an agglomeration of communities in which some of these communities, from time to time, can be targeted for harassment and even attack.

179

Communalism and the Media after Independence

While a section of the Indian media in the post-Independence period continued to look at religious minorities, especially Muslims, in a communalist manner—questioning their patriotism, their legitimate rights as citizens, their political wisdom and their social-cultural mores—mainstream sections of the media too sometimes contributed to this process of communalization. The sin, of course, was a derivative one. For in failing to transcend the community-centric approach to politics that had so divided society before 1947, the media was only following the lead of the country's political class. Thus, Muslims (and to a lesser extent, Sikhs) were ghettoized politically and various political personalities with links to 'mainstream' parties promoted by the media as 'leaders' of their respective communities. As products of a ghettoized polity, such leaders fully reflected the backwardness of their 'mainstream' mentors, with whom they negotiated the terms and conditions under which 'their' flock would be handed over at election time. What resulted from the media's uncritical acceptance of such a framework of politics was a low intensity campaign against the prospects for genuine secularization rather than a frontal assault against this or that religious minority, or against the formal ideology of secularism as espoused by the Indian state. It was only during communal riots—when the state and its organs themselves rebelled against this official ideology and allowed innocent citizens of the 'wrong' religion to be killed—that media communalism took on a higher intensity, with biased and sometimes inflammatory coverage predominating. At other times, the media's culpability was essentially limited to fostering the corrosive myth of 'Muslim difference'.

In the 1980s, however, two developments led to high intensity media communalism becoming more constant than episodic. First, the growing communalization of the state by successive Congress governments, and second, the strengthening of the Bharatiya Janata Party, which took the community-centric discourse of Indian politics to its logical conclusion by aggressively claiming to represent that 'most Indian of Indian' religious communities, the Hindus. Taken together, these two developments have led to some dramatic shifts in media coverage. A section of the press, especially of the Indian language press, has systematically communalized itself, while openly communalist notions and views have gained respectability all around and even find occasional expression in the relatively 'secular' English language press.[41] The way in which the Shah Bano case was covered by the media is highly instructive. In fact, the Shah Bano case—and Rajiv Gandhi's backward stance on the issue of maintenance for divorced Muslim women—was converted by the BJP and by a broad section of the print media into a symbol of the supposed Otherness, separatism and backwardness of the Muslim community as a whole. As Kalpana Sharma and Ammu Joseph have argued, the Shah Bano controversy was, essentially, a gender issue.[42] An indigent and aged woman had been divorced by her husband and left without any means of support; she approached the court as others like her—including Muslims—had done before and won a judgment in her favour. There the matter should have ended; certainly her case did not deserve the kind of publicity it received in the media, which incorrectly saw Justice Chandrachud's decision as having overruled Muslim personal law. The media's perception was, of course, fuelled by Justice Chandrachud's own wording, which emphasized the irrelevant fact that Shah Bano was a Muslim and converted what was essentially a question of women's rights into a diatribe against Muslims as a community. The media might have helped to clear the fog by shifting the debate away from the communal dimension; after all, it is not just Muslim women who suffer from unequal personal laws. Nevertheless, Shah Bano became a stick with which to beat Islam and the Muslims. In February 1986, the *Indian Express* ran a series of three-column advertisements by the Vishwa Hindu Parishad on the top right corner of its op-ed page which said, *inter alia*: 'Hinduism has the greatest respect for womanhood . . . Instances like Shah Bano (sic) case never arose in Hinduism. Women lost all their glory and liberty in the dark period when India was invaded by barbarians.' As Sharma and Joseph put it: 'Such a blatantly communal piece of writing was shocking in itself. What was worse was that a major national paper gave it an important editorial position, thereby silently endorsing it.'[43]

If the media was able to conjure up a communal issue out of thin air, this was largely because both the Congress and the BJP had an interest in the Shah Bano case being seen in that way. By presenting the Supreme Court's verdict as a 'setback' to Islam and to Indian Muslims in particular, the Congress could then strike a deal with self-styled leaders of the Muslim community. As for the BJP, the verdict and the Congress's subsequent legislative undoing of it could be used as proof that the Muslims were being 'appeased'. It didn't matter that fully one-half of India's Muslims—its Muslim women—had their rights curtailed as a result. In the popular perception, and in much of the media, it was the BJP's view which prevailed. As a manager of news, the BJP has proved to be much more skilful than the Congress or any other political formation in the country. In the run-up to the Ayodhya agitation, the party pioneered the use of press releases, leaks and press conferences, which took place on more or less a daily basis, thereby ensuring that the BJP and its activities and views received continuous and prominent coverage in the newspapers. According to the media analysts Charu Gupta and Mukul Sharma, the BJP's forte is the creation and management of the pseudo-event.[44] The pseudo-event is the product of the complex interplay of various factors, including the emergence of journalists as publicists of partisan causes and the presence of an issue, however remote, that can be exploited to put the party into the headlines. The textbook example of the way a pseudo-event was manufactured and sustained through the willing cooperation of the press, especially the Hindi press, was the agitation the BJP launched against 'Bangladeshi infiltrators' in the Capital a few years ago. The use of the word 'infiltrator' instead of immigrant or refugee (the words used for Nepalis or Bangladeshi Hindus in India respectively) is significant for it implies that as Muslims, their aim in coming to India is really to undermine the country from within. Not only did most of the Hindi media pick up the term 'infiltrator' (*ghuspetiya*) from the BJP but also the party's view that the presence of Bangladeshis in Delhi and India was somehow a question of vital national import, even a threat to national security. In Gupta and Sharma's words: 'The BJP or Madan Lal Khurana announces a campaign against illegal immigrants in South Delhi. It draws huge headlines. In the newspaper it acquires the colour of a campaign against crime and anti-national activities. They tell us it is a national problem, requiring a nationwide campaign. The editorials support it and give it a national perspective. The newspaper does no survey of its own. It does not search for any other source of information, except the BJP . . . It does not care about the citizens, groups, organizations and parties who are opposing the BJP campaign.'[45] So successful has this particular campaign been that virtually all newspapers today unthinkingly use the term 'infiltrator' to describe Bangladeshi Muslim immigrants. Another, less successful, example of the BJP's attempts to create a pseudo-event was its claim that hundreds of Hindu temples in Kashmir had been destroyed following the demolition of the Babri Masjid. To give the claim gravitas and legitimacy, party media managers even prepared a list of the 'destroyed' temples. Unfortunately for them, some journalists decided to verify the BJP claim and found it to be a total fabrication.[46]

For the BJP, however, the pseudo-event par excellence was

the fictitious martyrology it generated throughout the Hindi press in UP following its aborted assault on the Babri Masjid on 30 October 1990. So biased was the media coverage that the Press Council censured four Hindi newspapers—*Aaj, Dainik Jagran, Swatantra Chetna* and *Swatantra Bharat*—for 'gross irresponsibility and impropriety offending the canons of journalistic ethics to promote mass hysteria on the basis of rumours and speculation'.[47] According to the government, the assault on the Babri Masjid had led to the police opening fire. The UP government claimed nine people were killed, a figure that was subsequently revised to sixteen. But the BJP and its allied organizations like the VHP claimed the victims were in the hundreds. These claims, though unsubstantiated, were picked up and embellished by a section of the press.

So blatant was the distortion that different editions of the same newspaper chain gave widely varying figures. The Agra edition of *Aaj* declared the number of dead to be 100, Kanpur said 200, and Bareily 500.[48] Another newspaper, *Swatantra Chetna* of Gorakhpur, contradicted its own banner headline figure of 115 killed in the firing as the body of the report made no such claim. It emerged that the editor, unhappy at the death toll of fifteen, had added a '1' in front of the '15' even as the newspaper was going to press.[49] Another observer notes: 'In a more insidious fashion, a deliberate attempt was made by a large section of the Hindi press to force its readers to believe a majority of Muslims backed the VHP on the Ayodhya issue.'[50] Even the English language press echoed this view. On October 12, 1990, the *Pioneer* frontpaged a report which claimed the Muslim driver of L.K. Advani's chariot had been 'encouraging Muslims at several places to offer kar seva in Ayodhya'. Two days later, the same paper frontpaged a report headlined 'Five thousand Muslims to demolish Babri Masjid'. Even though the news was nothing but a report quoting the BJP leader Mukhtar Abbas Naqvi, the newspaper did not bother to put the headline in quotes.[51]

Demonizing the Sikhs

Although several observers have seen in the media's approach to the Ramjanmabhoomi campaign a sort of high water mark in communal coverage,[52] the tone was actually set a few years earlier by the biased and inflammatory manner in which sections of the mass media helped communalize the Punjab crisis. Once again, the sin was a derivative one, for the original sin was that of the Indira Gandhi and Rajiv Gandhi governments. Nevertheless, in the name of opposing terrorism and defending the unity and integrity of India, the media wittingly or unwittingly fostered the impression that the Sikh community as a whole was guilty for the crimes of a few. The media began by distorting the nature of the Akali demands against Indira Gandhi's government and misrepresenting the Anandpur Sahib resolution as some sort of a secessionist document. As the sociologist Dipankar Gupta wrote at the height of the crisis: 'The radio and television flood out by sheer cusecs of verbiage any possibility of a fair assessment of the Anandpur resolution.'[53] As a result, many Hindus came to the conclusion that Sikhs were looking to partition the country. By and large, the media also made no attempt to distinguish day-to-day political activity by Sikh leaders and organizations, much of which was anti-government, from 'extremism'.

Another critic of the way the Indian media covered the Punjab crisis is Patwant Singh, who argues: 'The irony of the events which propelled Punjab towards the abyss lay in the artful innocence with which the country's media helped ignite the communal keg.'[54] He ascribed the reasons for the media's failure to expose the Congress(I)'s 'disastrous moves in Punjab' to the fact that most of the major newspapers are owned by powerful business houses, which would hardly wish to alienate the government. But the media's role went beyond that: 'As the politics of north India polarized along communal lines, not without some canny manipulation by New Delhi, the national English newspapers became increasingly strident in their attacks on the Sikhs.' And there was plenty of that in supply at the time. For example, in a signed article provocatively titled 'The Sikhs are in Danger', one newspaper editor wrote: 'It is 11 p.m. in the history of the Sikh community. It must reverse the clock. It is still possible to do so. But time is running out. The community must demand that the agitation be called off. The Sikhs must heed the warning before it strikes midnight.'[55] Here, an entire community was being put on notice because of the crimes of a handful. Other media commentators ploughed history for roots of Sikh 'separatism'. One editor went back to 1857, when the Sikhs allegedly made common cause with the British against other Indians: 'It was during the Mutiny that Sikhs showed that, as a community, they had interests and motives of their own which differed from those of the Hindus and Muslims.'[56] In similar vein, a senior columnist argued: 'Our Sikh brothers remembered the old lesson, never really forgotten by them, taught them by the British, that they were different . . . Under the pressure of this psychology, grievances were manufactured, extreme slogans were put forward . . . In the last few years, even the politics of murder was introduced.'[57] Another editor (who has given more proof of his misplaced penchant for history since then) subjected his readers to a potted tour of the 1891 Punjab Census Report, a 1903 pamphlet by Macauliffe and the Cabinet Mission visit before concluding with this sweeping assessment: 'Every feature of Sikh politics has pushed the Sikh community towards internalizing a sense of deprivation, towards separateness, towards separation.'[58]

If the tendency towards separatism and extremism on the part of the Sikhs—and their betrayal of the nation as a community during British colonialism—were standard tropes in media coverage of the Punjab crisis, a derivative was the demand that every Sikh disassociate himself or herself from the activities of Bhindranwale and his accomplices. Of course, every Hindu is not so exhorted when his or her co-religionists do something nasty, a point forcefully argued by economic historian Dharma Kumar in a trenchant article for the *Times of India* shortly after the assassination of Indira Gandhi and the resulting massacre of Sikhs: 'Another sign of double standard is the widespread demand that Sikh intellectuals or "leaders" must denounce the assassination . . . I do not feel I have to rush into print and beat my breast in public when any Hindu does something dreadful (which is fortunate since I would then be doing nothing else). Why should every Sikh be responsible for the doings of all other Sikhs?'[59] Needless to say, her argument did not have much effect on newspaper editors.

In the print media and on television, all incidents of violence in Punjab were refracted through a political prism and reported as terrorism. The province, which was—and still is—notorious for all manner of violent disputes, suddenly became devoid of normal crime. For the media, every killing in Punjab was the handiwork of 'terrorists', 'Sikh extremists' or, sometimes, 'unidentified Sikh extremists'. In Dipankar Gupta's words, reportage of such events 'pivoted around the vivid prototype of the Sikh provocateur'.[60] At the height of the Punjab problem, the official media also contributed to the exacerbation of tensions by reporting normal incidents as if they were communal. Most newspapers, in fact, were guilty of a crime as serious as misreporting: relying on the police for news and information instead of conducting their own investigations. This affected reporting in three ways. First, as mentioned above, all crime was equated with terrorism and all terrorist crime with Sikhs.[61] Second, police claims about the death of alleged extremists in encounters were accepted at face value. (This provided some journalistic gems like the story of the Sikh extremist killed in a fierce encounter 'who upon medical examination by the police turned out to be Pakistani'.) Third, police information about terrorist threats, was uncritically transmitted, even when this information seemed contradictory and inconsistent. One Delhi newspaper ran on its front page the story 'Terrorist Alert in Capital' which reported: 'The police today released photographs of four terrorists who are suspected to be present in Delhi and are planning to create chaos by attacking individual targets and setting off explosions in the Capital.'[62] The report went on to say that one of the terrorists named is the dreaded 'Sukhdev Singh alias Sukha'. However, on the same day, the newspaper also carried the story 'Charge-sheet against Jinda' which mentioned, *inter alia*, that 'Sukhdev Singh alias Sukha' was currently lodged in Yarwada Central Prison, Pune!

The upshot of this kind of reporting, of course, was the creation of a fear psychosis among people, especially non-Sikhs. While every pronouncement of state functionaries was amplified and given wide publicity by the media, any news which challenged the government's version of events—or which cast the Sikhs as victims rather than perpetrators—was studiously ignored. On the same day that Punjab governor Siddhartha Shankar Ray's thousandth claim that normalcy was returning to Punjab received prominent coverage, for example, the press conference of an innocent young man, Avtar Singh Sandhu, who had been brutally tortured by the Punjab police, went virtually unreported. As one senior journalist lamented later, 'Even the sandwiches that the Punjab governor ate at his briefing received more publicity than Sandhu's story', which he had narrated at the Press Club in New Delhi.[63] Likewise, as Romesh Thapar observed, 'When the persons arrested (allegedly) for being involved in the (May 1985) transistor-bomb attacks were produced in a Delhi court, no newspaper had the integrity to comment on their poor physical condition.'[64]

In this communally vitiated atmosphere where the bulk of the media had forsaken its duty to inform and enlighten, the anti-Sikh riots which took place in the Karnataka town of

Bidar in September 1988 went virtually unreported in the national press for ten days. In fact, not a word came out until some of the affected Sikh students reached Delhi to tell their story. As the veteran journalist, Kuldip Nayar, wrote subsequently: 'Stringers of newspapers and news agencies in Bidar, it appears, were late in sending their despatches; and what is worse, press telegrams were not cleared for a few days . . . When reports did arrive at newspaper offices, the news desks also failed to appreciate the gravity of the situation— apparently because of delay, they tended to take the reports as "stale" news. The national press, it is true, cannot have staffers in every town in the country. But even when the story appeared in some regional newspapers, correspondents of big newspapers did not follow it up. I cannot say that this was because of any communal "prejudice" . . . But the national press cannot absolve itself of the initial lapse. How to ensure that it does not happen again is for the media to study.'[65]

In contrast to Bidar, where the media simply ignored the violence, newspaper coverage of the November 1984 massacre of Sikhs in Delhi was ample. However, this coverage was neither comprehensive nor entirely accurate. In some cases, there were elisions and even biases—both active and passive— which served to distort the nature of the violence and foster a sense of hopelessness and apathy. In particular, all the positive actions taken by the people of Delhi such as organizing relief and protection for the Sikhs, were more often than not consigned to the inside pages while tales of terror and gore were highlighted to inspire a paralysing fear amongst the victims and those ordinary Hindus who might have thought about coming to their rescue. Even when it reported the activities of citizens' committees, the media's obsession with party politics would lead reporters to focus on the big names and not on the heroic efforts made by ordinary people. 'When a peace march was organized by a group of concerned citizens in South Delhi on November 2, which was joined by the Janata leader Chandrashekhar and some of his followers, some newspapers the next day described it as a Janata Party march. This created temporary misunderstandings and hampered the effort of the non-party group to bring together citizens, many of whom did not want to identify themselves with any particular party.'[66]

If today it is common knowledge that the massacre was not a communal riot but a politically orchestrated pogrom, this is thanks to the citizens' groups which investigated the killings, and not so much to the media. This is not to say that Delhi newspapers ignored the evidence of police and political involvement. On the contrary, reporters who braved the violence and curfew to find out the truth did point to the inaction and, sometimes, active connivance of the police.[67] For obvious reasons, however, newspapers were more circumspect about highlighting the political dimension and amplified every official pronouncement of innocence despite the existence of basic evidence to the contrary. For example, a front page story in an important Delhi newspaper just as the killings were ending was headlined 'Cong-I refutes rioting charge'.[68] Yet it contained nothing other than an angry assertion from AICC-I general secretary Chandulal Chandrakar that party leaders and workers had 'been actively involved in saving the lives of those affected by the wrath of the hooligans and anti-social elements'. In this instance, the usual tendency of English-language journalism in India to use the word 'refute' when what is meant is 'deny' worked in the Congress party's favour. A reader who skimmed the headlines would well have thought that the Congress had convincingly disproved the charge of involvement in the massacres.

Given that the government's explanation for the violence was that a mass upsurge of Hindu sentiment following Indira Gandhi's assassination had led to revenge-taking against the Sikhs, the press did well to highlight the feelings of solidarity between ordinary Hindus and Sikhs. For example, one

190

newspaper wrote: 'Hindus in colony after colony decided to form their own protection squads . . . disgusted at the utter failure of the police and the government to protect the lives and properties of innocent Sikhs, Hindus assured their Sikh neighbours that they had nothing to fear and patrolled the areas throughout the night.'[69] Despite such evidence, however, the impression was sought to be created that the violence was not the result of political machinations but of enmity and suspicion between Hindus and Sikhs. Since a section of the media had, in fact, been fostering such suspicions for the better part of a year, the theory of 'Hindu-Sikh enmity' was an attractive one to offer readers as an explanation for the violence.

A number of critics have questioned the media's decision to identify Indira Gandhi's assassins as Sikhs. Thus the joint investigative report prepared by the Peoples' Union for Civil Liberties and Peoples' Union for Democratic Rights states: 'Evening bulletins brought out by different newspaper establishments on October 31 stated that there were "two Sikhs and one clean-shaven Sikh" among the assailants. The reporters did not clarify whether the news was from official or unofficial sources. Nor was it clear how a "clean-shaven Sikh" could be identified as a Sikh . . . But what is of immediate relevance is the question: should the media have described the assailants immediately as Sikhs? Given the background of the Punjab situation, such mentioning of a community by name was bound to excite communal passions and inflame communal hatred.'[70]

The argument is presumably that newspapers should have anticipated the danger that identifying Mrs Gandhi's assassins would lead to violence against Sikhs. Yet, the diffusion of news takes place in a variety of ways and even if the newspapers had blacked out the religion of the assassins, word would nevertheless have got around. While there can be two opinions about the choice made by newspaper editors, all observers were united in their condemnation of Doordarshan, which not only disclosed the religion of Mrs Gandhi's killers but also allowed the broadcast of highly provocative slogans like '*khoon ka badla khoon*' (blood for blood) by some Congress party supporters who had assembled at Teen Murti house to pay their last respects to their dead leader. So radical a departure was this coverage from the normally anodyne Doordarshan reports of such incidents that the respected civil libertarian Amiya Rao wrote angrily: 'One would like to know why this was done if not to inflame public opinion against the Sikhs.'[71] The Citizens' Commission report on the 1984 riots, authored by S.M. Sikri, Badr-ud-din Tyabji, Rajeshwar Dayal, Govind Narain and T.C.A. Srinivasavaradan, also had the following observations to make about the role of the media:

> It became immediately apparent that the coverage of the crisis by the official radio and visual media, beginning with the news of the assassination, had not been formulated with adequate care and foresight in relation to the psychological impact of their transmissions . . . As examples of impolitic broadcasts which had a damaging effect, we cite three: (a) premature disclosure of the religious identity of the two assailants; (b) the failure to monitor the provocative slogans raised by the crowds or to edit the over-emotional interviews with members of the public; and (c) earlier statements mistakenly describing the killings as being due to an 'exchange of fire', which gave the erroneous impression that there was fighting between the two communities.[72]

As for the print media, while the same report considered the reporting to be largely factual and detailed, it did accuse sections of the press of failing to exercise adequate care and restraint in their presentation, 'which at times had the effect of exacerbating feelings rather than assuaging them'.

Apart from some irresponsible reporting and editorializing—which turned the unsubstantiated rumour about Sikhs distributing sweets after hearing the news of Indira

Gandhi's assassination into a rationale for their massacre—the press was also guilty of allowing other inflammatory rumours to pass unchallenged. One of these was the whispering campaign (in which some policemen and Congress workers were involved) that Delhi's water supply had been poisoned. Tavleen Singh has also written about how the code of conduct for covering communal tension (under which the names of the communities should not be identified) helped fuel a dangerous rumour:

> Although it was only Sikhs who were killed on trains coming into the city, (the newspapers) kept reporting that trains filled with dead bodies were pouring in. Inevitably, memories of partition were evoked and rumours swept through the city that the trains were filled with dead Hindus. The rampaging mobs that were already looking for Sikhs to kill then went completely wild . . . Ironically, or perhaps typically, the newspapers that had shown the most hesitation about identifying the victims as Sikhs were the very newspapers who had shown no qualms about coming out with headlines like 'Indira Gandhi killed by Sikh guards'.[73]

Even if the newspapers provided enough details of police and political involvement in the rioting for the reader to draw her or his own conclusions about how such murder and mayhem was allowed to rule the country's Capital for several days, editorial analysts were reluctant to call a spade a spade. If at all the political role was conceded, this was ascribed to the nebulous phenomenon of 'goondaization' and not to the highest echelons of the government, without whose sanction such killings would have been unthinkable. To their credit, most newspapers did attack the government for refusing to appoint a commission of inquiry into the massacres; but eventually, as the demonization of the Sikhs resumed, this demand was no longer pressed with the same urgency. After all, the Sikhs had been taught a lesson for failing to follow the warning proffered them editorially during their 'eleventh

193

hour'. What had happened was that the clock had 'struck midnight'. Today, several years after the two hands of the clock came together to kill and burn citizens of the Sikh religion, November 1984 has all but been forgotten by the Indian media.

Reporting Riots

For a long time, newspapers in India have tended to follow a rather quaint code of conduct which prohibits the identification of the communities involved in communal disturbances. The curious manner in which this guideline is often implemented can be seen from the news item with the coy headline 'Sacrilege at Place of Worship' which the *Hindustan Times* ran on its front page a few years back. The report read: 'An incident took place at a place of worship in Lajpat Nagar where "pieces of flesh" were found in an envelope, along with a letter threatening a particular community and their place of worship. The priest, Mayaram, reportedly told police that he saw a young woman wearing a salwar kameez with a "chadhar" enter. Later they found the envelope containing the "flesh pieces".'[74] Nowhere are the two 'communities' named, yet it is clear from the naming of the priest and the description of the young woman's clothes (salwar kameez with a 'chadhar') that the reader is being encouraged to assume we are talking about Hindus and Muslims. In fact, reports of this type are particularly insidious for whenever the victim of an outrage is a Hindu and the perpetrator a Muslim, helpful clues such as names, dress and type of facial hair are often supplied, even as the fiction of not naming the two 'communities' is maintained; but when a Muslim is the victim, more often than not the news reports will be terse and lacking in nomenclatural or other clues. The media's strategy of providing selective markers leads, of course, to an extremely distorted picture of communal violence. Even though 90 per cent of victims in a riot are Muslims, the fact that their names are not reported when the names of a few Hindu victims are, can create a false and dangerous impression of Muslim aggressiveness. Likewise, the majority of those indulging in murder and looting may be criminals who happen to be Hindus but the seemingly harmless naming of just one Muslim can, within a communally vitiated atmosphere, contribute to the fiction of Hindu victimhood: 'More than a dozen shops were burnt in the night's incidents', one newspaper report read, adding: 'According to the police inspector of Hapur, the police have arrested a rioter called Sikander'.[75]

During the communal killings of 1926 and 1946, the Bengal press played an extremely negative role, fanning the flames of hatred by biased, misleading and even fictional reports.[76] With some exceptions, the Bengali language press was divided on the basis of religion, with most newspapers aimed exclusively at either Hindus or Muslims. The *Asr-e-Jadid* reminded the Muslims of their domination over Hindus for 'thousands of years' and exhorted them to face the 'challenge that has been thrown at living Islam by paganism'. The *Mohammadi* wrote, after the first phase of the 1926 Calcutta riot, that 'Mohammedans have proved . . . that however inferior they may numerically be they can fight against people ten or eleven times as numerous'. Not to be left behind, Hindu newspapers such as the *Matwala* declared: 'If Malaviyaji gives a signal then Hindus can tear out every hair on the beard of those Moslem goondas.' The hugely influential *Ananda Bazar Patrika* asked the Hindus is a leading article on 5 May 1926: 'Will you receive the news of the desecration of temples hanging . . . your heads in shame and disgrace and remain silent? . . . Let the eternal youth of Bengal come forward. Let the wild dance put fury and seize the soft feet of the youth and hoods of viciousness break and fall to the ground at every stroke of their feet.' Though most of the rioters were 'illiterates', they drew their information from these newspapers read aloud to them by their leaders.

During the 1940s, the Dhaka and Calcutta press worked to inflame communal passions. Nearly a month before the outbreak of riots, the *Star of India* on 4 March 1941 warned the Hindus: 'The time has come for the little rats (Hindus) to know that the lion (Muslims) is not dead, only sleeping; the challenge is to be accepted; . . . the Hindus will see to whom Bengal belongs; they shall be taught the lesson they need.' Once the riot began, Muslim papers circulated exaggerated stories to incite their readers. The *Azad*, which had a wide circulation among the Muslims of Dhaka, fabricated an episode of the stripping of Muslim women. In the Hindu press, a role similar to that of the *Azad* was played by the *Amrita Bazar Patrika, Ananda Bazar Patrika* and *Basumati*, which invented stories about the molestation of Hindu women on their way back from a temple.

Stories about the molestation of 'our' women is a recurring theme in communal media coverage. During the Ahmedabad riots in 1969, a widely circulated evening daily carried on its front page lurid but fictitious details about the molestation of Hindu women in the Lal Mill area; worse, in that communally charged atmosphere, All-India Radio broadcast a false rumour about the poisoning of the city's milk supply.[77] The Madon Commission which investigated the circumstances relating to the Bhiwandi riots of 1969 found that newspaper coverage of the disturbances contributed to the heightening of tension. The Commission went on to recommend pre-censorship of news relating to communal disturbances. As for the Meerut riots of 1982, what appeared in the national press was, according to Asghar Ali Engineer, 'hardly a tip of the proverbial iceberg'. More than 100 people died, mostly Muslims, including at least forty-two who were killed in cold blood by the Provincial Armed Constabulary. Yet, the Delhi press hardly gave the matter any coverage. The local Hindi newspapers 'acted as the mouthpiece of the RSS (and) played havoc by publishing inflammatory material against minorities'. Among the newspapers responsible were *Prabhat, Meerut Samachar* and *Hamara Yug.*[78]

A similar pattern could be observed in media coverage of the 1989 Bhagalpur riots. English and Hindi dailies gave extensive coverage to unsubstantiated and totally fictitious reports about the murder of hundreds of Hindu students by Muslim lodge owners in Parbatti mohalla. A few days later, when a number of dead bodies were found at a well nearby—all the victims turned out to be Muslims—the Bhagalpur and even Patna press continued to imply that Hindu students had been killed. 'In the initial days of the riots, an image was built that the riots were a "Hindu backlash" to the incidents at Tattarpur. The incidents themselves were distorted beyond recognition. Some correspondents even attributed a history to the locality, tracing its role in the 1946 riots when, as a matter of fact, the locality did not even exist at that time.'[79] Once again, newspaper reports conformed to the usual communal style: Hindu victims were named while Muslim victims remained nameless, and the numbers of the former were inflated while the latter were underplayed.

The riots which took place in Bhopal following the demolition of the Babri Masjid were also reported locally as a Muslim plot.[80] Even before the violence broke out, rumours had been put into circulation about how atrocities were being committed on Hindus. On 9 December 1992, these rumours found their way into print: The *Dainik Bhaskar* claimed that rioters had entered Hamidia hospital and beaten up injured patients after identifying them; and *Nav Bharat* carried three separate items on its back page about young Hindu girls being abducted, attacked and raped. The reports were baseless but the newspaper nevertheless supplied the names of the girls. The same day, the eveninger *Jan Charcha* quoted a lieutenant of Arjun Singh as saying 'breasts of seventy Hindu women were cut off in Old Bhopal' and claimed some 25,000 people had died in rioting nationwide. In one of the few quantitative assessments of the damage a communal media can do, a senior official of the state administration was quoted as admitting that 'at least forty murders in the city should be attributed to the 9th morning *Nav Bharat*'. As for the complicity of the state administration itself, the Sanskritik Morcha-PUDR report states: 'Throughout the first few days one of the most inflammatory rumours in circulation was that the Laxmi Narayan Mandir had been set on fire. A visual on Doordarshan could have nipped it in the bud. Instead, the government let these rumours circulate.'[81]

More recently, in Gujarat, a section of the Gujarati language press has directly contributed to the anti-Muslim and anti-Christian campaign of the Sangh parivar. Consider some of the headlines: 'Muslims retaliate in Gujarat: Disgusting attempt to set fire to three small children. Attempt to rape woman, idol of Ganapati broken';[82] 'Riots break out in Bardoli as stones were thrown from the mosque at rally of Hindus';[83] 'Terror of Christians in Zankhav: Attacks on Shops, Homes of Hindus'.[84] One newspaper ran two inflammatory headlines under the guise of reporting a speech: 'Muslims should be stripped naked and beaten' and 'Crush like mosquitoes those Muslims who kidnap Hindu women'.[85] Once again, we see the appearance of the pseudo-event: several newspapers ran similar unsourced stories on the same day about an alleged Muslim plot to corrupt Hindu womanhood. One newspaper wrote: 'It is believed that there is an international conspiracy that a Muslim who marries a virgin Hindu girl receives sixty thousand rupees and a Muslim who marries a married Hindu girl gets one lakh rupees.'[86] On the same day, *Dabkar* gave the news: 'Four lakh Hindu women have been victims of this conspiracy.'

The English language newspapers, on the other hand, have reported the events in Gujarat—and the anti-Christian tirade of senior BJP, VHP and RSS leaders—comprehensively and accurately. The tenor of this coverage has hardly been sympathetic to the Sangh parivar and all the major national dailies have run editorials roundly condemning the targeting of the Christians. Thanks to the national press, the Gujarat government's controversial religious census of Muslims and Christians was stopped.[87] Predictably, the BJP has accused the English language media of exaggerating the extent of the violence and blowing a few incidents out of proportion, a charge which has drawn a sharply worded rejoinder from the editor of the *Indian Express*: 'It's difficult to defend the English media at the best of times. God knows, we do commit crimes each day, on each page, including the rape of Queen's English. But on this one, our only crime is reporting faithfully the pearls of wisdom that leading lights of the Sangh parivar have been spreading so liberally.'[88]

Despite overwhelming evidence to suggest Muslims are the main victims of communal violence, why is it that the standard riot narrative as propounded by the bulk of the print media continues to revolve around the alleged aggressiveness of the Muslim? There are three reasons. First, the average newspaper's over-reliance on the police for news and information. Given the communal bias of the police force, especially in riot situations, something which has been amply documented by the scholar-policeman Vibhuti Narain Rai,[89] it is extremely dangerous for newspapers to rely on police handouts for information about the sequence of events or the course of the violence. For example, during the Seelampur riots in Delhi which started on 11 December 1992, most newspapers uncritically accepted the version of the authorities without bothering to ascertain the facts through their own means. Since the official version was aimed at whitewashing the role of the police, Muslims were cast as aggressors.

Second, due to the high financial and logistical costs, most newspapers cannot afford to maintain full-time news bureaux all around the country capable of making it to a potential or actual trouble spot in time to file a credible despatch. The result is that newspapers maintain a large roster of underpaid stringers, who get paid on the basis of stories printed. Since being a stringer is not directly remunerative, there is a temptation to use one's status as a 'press reporter' in order to please (or threaten) local big-wigs. To the extent this means compromising on the integrity of news despatches, a variety of biases can creep in, including communal ones, depending on the particular constellation of political interests operating at the local level.

The third reason why riot coverage tends to be biased against Muslims is the prevalence of biases and unprofessionalism within the news desks of newspapers. Finally, the pressure of space and deadlines can also lead to communal stereotyping:

> If both journalists and a majority of readers associate Muslims with 'threat', then reporters and editors, pressured by deadlines and constrained by the limited space available, may simply treat the news about riots in a way which conforms to this. In other words, what they are doing is to present unfamiliar events in as familiar and easily digestible a fashion as possible. This leads to obvious distortion, as does the tendency to neglect background and context. Riots are likely to appear as sudden, dramatic and unexplained, or as having only direct and immediate causes. The underlying state of affairs is ignored and easy assumptions, instinctive associations, are upheld.[90]

In his comparative analysis of communalism and collective violence in South Asia, Stanley Tambiah considers the processes of 'focalization' and 'transvaluation' as key to the development and normalization of riots.[91] Focalization occurs as local incidents—a property dispute, a fight between neighbours—are progressively denuded of their local contexts; transvaluation is the parallel process of assimilating particulars to a larger, collective, more enduring and therefore less context-bound cause or interest. Thus, local incidents and physical disputes can be cumulatively built up into larger and larger clashes between growing numbers of antagonists who were only indirectly or peripherally involved in the original disputes. Central to this process is propaganda which aims to distort and inflate the 'substantive nature of micro-events', stripping them of their local contexts and translating them into contextless and unchanging principles of communal identity, interests and entitlements.[92] This is the role that the media tends to play in India, before, during and after incidents of communal violence.

At a more abstract level, it must be stressed that communalized reporting flows inevitably from the very discourse of communal riots. 'Communal riot' is a rather infelicitous term that one has been conditioned into using in order to describe the killing of persons on the basis of their religion. What makes it particularly misleading is the fact that more often than not such events resemble pogroms rather than riots. Secondly, the qualifier 'communal' would suggest that ordinary members of various religious communities occasionally come together to riot and kill with no basis for unity among themselves other than their Hinduness or Muslimness. The discourse of 'communal riots' has no room to acknowledge that some Hindus who get together due to political or economic motivation to attack Muslims at large cannot really be referred to as 'the Hindus' or even as 'some Hindus'. It is not necessary to grant the Shiv Sena activists who attacked Muslims in Mumbai in 1993 (or the Congressmen who attacked Sikhs in Delhi in 1984) the appellation 'Hindu' in order to recognize that their victims all belonged to one particular religion. By what logic can a politically instigated mob that enjoys the tacit backing of the state law enforcement machinery be labelled a 'Hindu mob'? And what purpose does such a label really serve other than to mask the *political* nature of the violence which was perpetrated?

An anti-communal magazine recently ran a cover story

with the headline 'Why don't Muslims and Christians Unite?'[93] But unite against whom? Hindus? There is a smaller headline on the side: 'The coming together of the country's largest religious minorities—both targets of Hindutva—is in their own and the nation's interest, says a Christian priest.' Even if the enemy is Hindutva and not Hindus, the first headline implicitly suggests that the Hindus are for Hindutva. The cause of secularizing the mass media's coverage of riots and related subjects will not be advanced merely by inverting the matrix of victims and perpetrators. If the media today blames 'the Muslims' for starting communal riots, nothing will be served by insisting that it is really 'the Hindus'. In truth, neither one or the other is responsible, though the Muslims form the bulk of the victims. Moreover, both must suffer the consequences of a polity that can be so easily and frequently diverted from the task of dealing with its fundamental problems.

Communalism and the Airwaves

Even before Independence, the airwaves' potential to mobilize public opinion on a hitherto unimagined scale made All-India Radio a battleground for competing political interests. Though the content of news broadcasts was controlled by the government and was, in fact, prepared in English, there was considerable scope for linguistic licence. When words can be transmitted to millions of listeners around the country in a matter of seconds, the language those words are uttered in becomes intensely political. Turkey today, for example, does not allow broadcasts in Kurdish for fear that this will encourage separatism; on the other hand, one of the first concrete steps taken by the regional governments of Catalonia and the Basque country in Spain after the post-Franco Constitution granted them wide-ranging autonomy was to launch radio and television stations in the Catalan and Basque languages respectively. In pre-Partition India, with the political atmosphere already vitiated by religion, AIR's language policy became a proxy through which competing communal (i.e. political) claims were staked and contested. Though the conflation of religion and language in north India had been underway for several decades, a full-blown linguistic partition between Hindi and Urdu could not occur, *inter alia*, due to low literacy levels. By standardizing the spoken language on a mass scale, however, radio had the potential to either drown Hindi in Urdu or vice-versa, develop an idiomatic Hindustani that drew equally from both, or ensure that both languages developed in a separate, mutually incomprehensible direction. Hence, various political lobbies tried their best to ensure AIR's language was in sync with their own narrow agendas.

In 1940, the Director-General of AIR, Ahmad Shah Bukhari, set up a committee to resolve the Hindi-Urdu question once and for all. The committee had two members—the well-known Hindi writer S.H. Vatsyayan 'Agyeya' and Urdu litterateur Chaudhuri Hassan Hasrat—and they were charged with the task of compiling an authoritative lexicon that AIR could use for translating its news broadcasts from English to Hindustani. As David Lelyveld describes it, 'the procedure was to list English words from the original news copy from which the vernacular news translations were prepared. The Hindi poet then made a list of Hindi equivalents, the Urdu essayist set down his Urdu counterparts; then the two sat down and worked out a compromise based on what they considered most common, precise, and, if possible, neutral.'[94] Five years later, the committee produced a comprehensive lexicon, but it was already too late. The impending division of the subcontinent along religious lines meant that the language known as Hindustani had no chance of remaining undivided. The lexicon was quickly forgotten and separate Hindi and Urdu radio broadcasts soon began—the partitioning of the airwaves, as it were, presaging the partitioning of the land below.

After Independence, All-India Radio did more than merely finalize the rupture between Hindi and Urdu. After all, Hindi and Urdu were thinly disguised proxies for 'Hindus' and 'Muslims'; under Sardar Vallabhbhai Patel (who was information and broadcasting minister till 1950) and B.V. Keskar (who ran the ministry from 1950 to 1962), AIR moved to shut out not just Urdu but other aspects of 'Muslim' influence as well.[95] According to the veteran AIR broadcaster P.C. Chatterji, Sardar Patel sent a note to Bukhari demanding that singers and musicians from the *tawaif* culture—all 'persons whose private lives were a public scandal'—be taken off the air. Bukhari replied that these women had no private lives and, therefore, could not be a public scandal, but Patel had his way and soon the AIR DG had to quit.[96] In Lelyveld's view, 'the distinction between amateur and professional was called into question so that greater room could be made for performers who had come out of music schools rather than Muslim-dominated *gharanas*'.[97] Keskar himself believed that Indian music had been damaged not just by the British but by India's Muslim rulers. In particular, he blamed Muslim musicians through the centuries who, in his view, 'had appropriated and distorted the ancient art, turning it into the secret craft of exclusive lineages, the *gharanas*, and, ignorant of Sanskrit, divorced it from the religious context of Hindu civilization . . . Just as the British had no great place for music in their scheme of things, neither did Islam. In Muslim hands music was no longer "spiritual"; it had become merely "erotic", the special preserve of "dancing girls, prostitutes and their pimps".[98] His pathological aversion to this 'alien' influence also led him to shut out Hindi film songs from AIR altogether. For Keskar, these songs—with their Urdu lyrics, Western melodies and rhythms, and 'erotic' sentiments—were the main enemy to his project of rejuvenating an authentic 'national' culture through 'pure' *shastriya sangeet* and light orchestral music. He began by restricting the amount of airtime for *filmi* songs and then banished them altogether. It was not until 1957 that 'Muslim' music was allowed back on AIR via the Vividh Bharati service. A decade later, thanks to the arrival of mass-produced, cheap transistor sets, advertisements were also introduced.

For the airwaves, the moment of 'secularization' was, ironically, the moment of commodification as well. Though the subtle communalism of the Keskar era has thankfully long since passed, Indian radio continues to suffer from rigid state control and creeping commericialization. Despite the technological potential of the medium—dozens of stations catering to a variety of interests and tastes could easily be established by public, private and community organizations—radio remains woefully underutilized. The proposed Broadcasting Bill would liberalize matters somewhat but contains no provisions for non-state public broadcasting. As for autonomy for AIR and Doordarshan, it is already obvious that the creation of a supposedly independent Prasar Bharati has not hindered the government from influencing the content of public broadcasting. In the 'bad old days' before Prasar Bharati, an information and broadcasting minister could assert with impunity that he was not in the least bit bothered about whether radio and television were credible or not: 'Credibility is the dubious preoccupation of the cocktail party circuit. Ask a villager what it means and he will not know.'[99] Today, few ministers would dare to be so blatant but the old urge to interfere in news and programming operations has not diminished. In most cases, such interference is mundane, aimed at nothing more than increasing the visibility of a minister or highlighting the 'achievements' of the ruling party or coalition. But television is an extremely powerful medium and sometimes it has been used towards more strategic political ends, as in the case of *Ramayana*.

From *Ramayana* to *Fire*

Though the emergence of a mass nationwide viewership for

television is closely linked to the serialization of epics like the Ramayana and Mahabharata, mythological and religious themes have tended to fade in popularity as subjects for television programming in recent years. Thanks to cable channels, crime and horror themes have begun to proliferate, as have 'family-oriented' soap operas. Many theorists have long held both fictional genres to be alienating. For Adorno, the setting of 'spectacular' crime and horror in locales that are familiar and everyday such as the workplace, university or residential neighborhood 'creates an atmosphere of fear in the presence of daily objects on the streets, stimulates distrusts for strangers, alienates people, and pigeonholes them within their family life or the small world of the office or workshop.'[100] Soap operas generate their own pathologies—consumerism, the subordination of women, domesticity, and, in the Indian context, a rather narrow, upper caste 'Hindu' view of what constitutes the 'normal' family. These themes are much more well developed in Bollywood where popular films such as *Hum Aapke Hain Koun . . .!* and *Dilwale Dulhaniya Le Jayenge* help to perpetuate certain reactionary notions of 'family values' and what Uberoi has called the 'tyranny of tradition'.[101] However, the need to cater to a culturally segmented market both within India and abroad (the average satellite footprint means programmes beamed to India can typically be watched in an area stretching from the Gulf to Malaysia) has led some channels to move away from exclusive reliance on the stereotypical Hindu family as the focus around which soap themes are built. According to one TV critic, Shailaja Bajpai, the 'need to cater to niche audiences' has led to serials such as *Adhikaar* and *Tanha*, which deal exclusively with Muslim families and 'depict them as modern and urban in much the same way as Hindus'.[102] At the same time, she takes issue with *Shaktimaan*, the highly popular Doordarshan programme based on the exploits of a comic book superhero of the same name. The serial, she argues, is a 'worrying expression of Hindu ideology . . . (which) propagates the Hindu way of life among children, passing it off as the true Indian way of life'.[103] Another recent development is the advent of vernacular cable channels, which have led viewers to switch from Doordarshan to Tamil, Telegu, Kannada and other language programming. Divya McMillan argues that to the extent to which Doordarshan propagates a Hindu-centric and Hindi-centric notion of nationhood, these channels, which are also highly commercialized, serve to provide alternative, language-based, communities of consumption.[104]

While one must guard against reading too much into this or that television programme or serial, there is a need for systematic research into the social and political impact of Indian television programming. In particular, how has the 'inter-ocular field'[105] generated by television in combination with other visual and cultural fields facilitated the communalization that has occurred over the past decade? The role of TV in either promoting (or countering) communalist politics came under intense scrutiny in the late 1980s when three serials—*Ramayana*, *The Sword of Tipu Sultan* and *Tamas*—were shown on Doordarshan's national network. Although the first was mythological, the second historical, and the third fictional-cum-historical, each straddled the controversial terrain of religion and nationalism and was considered by critics and supporters alike to be of great political importance, not least because the use of the mass media gave the programmes unprecedented reach. Although at the time, not many analysts were prepared to make the link between the televised version of the Ramayana—which Rajiv Gandhi's government gave prime time space to on Doordarshan—and the feverish propaganda campaign for a Ram temple in Ayodhya, subsequent events, including the demolition of the Babri Masjid on 6 December 1992, do suggest a strong link. For Tapan Basu et al, 'the serialized "Ramayana" . . . reduced Hinduism to its mythology which was then presented as the

essence of nationhood . . . It provided to the new aggressive
social class spawned in the '80s a packaged, collective self-
image which, with the mobilizing by Hindutva, became the
motivating force for changing, by force and violence, the
image of the country itself.'[106] Elsewhere, Appadurai and
Breckenridge have argued that 'the entire nation viewed (the)
local battle (for a Ram temple at the site of the Babri Masjid)
in the context of its feverish recent consumption of the
televised Hindu epic, the *Ramayana*. While the televised epic
was not openly incendiary in regard to religious sentiments
. . . there can be no question that the electronic rediscovery
of the Hindu epics gave tremendous leverage to Hindu religious
nationalists as they escalated the communal stakes in places
like Ayodhya.'[107]

Lutgendorf, however, has criticized the critics of the
teleserial for believing Ramanand Sagar's narrative and
performative idioms would be hegemonic, and for assuming
that it represented an 'assault on a hitherto pristine and
incommercial tradition'. He argues that this was not the first
time the Ramayana had been 'marketed' and points to the fact
that the epic has 'clearly been supporting a large (if
decentralized) industry on the subcontinent for many years'
and that this 'marketing' has always been inseparable from the
dissemination and performance of the epic'.[108] Accepting that
the Ramayana has always been a 'national' and even political
epic, van der Veer argues that 'in the age of nationalism, the
politics of Rama devotion has been transformed, so that the
legitimation of a royal dynasty has been replaced by that of the
'Hindu nation'.[109] Thanks to its reach and fantastic special
effects which made mythology seem ever so real, television
gave the epic a potency it never had before, and the state
knew this. The Faizabad court's decision to open the padlocks
which had kept the Babri Masjid away from the public eye for
more than four decades—and the joyous televised coverage of
this act of 'liberation'—were blatant attempts by the ruling

Congress to manipulate the politics of Rama devotion in its favour. However, the BJP proved it could play the game better. With hindsight it is obvious that the TV *Ramayana* benefited the Sangh parivar much more than it did the Congress. Of course, the benefits were more in iconic than ideological terms. Rather than Rama espousing Hindutva, BJP leaders fully exploited the popularity of the televised epic, even going so far as to strike godly poses for propaganda photographs and using Sagaresque decor for their raths and stages at political rallies. Actors who had played key roles were recruited to campaign and even stand for election.[110] As van der Veer argues, 'It is difficult to imagine the "naturalness" of L.K. Advani's impersonation of Rama in his campaign without taking the recent telecast into account . . . In the VHP's iconography, Rama is a heavily armed warrior. The devotional movement towards sweetness and femininity in the worship of Rama seems to have been jolted towards militancy as a result of (Doordarshan's) more martial portrayal of Rama and his actions in the *Ramayana*. Moreover, through the power of television, Ayodhya and Rama's life in and return to that city are brought very close to the viewer . . . There can be little doubt that Ayodhya, as a real, historical place in Uttar Pradesh, has been effectively connected by the VHP and BJP campaign to the Ayodhya of television.'[111]

An early and perceptive critic of the serial was the historian Romila Thapar, who linked the televised epic to the Indian state's desire to iron out sociocultural diversities and fabricate a homogenized culture that would be easier to control. After all, 'to concede that a nation's culture may be constituted of a variety of cultural systems would require that the functionaries of the state be sensitive to these multiple cultural systems and respond to their political implications.'[112] This was something the Congress party under Rajiv Gandhi was unwilling to do, especially since it had visions of utilizing a politicized Hinduism to split the polity and cling to power. By abusing the power and reach of television, however, the Congress was doing something more: it was fostering a culture that was not just monolithic but intolerant of dissent as well. To quote Thapar: 'If the state has taken on the role of the main patron of culture and if it should then withdraw from innovations in creativity on the grounds that it will hurt the sentiments of a "religious community", culture will tend to be reduced to the lowest common denominator.' This is precisely what happened a few months later when, during the V.P. Singh government's tenure, a controversy broke out over the telecast of *The Sword of Tipu Sultan*. Based on the best-selling and classic book of the same name by Bhagwan Gidwani, the multi-episode serial directed by Sanjay Khan was all set to be shown on Doordarshan when some organizations linked to the BJP began to protest. These organizations claimed that Tipu Sultan, one of the outstanding personalities of India's freedom struggle, was an 'Islamic fundamentalist' who was 'anti-Hindu'. They recycled an old British canard that he had forcibly converted Hindus to Islam and said that to glorify such a personality on TV would be a 'gratuitous insult to every Hindu'. Unfortunately, the government began to prevaricate on the issue and refused to clear the serial's telecast. Since Gidwani's assessment of Tipu Sultan was at the heart of the controversy, the author— a retired international civil servant who is based in Montreal— flew to New Delhi to meet the information and broadcasting minister at the time, P. Upendra. In an interview to the Indian Progressive Study Group in New York a few months later, Gidwani revealed what transpired during that meeting. The conversation between the two men was surreal and bears quotation in full as a telling testament of what happens when the government not only controls television but also attempts to dominate the interpretation of culture and history as well:

'Upendra said: "I am sorry there are so many protests." He showed me a number of cases. "Well," I said, "if the book is communal, you show me one word or paragraph, one comma or full stop that is communal. I shall have the book burnt and I shall never write again." He looked at me and said, "I will read the book." I was surprised that he had not read the book. After forty-eight hours we met again. Then he told me that the book was not communal but that this man—Tipu Sultan—was communal himself.

'Then the minister made the point, "There are so many demonstrations . . . there are protests." I replied, "When you succumb to this kind of pressure, you encourage these forces." He said, "No, but I will appoint a historians' committee to look into this book." "A historians' committee for what," I asked. He said, "A historians' committee will see whether you have glorified Tipu Sultan or not." "I haven't glorified Tipu Sultan and who can decide whether I have unduly glorified him or not?" I asked him. But he did not want to discuss these things in detail. He said, "No, no, Mr Gidwani, if you want the serial to come out you should appear before the committee." I replied, "I don't think any historian must come and tell me how I should view Tipu Sultan . . ."

'Later on he told me, "If you are taking this attitude . . . then your serial will not come out." My answer was simply that I am not bothered. "My historical perspective, the memory of Tipu Sultan will outlive this government and many other governments." '[113]

Prophetic words indeed. In any event, because of public pressure, the V.P. Singh government finally agreed to allow the serial's telecast. But a disclaimer was attached after each episode telling viewers that what they had just seen was merely a 'fictionalized version' of history, and not the real thing. Of course, no such disclaimer was tagged on to *Ramayana* or *Mahabharata* when they were shown on Doordarshan.

While *Ramayana* and *The Sword of Tipu Sultan* raised questions about the impact of myth and history on modern politics, the controversy surrounding *Tamas* was of a slightly different nature. The serial, which was based on the Hindi

novel of the same name by the celebrated writer Bhisham
Sahni, contained several scenes of graphic communal violence.
It also depicted the negative role played by political
organizations like the RSS in inciting violence and hatred.
Since a claim about the innocence of the RSS's role carried
with it the potential for a troublesome can of worms to be
opened, opponents of the telecast decided to focus on the
'inflammatory' nature of the scenes depicting violence. Does
the depiction of communal violence in a television programme
or film incite communal hatred? Judging by the recent
censorship of the Bollywood film, *Zakhm*, directed by Mahesh
Bhatt, this is still a controversial subject. In the case of *Zakhm*,
the censor board (or rather the Union and Maharashtra
governments) decided that scenes of 'mob' violence could be
shown but excised two scenes: one showing a mob wearing
saffron headbands and the other showing a (Hindu) police
inspector who is in league with the communalist *sangathan*
killing a Muslim prisoner in a staged encounter.[114] Even if we
assume that mass media portrayals of communal violence
incite communal hatred, surely it is 'better' to show that the
violence is instigated by political groups and the police (which
is the truth, in any case) rather than by ordinary 'Hindus' or
'Muslims'. In reality, the state tends to be more concerned
about its own image and hence adopts a convenient definition
of the phrase 'threat to law and order'. Inflammatory articles
and even broadcasts are allowed so long as they do not sully
the image of the state; but anti-communal programming
which shows the state or ruling party in poor light can be
cancelled or indefinitely postponed, as was the case with
Anand Patwardhan's 1992 documentary on Ayodhya, *Ram ke
Naam*. It was only after the Babri Masjid had been demolished
that Doordarshan finally agreed to telecast it, that too at a
time when most viewers would be fast asleep.

In *Ramesh v. Union of India and others* (1988),[115] otherwise
known as the *Tamas* case, the Supreme Court sought to define

a yardstick by which media depictions of communally sensitive situations—especially communal violence—could be judged to be inflammatory or not. *Tamas* is set in Punjab during Partition and explores the manner in which communal animosity and violence was incited by extremist political forces claiming to represent Hindus, Muslims and Sikhs. It also highlights the role of the British in first encouraging these forces and then turning a blind eye when violence occurs. Since the very first episode portrayed a none-too-flattering image of the RSS—a *pracharak* is shown initiating young boys into the 'art' of violence—the Sangh parivar was particularly exercised by the serial. In his submission to the Court, the petitioner contended that the broadcast of *Tamas* was against public order and was likely to incite people to indulge in violence. He also contended that the serial attempted to promote feelings of enmity and hatred on the grounds of religion, caste and community. In considering the petition, the Court (*coram* Sabyasachi Mukharji and S. Ranganathan, JJ.) noted that since *Tamas* had been given a 'U' certificate by the Central Board of Film Censors and since there was no allegation of mala fide or bad motive on the part of the authorities concerned, 'the only question, therefore, is whether the film has been . . . wrongly judged and allowed to be . . . serialized on TV on a wrong approach.'According to the Court, 'the film indubitably depicts violence. That violence between the communities took place before the pre-Partition days is a fact and it is the truth. (But the petitioner's counsel) submits that truth in its naked form may not always and in all circumstances be desirable to be told or exhibited.' In other words, what criteria should be used to judge when it is prudent to show the truth or censor it? In answering this problem, the Court drew upon the celebrated 1946 Nagpur High Court judgment of Justice Vivian Bose in *Bhagwati Charan Shukla v. Provincial Government* in which it was held that the effect of the words must be judged 'from the standards of reasonable, strong-willed, firm and courageous men, and not those of weak and vacillating minds, nor of those who scent danger in every hostile point of view.' Justices Mukharji and Ranganathan ruled. that this was the correct approach in judging the effect of reading a book or exhibiting a film. 'It is the standard of an ordinary reasonable man; or as they say in English law, "the man on the top of a Clapham omnibus".' The learned judges also drew on the 1970 judgment of Chief Justice Hidayatullah in *K.A. Abbas v Union of India*, in which he asked: 'If Nadir Shah made golgothas of skulls, must we leave them out of the story because people must be made to view a historical theme without true history?' Hidayatullah had gone on to observe that the standards of evaluation must be framed in such a way that 'we are not reduced to a level where the protection of the least capable and the most depraved amongst us determines what the morally healthy cannot view or read.'

From this standpoint, the Court concluded that the average man would 'learn from the mistakes of the past and realize the machinations of the fundamentalists.' *Tamas*, it held, 'takes us to a historical past—unpleasant at times, but revealing and instructive . . . Naked truth in all times will not be beneficial but truth in its proper light indicating the evils and the consequences of those evils is instructive and that message is there in *Tamas*.' Far from affecting public order, the Court held, 'it is more likely that it will prevent incitement to such offences in future by extremists and fundamentalists.' The judges then made some broad observations about the potency of depicting communalism in pictures and serials in general. 'If some scenes of violence, some nuances of expression or some events in the film can stir up certain feelings in the spectator, an equally deep, strong, lasting and beneficial impression can be conveyed by scenes revealing the machinations of selfish interests, scenes depicting mutual respect and tolerance, scenes showing comradeship, help and kindness which transcend the barriers of religion.'

The Supreme Court returned to the theme of the possible public reaction to potentially inflammatory films in its ruling in *S. Rangarajan v P. Jagiivan Ram and others* (1989).[116] The petitioner had challenged a High Court decision to withdraw the 'U' certificate granted to the Tamil film *Ore Oru Gramathile*, which deals with the reservation issue and argues that reservation should be on the basis of economic criteria and not caste. The Tamil Nadu government held that the film was bringing its reservation policy into disrepute; it also argued that if the film were to be exhibited, there would be protests and a potential threat to law and order. Though the Supreme Court gave various arguments in justification of its decision to allow the film to be screened, one of its points is worth remembering, especially because of the bearing it has on certain unpleasant events that have occurred recently, such as the attempt by the Shiv Sena to violently force the film *Fire* off cinema halls in Mumbai and Delhi. The Court held that 'freedom of expression which is legitimate and constitutionally protected, cannot be held to ransom by an intolerant group of people . . . (The) freedom of expression cannot be suppressed on account of threat of demonstration and processions or threats of violence. That would be tantamount to negation of the rule of law and a surrender to blackmail and intimidation . . . The State cannot plead its inability to handle the hostile audience. It is its obligatory duty to prevent it and protect the freedom of expression.' When Shiv Sena activists attacked cinema halls showing *Fire*, however, this is precisely what the state failed to do. Instead of protecting the exhibiting theatres and their patrons, the Vajpayee government ordered the film to be sent back to the Censor Board for re-examination.

The reason the *Fire* controversy is of particular interest to us is because of the manner in which the Shiv Sena was able to use the media to publicize its act of vandalism. This is especially true of their violent attack on the Regal theatre in New Delhi. As Sidharth Bhatia has argued, 'The protest started only after TV journalists landed up. Viewers saw a handful of miscreants breaking glass showcases, tearing posters and generally making a nuisance of themselves. It was live and exciting television. But was it journalism?'[117] In fact, by alerting TV stations several hours before hand, the Shiv Sena had demonstrated its awareness of the key difference between the print media and television: the latter's weakness for a good 'visual'. In Bhatia's words: 'The entire effort of a TV journalist is to get the visual to back the story. But that is not always possible, at least not as soon as news breaks. Since, unlike newspapers, TV channels cannot wait till the next day's edition, they have constantly to churn out news and anything visually dramatic becomes news.'[118] The Shiv Sena understood this dictum very well and knew that the lure of dramatic visuals would pull in the TV crews.

At the same time, the preceding analysis should not be read as an argument for censorship, precensorship or self-censorship. The television stations who covered the Regal incidents would argue that the subsequent broadcast of their footage actually increased public revulsion towards the Shiv Sena. They would also argue that the messenger must not be shot, and that if anyone is to be held responsible for the vandalism, it is the police and the state which allowed the violence to continue, failed to arrest all of those responsible and didn't bother to prosecute those whom they did apprehend.

Conclusion

In this chapter, we have looked at the mass media as a factor in the process of communlization. A constant theme has been the way in which the media, at different times, has incited and disarmed people. The technology of incitement is fairly simple and has remained more or less unchanged for the better part of a century. It involves the transmission of rumours, coupled with biased or tendentious reporting in which passions are inflamed and prejudices freely indulged. There are particular moments when incitement goes into high gear, such as before and during riots or when journalists, editors or proprietors get involved in communalist campaigns waged by political parties. At other times, incitement remains at a low intensity. Grievances are manufactured, myths of difference are nurtured, bonds of solidarity cutting across community lines are corroded.

The technologies of disarmament are more complex but the bottom line is the evasion of politics. Whether it is the fracturing of the polity along communal lines, the devaluation of a secular notion of citizenship, the promotion of diversionary agendas or the very process of news dissemination, the media often serves to depoliticize the citizenry. As Habermas put it in his seminal work, *The Structural Transformation of the Public Sphere*, the public, instead of critically reflecting on its culture, ends up merely consuming it.[119] Or, reworking this, we may say that thanks to the tranquilizing effect of the mass media, the public, instead of critically reflecting on and participating in politics, ends up as a passive observer.

At this turning point between two centuries, the prospects for the Indian media transcending the limits of its coverage and serving as a genuine vehicle for enlightenment are not especially good. In smaller media establishments, professional standards of news gathering and dissemination are not usually maintained; even bigger newspapers tend sometimes to make appalling errors of judgment. The fact that the laws are rarely applied does little to help matters. As per the provisions of the Indian Penal Code and Criminal Procedure Code, the incitement of communal hatred is an offence. Yet, newspaper editors and proprietors are rarely hauled up for printing false and inflammatory news. Whenever they are, the authorities show little interest in the prosecution. In the case of the Marathi dailies *Saamna* and *Navakal*—which were taken to court for publishing communal propaganda during the

Mumbai riots of 1992-93—the Shiv Sena-BJP government in Maharashtra simply withdrew all criminal charges filed against them. Which is not to say that the Congress administration which preceded it was particularly keen to prosecute.

Although the prognosis generally appears pessimistic, one must also bear in mind the lage number of journalists who are genuinely objective and sensitive in their treatment of communal violence. Often working against difficult odds, such journalists have brought to the attention of the public shocking details of how riots are engineered and conducted. Unfortunately, it is not uncommon for such journalists to be subjected to threats and intimidation. After the BJP's failed assault against the Babri Masjid in October 1990, for example, the editor of *Jan Morcha*, a leading daily of Faizabad, was threatened for refusing to exaggerate the number of kar sevaks killed in police firing. The editor of another Faizabad daily, *Hum Aap*, told a correspondent that he had begun to inflate the number of dead for fear of being lynched.[120] But by far the most systematic campaign of harassment against journalists anywhere in the country has been in Maharashtra in the past few years. There, the ruling Shiv Sena-BJP alliance is so intolerant of dissent that newspaper offices, especially of Marathi language dailies, have frequently been made the target of attack. The editors of three highly influential newspapers—Kumar Ketkar of *Maharashtra Times*, Arun Tikekar of *Loksatta* and Nikhil Wagle of *Apla Mahanagar*—have been threatened for their criticism of the government and of Sena leader Bal Thackeray.[121] The three are frequently denounced by Thackeray in the editorial columns of his organ, *Saamna*. In one famous editorial, '*Loksatta*'s mad editor', he virtually called for Tikekar to be beaten, writing that 'every 1000 slaps should be counted only as one'. The threats and attacks have not been confined to Mumbai. In Amravati, the offices of the daily *Pratidin* were attacked by a mob led by the city's BJP mayor. In Akola, a relative of a Shiv Sena minister was arrested for the attack on *Deshunnati*. In Thane, the *Maharashtra Times'* chief sub-editor, Anand Dighe, named a Sena man as responsible for an attack on him. In Aurangabad, 150 Sainiks ransacked the *Mahanagar* office and blackened the face of the editor, Nishikant Bhalerao, because he had carried news critical of Thackeray.[122]

The Press Council, which does a reasonable job monitoring such instances of intimidation as well as communal bias in print media coverage, is nevertheless hampered by the fact that it lacks the ability to enforce its recommendations. Unless it is made a statutory body, it will continue to have little practical impact on newspaper coverage. In any event, its model code of conduct—which says that the religious affiliation of riot victims and participants should not be mentioned—is itself highly problematic, as we have seen above. While there is no logical reason for the religion of riot victims not to be identified, I still believe there is merit in not identifying assailants by community. My hesitation does not stem from the fear that passions will be aroused but rather that one needs to make a break with the very discourse of the 'communal riot', which sees 'Hindus' and 'Muslims', for example, as monolithic and mutually antagonistic communities. In fact, a riot is rarely a clash between 'communities'. By what yardstick can the Bajrang Dal or the Hindu Jagran Manch in Gujarat be equated with the so-called 'Hindu community', if there is even such a thing? And why should the Congress-organized pogroms against the Sikhs in Delhi and other cities in November 1984 be described as 'Hindu-Sikh' violence? In each instance, the victims were targeted because of their religion and this fact must be highlighted by the media. But the perpetrators were not representatives of the Hindu 'community', even if they sought to act in its name.

While issues of day-to-day coverage are extremely important, the best antidote to the pressures of communalization is to strive for what Brecht called the 'functional transformation' of the media. Communalism in the media is a problem but it is only an instantiation of the largely undemocratic nature of the mass media. What we need, therefore, is journalism which raises the level of discussion in society by addressing the concerns of the people. In modern market economies, two obstacles need to be overcome. The first is the market mechanism itself. The inability of small and medium-sized media organizations to remain profitable has led to a growing degree of concentration in all sectors of the mass media around the world. In India, this trend has been late in arriving, in part because of the diversity of the language press, but it is evident that a process of concentration is already underway. As Michael Gurevitch and Jay Blumler argue, competition between large media organizations for a large and heterogeneous mass audience has a negative effect on the public sphere. This is because such circumstances 'are likely to generate pressures to limit the amount of public affairs coverage, shift its style from the serious and extended to the entertaining and arresting . . . (and) impose rigid formats'. The second obstacle is the state, which, together with other powerful institutions in society, is able to mould media coverage thanks to its position of authority. In India, for example, the police and paramilitaries are considered to be the authority on questions of law and order, the Reserve Bank of India, the Union finance ministry and investment banks on the economy, and the defence ministry and quasi-government think-tanks like the Institute for Defence Studies and Analyses the last word on issues of defence and national security. Journalists looking for an objective assessment turn mostly to officials from such institutions. 'Media professionals do not see this practice as a violation of the canon of objectivity . . . Alternative definitions of social issues are then disadvantaged—either not represented at all, given short shrift, or labeled as "interested" and "biased".'[123]

If the mass media are constantly seeking to place limits on

220

public discussion, the only way of ensuring democratic political communication is to provide people with actual access to the means of communication. Utopian though this sounds in the present context, there is ultimately no alternative to Phillip Green's argument that what is required is the 'dismantling (of) the entire structure of monopolised mass communication—newspaper chains, nationwide network television, mass-market book publishers—that we have come to take for granted as the very heart of consumer civilization itself'.[124] There is a need for genuine pluralism of access which only different forms of ownership—community, private and public—can provide. Unfortunately, there is little chance of the existing patterns of ownership becoming more democratic in the near future. If at all, things are only going to get worse. However, the struggle for new journalism—journalism which speaks to the concerns of citizens, makes them conscious of their rights, and assists them in their striving for empowerment—will have to go on regardless.

Notes

1. The reference, of course, is to Prime Minister Atal Behari Vajpayee's call for a national debate on conversions. See the *Times of India*, 11 January 1999.
2. Quoted in Amrit Srinivasan, 'The Survivor in the Study of Violence' in Veena Das, ed. *Mirrors of Violence: Communities, Riots and Survivors in South Asia*, New Delhi, 1990, p. 316.
3. Anoop Babani, 'Index on Media,' *Seminar*, October 1997, p. 56.
4. Robin Jeffrey, 'Indian-language Newspapers,' *Seminar*, October 1997, p. 24-28.
5. 'Internet and Rock Music Help Rightist Extremists, Bonn Says,' *International Herald Tribune*, 26 March 1999, p. 6.
6. Peter Manuel, *Cassette Culture: Popular Music and Technology in North India*, Chicago, 1993, p. 250-56.
7. Walter Benjamin, ibid, p. 224-26.
8. Fredric Jameson (ed.), *Formations of Pleasure*, London, 1983, p. 1-14.

9. Jürgen Habermas, *Between Facts and Norms: Contributions to a Discourse Theory of Law and Democracy*, Oxford, 1997, p. 376.
10. Ibid.
11. Praful Bidwai, 'Media in the Service of Communalism', *Communalism Combat*, August 1997, p. 14-15.
12. Habermas, op. cit., p. 377.
13. Herbert Schiller, *The Mind Managers*, Boston, 1973, p. 24. Fragmentation, he adds, did not originate as an end in itself; rather it arose from the market economy's need to fill all communications space with advertising.
14. George Ritzer, *The McDonaldisation of Society: An Investigation into the Changing Character of Contemporary Social Life*, Thousand Oaks, CA, 1993, p. 57-8.
15. June Jordan, *Naming Our Destiny: New and Selected Poems*, New York, 1989, p. 141.
16. Benedict Anderson, *Imagined Communities: Reflections on the Origins and Spread of National Consciousness*, London, 1984, p. 37-46.
17. S Natarajan, *A History of the Press in India*, London, 1962, p. 14.
18. S. Cromwell Crawford, *Ram Mohan Roy: Social, Political and Religious Reform in 19th Century India*, New York, 1987, p. 135.
19. Quoted in Jatindra Kumar Mazumdar (ed.) *Raja Rammohun Roy and Progressive Movements in India*, Calcutta, 1941, p. 299.
20. See Frank Conlon, 'The Polemic Process in Nineteenth-century Maharashtra: Vishnubawa Brahmachari and Hindu Revival', in Kenneth W. Jones (ed.), *Religious Controversy in British India: Dialogues in South Asian Languages*, Albany, 1992, p. 15, 19.
21. Barbara Daly Metcalf, 'Imagining Community: Polemical Debates in Colonial India', in Jones, op. cit., p. 236.
22. Sajjan Lal, *Delhi Urdu Newspapers and the Freedom Struggle*, New Delhi, 1955.
23. Mahdi Husain, *Bahadur Shah II and the War of 1857 in Delhi with its Unforgettable Scenes*, New Delhi, 1986, p. 299-300.
24. Ibid., p. 46.
25. Reproduced as the 'Azamgarh Proclamation' in Rudrangshu Mukherjee, *Awadh in Revolt*, New Delhi, 1985, p. 173.
26. 'The Indian Mutiny', Letter to the Editor, The *Times* (London), 25 July 1857. 'Akhbar' then went on to advocate that Her Majesty's Government 'abandon the old custom of forming regiments of Hindoos and Mahomedans promiscuously, and

keep them distinct and wholly separate . . . never located at the same stations, nor within a short distance of one another'.

27. *Sambad Prabhakar*, 20 June 1857. Quoted in Dilip Simeon, 'Communalism in Modern India: A Theoretical Examination', *Mainstream*, 13 December 1986.

28. See Kenneth W. Jones, *Arya Dharm: Hindu Consciousness in Nineteenth Century Punjab*, Berkeley, 1976, and 'Ham Hindu Nahin', *Journal of Asian Studies*, 1973, p. 457-75.

29. Sudhir Chandra, 'Communal Elements in Late Nineteenth-century Hindi Literature', *Journal of Arts and Ideas*, January-March 1984. All quotations in this section are from his article.

30. Quoted in ibid, p. 13-14.

31. See Chris Bayly, *Local Roots of Indian Politics: Allahabad, 1880-1920*, Oxford, 1975.

32. Cited in Sudhir Chandra, op. cit. Mahatma Gandhi's tendency, in his capacity as a Congress leader, to use 'we' and 'us' when referring to Hindus has also been criticized for its alienating effect on Muslims. See R. Palme Dutt, *Inside India Today*, London, 1940, p. 326.

33. Milton Israel, *Communication and Power: Propaganda and the Press in the Indian Nationalist Struggle, 1920-47*, Cambridge, 1994, p. 8.

34. Sandria B. Freitag, *Public Arenas and the Emergence of Communalism in North India*, Delhi, 1990, p. 209.

35. Barbara Daly Metcalf, op. cit., p. 231.

36. Israel, op. cit., p. 8.

37. Gyanendra Pandey, *The Construction of Communalism in Colonial North India*, New Delhi, 1990, p. 210.

38. *Pratap*, 17 November 1924, translated and quoted by Pandey, op. cit., p. 238-9.

39. See Israel, op. cit., and Aurobindo Mazumdar, *Indian Press and Freedom Struggle, 1937-42*, Calcutta, 1993, for an analysis of the newspapers of this period.

40. Paul Brass, 'Secularism Out of its Place,' in *Contributions to Indian Sociology*, July-December 1998, p. 485-505.

41. A senior and respected journalist like Arun Shourie, for example, has written countless columns in leading newspapers attacking Islam as a religion. See his book, *The World of Fatwas, or the Shariah in Action*, New Delhi, 1996, for a collection of some of these.

42. Kalpana Sharma and Ammu Joseph, 'The Shah Bano Controversy: A Question of Maintenance,' p. 52 ff. In Ammu Joseph and Kalpana Sharma, *Whose News? The Media and Women's Issues*, New Delhi, 1994.

43. Ibid, p. 61. In their assessment, 'while the overall coverage of the issue was not overtly communal, there was an underlying bias in some of the editorial comment. For instance, the insistence that a Universal Civil Code was the best solution reflected an unquestioning belief that what was acceptable to the majority community should also be acceptable by all minorities, especially Muslims'.

44. Charu Gupta and M.K.S., 'From News Gathering to News Making: The Creation of Pseudo-Events,' *Mainstream*, 12 June 1993, p. 27-32.

45. Ibid.

46. See B.G. Verghese, 'Fact and Fiction,' *Mainstream*, 13 February 1993; Harinder Baweja, 'Kashmir Temples: Damaging Lies,' *India Today*, 28 Febraury 1993, p. 24-28.

47. Press Council Report of 21 January 1991, quoted in A.G. Noorani, 'Reporting Riots: Need for Precise Formulation,' The *Statesman*, 18 July 1995.

48. Charu Gupta and Mukul Sharma, 'Communal Constructions: Media Reality vs Real Reality', *Race & Class*, 38, 1 (1996), p. 16.

49. *Swatantra Chetna*, 2 November 1990. Cited in ibid.

50. Radhika Ramaseshan, 'The Press on Ayodhya', *Economic and Political Weekly*, 15 December 1990, p. 2701-2704.

51. Ibid.

52. See, for example, Charu and Mukul, *Print Media and Communalism*, New Delhi, 1990.

53. Dipankar Gupta, 'The Communalising of Punjab, 1980-1985,' *Economic and Political Weekly*, 13 July 1995, p. 1188.

54. Patwant Singh, 'The Distorting Mirror', in Patwant Singh and Harji Malik (ed.), *Punjab: The Fatal Miscalculation*, New Delhi, 1985, p. 9-32.

55. Girilal Jain in the *Times of India*, 7 March 1984.

56. M.J. Akbar, *India: The Siege Within*, New Delhi, 1985, p. 130.

57. Ram Swarup, 'Concept of a Sikh Nation' and 'The Hindu-Sikh Cleavage,' the *Times of India*, 19 and 20 December 1984.

58. Arun Shourie, writing on 12, 13 and 14 May 1982 in the *Indian*

Express. Quoted in Patwant Singh, op. cit.

59. Dharma Kumar, 'A Voice from the "Rest of India",' the *Times of India,* 14 November 1984.

60. Dipankar Gupta, op. cit.

61. It was only in 1988, for example, that it was revealed that some of the terrorist groups operating in Punjab were not 'Khalistani' but police-funded 'counter-insurgents'. See Sanjoy Hazarika, 'The Gambit,' *Illustrated Weekly of India,* 10 July 1988 for an account of the activities of one such terrorist, Santokh Singh Kala.

62. *Hindustan Times,* 25 June 1987.

63. Tavleen Singh, 'In a State of Terror', *Indian Express,* 7 May 1989.

64. 'The Making of a Lawless Society', *Economic and Political Weekly,* 1 June 1985, p. 943. Thapar adds: 'When one of the leading accused died in hospital, we were told that it was the result of injuries sustained when struggling against the police. The doctor's report was the most unsatisfactory document that I have read in a long while'.

65. 'The lessons from Bidar', *The Tribune,* 6 October 1988.

66. People's Union for Democratic Rights and People's Union for Civil Liberties, *Who are the Guilty? Report of a Joint Inquiry into the Causes and Impact of the Riots in Delhi from 31 October to 10 November,* Delhi, November, 1984, p. 13-14.

67. 'The Police Commissioner was present at one of the earliest trouble spots, a place of worship in Sadar Bazar. It was in his presence, and in the presence of other senior officers . . . that the place of worship was set on fire'. (*The Statesman,* 7 November 1984); 'A shopkeeper in Kamla Nagar, Pritam Singh, watched helplessly as his shop was looted. Policemen encouraged the mob to do so and were themselves a party to it'. (*The Statesman,* 5 November 1984).

68. *Hindustan Times,* 8 November 1984.

69. 'Ray of Sunshine in Darkness,' the *Times of India,* 3 November 1984. 'Stories of Hindus and Muslims saving their Sikh neighbours and friends were heard at almost every relief camp and riot-hit locality this reporter visited' (*The Statesman,* 10 November 1984). See also 'Sikhs are all praise for Hindu neighbours,' *Hindustan Times,* 7 November 1984.

70. PUDR-PUCL, op. cit., p. 13-14.

71. 'When Delhi Burnt,' *Economic and Political Weekly,* 8 December 1984, p. 2066.

72. *Delhi, 31 October to 4 November 1984: Report of the Citizens' Commission,* Delhi, 1984, p. 33.
73. Tavleen Singh, 'Self-imposed,' *Seminar,* November 1986.
74. *Hindustan Times,* 12 March 1987.
75. *Jansatta,* 2 November 1990. Cited in Charu Gupta and M.K.S., 'The Muslim and the News,' *Mainstream,* 13 February 1993, p. 15-19.
76. See Suranjan Das, *Communal Riots in Bengal, 1905-1947,* Delhi, 1991. The examples in this paragraph and the next have all been drawn from his study, p. 79-80, 146 ff, 168 ff.
77. Cited in Satish Saberwal and Mushirul Hasan, 'Moradabad Riots, 1980: Causes and Meanings' in Asghar Ali Engineer, (ed.) *Communal Riots in Post-Independence India,* New Delhi, 1991, p. 214.
78. Asghar Ali Engineer, 'An Analytical Study of the Meerut Riot' in Engineer, (ed.), ibid. p. 280.
79. Peoples' Union for Democratic Rights, *Bhagalpur Riots,* Delhi, 1990, p. 16.
80. Sanskritik Morcha and People's Union for Democratic Rights, *Bhopal Riots: A Report,* Delhi, 1993. The details of press coverage of the riots which follow have been taken from this report.
81. Ibid.
82. *Gujarat Samachar,* 27 July 1998. Cited in CPI(M-L) (New Democracy), *Gujarat: Minorities in the Storm of Communal Attacks—A Report from the RSS Laboratory of Religious Cleansing,* Delhi, 1999, p. 17-20. The other examples have been drawn from this source.
83. *Gujarat Samachar,* 26 June 1998.
84. *Nav Gujarat Times,* 18 July 1998.
85. *Dabkar,* 26 June 1998.
86. *Gujarat Samachar,* 29 June 1998.
87. Virender Kumar, 'Orwellian "census" raises eyebrows and tempers in Gujarat,' *Indian Express,* 15 February 1999.
88. Shekhar Gupta, 'Anti-Christian violence and the English media: No Printer's Devil Here,' *Indian Express,* 28 January 1999.
89. See Vibhuti Narain Rai, *Combating Communal Conflicts: Perception of Police Neutrality During Hindu-Muslim Riots in India,* New Delhi, 1998. The author is a serving IPS officer.
90. Charu Gupta and Mukul Sharma, 'Communal Constructions:

Media Reality vs Real Reality,' *Race & Class*, 38, 1 (1996), p. 8.

91. Stanley J. Tambiah, *Leveling Crowds: Ethnonationalist Conflicts and Collective Violence in South Asia*, New Delhi, 1996.

92. Ibid., p. 192-93.

93. *Communalism Combat*, July 1998.

94. David Lelyveld, 'The Fate of Hindustani: Colonial Knowledge and the Project of a National Language,' in Carol A. Breckenridge and Peter van der Veer (ed.) *Orientalism and the Postcolonial Predicament: Perspectives on South Asia*, Philadelphia, 1993, p. 208.

95. David Lelyveld, 'Upon the Subdominant: Administering Music on All-India Radio', in Arjun Appadurai and Carol Breckenridge, *Consuming Modernity: Public Culture in a South Asian World*, Minneapolis, 1995, p. 57-59. The rest of this paragraph draws heavily on Lelyveld's work.

96. See P.C. Chatterji, *The Adventure of Indian Broadcasting: A Philosopher's Autobiography*, New Delhi, 1998.

97. Lelyveld, *supra* n. 97.

98. Ibid.

99. One-time Rajiv Gandhi loyalist and senior Congress functionary K.K. Tewary, quoted in *Indian Express*, 30 April 1989.

100. Theodore Adorno, 'Television and the Patterns of Mass Culture' in W. Schramm, (ed.) *Mass Communications*, Urbana, 1960.

101. See Patricia Uberoi, 'The Diaspora Comes Home: Disciplining Desire in DDLJ,' in *Contributions to Indian Sociology*, July-December, 1998, p. 305-336, and 'Imagining the family: An ethnography of viewing '*Hum aapke hain koun . . .!*,' in Rachel Dwyer and Chris Pinney, (ed.), *Pleasure and the Nation: The History and Politics of Popular Culture in India* (forthcoming).

102. Shailaja Bajpai, 'Culture and Television,' *Seminar*, March 1999, p. 52-57.

103. The programme—which is produced by (and stars) a BJP politician, Mukesh Khanna—is controversial mainly because several children have died trying to emulate Shaktimaan's stunts. If media comment is to be believed, the programme has not been pulled off the air by Doordarshan mainly because of Khanna's political connections. See Sidharth Bhatia, 'Shaktimaan, Children and the Parivar,' the *Pioneer*, 23 February 1999.

104. Divya C. McMillan, 'Communities of Consumption: Television and Audiences in India,' Paper presented to the University of

Victoria Conference on South Asian Popular Culture, 22-24 April 1999.

105. According to Appadurai and Breckenridge, 'this interocular field is structured so that each site or setting for the socialising and regulating of the public gaze is to some degree affected by the experiences of the other sites'. See Arjun Appadurai and Carol Breckenridge, 'Public Modernity in India,' in Appadurai and Brackenridge (ed.) *Consuming Modernity: Public Culture in a South Asian World*, Minneapolis, 1995, p. 11-13.

106. Tapan Basu et al, *Khaki Shorts, Saffron Flags: A Critique of the Hindu Right*, New Delhi, 1993, p.107, 109.

107. Appadurai and Breckenridge, op. cit.

108. Philip Lutgendorf, 'All in the (Raghu) Family: A Video Epic in Cultural Context' in Lawrence A. Babb and Susan S. Wadley, *Media and the Transformation of Religion in South Asia*, Philadelphia, 1995, p. 239.

109. Peter van der Veer, *Religious Nationalism: Hindus and Muslims in India*, Berkeley, 1994, p. 177-78.

110. This was a tactic the Congress also tried, besides launching its 1989 election campaign from Ayodhya's twin city, Faizabad, with Rajiv Gandhi promising 'Ram rajya'.

111. van der Veer, op. cit.

112. Romila Thapar, 'The Ramayana syndrome,' *Seminar*, January 1989, p. 72.

113. K.S. Raghavan, 'The Sword of Gidwani and the Tipu Sultan Controversy: A Conversation with Bhagwan Gidwani,' *IPSG Newsletter*, Columbia University, New York, September 1990.

114. *Communalism Combat*, December 1998, p. 11. The documentary film-maker, Shohini Ghosh, has also reported that a privately edited version of *Zakhm* is being circulated on video and shown on cable which plays down certain aspects of the Hindu-Muslim theme and the complicty between the police and the *sangathan*. See 'The Wounding of *Zakhm*,' *Communalism Combat*, February 99, p. 38-39.

115. 1 SCC 668. Subsequent quotations are from the judgment.

116. 2 SCC 574. Subsequent quotations are from this judgment.

117. Sidharth Bhatia, 'For the Sake of a Story,' the *Pioneer*, 8 December 1998.

118. Ibid.

119. Jürgen Habermas, *The Structural Transformation of the Public Sphere*, Cambridge, 1989, p. 175.

120. See Radhika Ramaseshan, 'The Press on Ayodhya,' *Economic and Political Weekly*, 15 December 1990, p. 2701-2704.

121. See Javed Anand, 'Held to Ransom,' the *Pioneer*, 11 November 1997. The following details are from this article.

122. *Asian Age*, 18 December 1996.

123. Michael Gurevitch and Jay G. Blumler, 'Political Communication Systems and Democratic Values,' in Judith Lichtenberg, *Democracy and the Mass Media*, Cambridge, 1990, p. 276-7.

124. Phillip Green, *Retrieving Democracy*, Totowa, NJ, 1985, p. 219.

Afterword

A communal agenda is now before the nation, initially conceived by the ideologues of Hindutva and later elaborated and foregrounded by its politics. The main thrust of the agenda is the construction of a socio-political order that would privilege the culture and religion of the Hindus, legitimized by what is euphemistically called 'cultural nationalism'. The BJP's access to state power, though brief and without a majority in the Parliament, occasioned an unprecedented opportunity to advance at least some aspects of the agenda through official patronage and support. The government's achievements in this respect, bridled by the limitations of coalition politics, did not fully meet the expectations of the Parivar; issues like the construction of the Mandir at Ayodhya, the enactment of a common civil code and the abrogation of Article 370 of the Constitution could not even be included in the 'national agenda'. Nevertheless, the government took initiatives in several fields of governance, particularly in culture, education and defence, to further a Hindu communal programme.

The BJP's control over the apparatuses of the state also facilitated a more aggressive pursuit of the agenda by other members of the Parivar. For, they could now rely on official patronage and support, which enabled them to negotiate the administrative hurdles with greater ease. They focussed on what the government could not undertake on its own due to the constrains of coalition politics. The different constituents the Parivar and the government were thus complimenting each other in the pursuit of a common goal; collaboration rather than contradiction characterizing their relationship. The consequences of this collaboration quite adversely impinged upon the national life: the broad consensus and harmony, which for long characterized the religious and social life were unsettled; the democratic and secular commitments and practices of the state were undermined; and the social and political life was vitiated and brutalized.

I

While the political philosophy of Hindutva has emerged out of authoritarian convictions, its practice has increasingly adopted anti-democratic methods. The notion of Hindutva itself was influenced by the racial theories of German thinkers, whose works Savarkar had read during the period of his transition from a revolutionary to a Hindu communal ideologue. Golwalkar was a great admirer of Hitler and several of his formulations have the unmistakable imprint of the ideas of the Führer. The racial hatred, cultural arrogance and obsession with discipline and physical strength that the RSS professes are reminiscent of the ways of European fascism. If the political practice of the Parivar is an indication, it shares the fascist attitude towards democratic institutions. The seizure of power by the Nazis in Germany was by instrumentalizing the democratic institutions and practices and then subverting them by establishing an authoritarian regime. Such tendencies are conspicuous in the political record of Hindutva, even if its emergence is in substantially different economic and political

231

contexts, as well. The BJP governments, both at the Centre and the states, have placed their partisan political interests above their constitutional obligations. The BJP government in Uttar Pradesh, for instance, neither discharged its constitutional duties nor respected the directives given by the judiciary. It did not take the necessary steps to protect the Babri Masjid as instructed by the courts, and worse still, it chose to collude with the karsevaks in the demolition of the monument, for which the chief minister, Kalyan Singh, was censored and punished by the Supreme Court. The recent political crisis at the Centre, when the BJP-led government lost its majority, has further demonstrated that power rather than principles is the Parivar's prime concern. Some of its leaders then tried to circumvent the well-established democratic principle of seeking a vote of confidence and the prime minister took the unprecedented step of criticizing the President for upholding the constitutional principles.

The Constitution itself is not to the liking of the Parivar, particularly its liberal-democratic character and provisions to protect the rights of the minorities. Several members of the Parivar have demanded fundamental changes in the Constitution. In fact, the VHP had set up a committee in the early nineties to draft a new constitution. The steps are now on, initiated by the BJP-led government to introduce basic changes in the Constitution, which include the introduction of a presidential form of government and the abrogation of Article 370 that provides greater autonomy to Kashmir. Some provisions regarding the minority rights like Articles 29 and 30 have already been proposed for deletion.

The marginalization of the minorities, if not their total exclusion from the nation, is central to the tenets of cultural nationalism advocated by Hindutva. The discrimination against the minorities by the BJP government was, therefore, not altogether unexpected. But large-scale violence against them as happened in Gujarat and the inhuman brutality in Orissa, however, came as a rude shock to many. More so the government's abdication of its primary responsibility of protecting the life and property of the citizens. The government took no steps either to prevent the atrocities or to punish the guilty, as its attitude was coloured by communal considerations. The bureaucracy, rather than playing an impartial role, turned collaborator to support the leaders who aided and abetted these crimes. This has raised a serious question about the future of democratic governance, if and when the BJP gains full control of the administration, particularly because the Parivar has taken steps to ideologize the bureaucracy in the states under its rule. A possible consequence of such administrative partisanship is the alienation of the minorities from the mainstream political life, leading to the emergence of secessionist tendencies. Given that ghettoization of the minorities has already occurred during the post-Babri Masjid period, the BJP's record of administration spells serious danger to peaceful community life.

The nuclear adventurism of the BJP government is yet another face of the Hindutva agenda. Despite the claims of the government, the nuclearization has not enhanced the security of the nation. If anything, it has only imperiled it. The nuclear weapons are no guarantee against aggression, as evident from the recent developments in Kargil. It has only intensified the tension in the subcontinent and has raised the spectre of another war. It is paradoxical that a government, which develops nuclear weapons in the name of national security, is not adequately equipped even to prevent the intrusion of infiltrators! The testing of the nuclear bomb, the prime minister had assured the American authorities, was directed against the two neighbours, Pakistan and China. The immediate consequence of this step is an armament race with a disastrous impact on the region as a whole. It is unlikely that the BJP leadership is not alive to the consequences—Atal Behari Vajpayee himself was earlier a sensitive critic of the nuclear bomb. As such the political advantages rather than the requirements of national security appears to have influenced the government. If the Parivar has a secret agenda the nuclear weaponization is certainly one, for it was undertaken without a national consensus or the knowledge of its own allies—it is reported that even the defence minister was not privy to the decision to test the bomb. Only the RSS knew about it in advance. While the defence strategists and military experts are debating the wisdom behind such a move, many of them very critically, the Hindu nationalists celebrate it as a long desired assertion of national i.e. Hindu prowess. The Parivar's political and organizational philosophy has been based on recovering and harnessing this prowess, as evident from the programmes of the RSS, dressed, drilled and discipled in a paramilitary fashion. The nuclear weaponization, attempted so quickly after the BJP came to power, was an attempt to regain the prowess, which the Hindus supposedly lost due to foreign subjugation. It is essentially a partisan political project— intended to recover the long lost self-confidence of the Hindus and bind them together by imparting a common aggressive self-image. The national security is only a convenient surrogate to advance the politics of Hindutva.

The internal consolidation of the Hindus attempted through a variety of strategies is informed by a common concept of cultural nationalism, rooted in an identity between religion and culture. The cultural engagements of the Parivar generally underlined this conflation by imparting religious attributes and meaning to quotidian cultural practices and by tracing the origin of cultural forms to religious sources. Since religious and cultural developments are historically intertwined in all societies, the cultural and religious practices converge at some point in their evolution. Such a convergence is neither universal nor absolute, yet the Parivar invokes it to underline the religious identity of cultural practices, thus creating a cultural common sense rooted in religious consciousness. The mode and means of communication the Parivar employs considerably aid in effecting this change. Both draw upon religious sources: its language and vocabulary, its metaphors and symbols and its institutions and infrastructure. They foreground the religious in tradition and culture and render the communal discourse both easily accessible and emotionally acceptable. The BJP governments have considerably furthered this cultural project by ensuring communal control over cultural and research institutions and by initiating several steps to impart a Hindu character to education.

The politics of Hindutva is now well entrenched, even if its record of administration has been rather dismal. Regardless of electoral defeat in the states in which the BJP was in power, its organizational strength and social base have largely remained undiminished. The sources of its strength are several. The long-term social, ideological and cultural work, spanning about eighty years, has created a large institutional network and a committed cadre. They relentlessly pursue the dissemination of Hindutva, setting aside the distinction its progenitor, Vinayak Damodar Savarkar, had made from Hinduism in order to project it as the real faith and ideology of the Hindus. The recent access to state power is an important marker in its progress, as it seized the opportunity to advance its agenda and to establish its political legitimacy.

II

The rise of Hindu communalism to a position strong enough to control the government is a reflection of the weakness and discomfiture of the secular forces: their internal fissures, fragile ideological commitment, lack of creative initiatives and failure to correctly gauge the political situation. The combined strength of secular formations is far greater than that of the communal, yet the communal forces threaten to dominate both polity and society. This is primarily because of the weak secular convictions of many and the dissension within the secular camp. At the political level the secular initiatives are mainly limited to alliance of secular parties, which has proved to be quite inadequate to stem the communal upsurge. Most political parties, with the exception of the Left, hardly do anything to defend or recover the secular space in civil society. Their perspective is focussed on the electoral battle, which in the absence of organized social support, they seem to be increasingly losing to the advantage of the communal forces.

Outside the political parties, however, there are innumerable small but active voluntary organizations engaged in combating communalism. So far they have been mainly involved with reactive, sporadic and short-term activities. Plagued by mutual differences and hence unable to co-ordinate the activities, their impact and success have been rather limited. Conscious of these limitations, they are now engaged in evolving a new perspective, which would lead to more constructive and effective action. Several ideas are under their active consideration, three of which are particularly important: how to effect a change of focus from anti-communalism to secular action which would help in creating secular consciousness in society; how to make secular action integral to their main concern; and how to create common platforms to share experience and resources and thus make joint struggles possible.

There is increasing feeling among voluntary organizations that an anti-communal campaign is not constructive enough to sustain secular consciousness, as the popular participation in it is either passive or sporadic. Only active and continuous engagement can ensure the sustenance of consciousness, for which a change from an anti-communal campaign to secular mobilization is imperative. While the former, being reactive is negative in perspective and programme, the latter is conceived as a positive step with its own agenda. These organizations are conscious that there is no universally applicable prescription for mobilization, as ground realities are different from one locality to the other. Therefore they plan to work through small local communities organized around secular issues.

The cultural engagement of most of these organizations have not been effective enough to imbibe a secular ethos in society and thus to counter the communal threat. Both the content and mode of their cultural action suffer from a static view of culture and hence overlook the processes of interaction and integration of various cultural elements. The secular cultural action is, therefore, generally confined to invoking, highlighting or celebrating the secular in tradition, without emphasizing how this tradition was constantly evolving through interaction with the religious. The failure to interrogate this relationship between the secular and the religious has given an opportunity to the communal forces to appropriate and sacralize the cultural tradition. Some cultural organizations have become sensitive to the importance of this relationship for reaching out to the masses by evolving a mode of communication easily accessible to them.

The form and message of secular cultural communication, despite the support of some of the best cultural practitioners of the country, are repetitive and uninspiring. Over the years they have largely remained the same. Either an exhortation for communal harmony or an idealization of the syncretic tradition makes up the content of most secular cultural interventions. This is too simplistic to comprehend the complexities of the tradition or the contradictions in contemporary life. As such the secular cultural action remains at a predictable terrain and hence its effectiveness either to counter the communal or to advance the secular consciousness is only marginal. The attempts to overcome this weakness, still being at the level of experimentation, tends to be so abstract that it is not comprehensible to many. Either way, the secular cultural interventions fail to forge the necessary links with people.

The voluntary organizations in their efforts to incorporate a conscious struggle for secularism in their activities are now engaged in redefining the scope and meaning of cultural action. Out of their considerations two solutions seem to have emerged. The first is the need to enlarge the scope of cultural action by incorporating all issues germane to social life. This has led to the formation of a large number of small secular communities involved with matters of local interest like water, cleanliness, environment, regional history, cultural forms and so on. These are conceived and developed as focal points of secular action, with a wider meaning and greater reach.

The second area of concern is the lack of a mutual rapport between secular action and democratic struggles. The activities of voluntary organizations are generally confined to their chosen fields and despite their secular character and convictions are not sensitive to the secular demands. The relationship between secular action and democratic struggles therefore remains very tenuous and, as a result the members of voluntary organizations often fail to internalize secular values. At times of crisis the secular commitment of such organizations tends to be fragile, as happened to some trade unions in Mumbai during the Ramjanmabhoomi campaign. The voluntary organizations are now conscious of the importance of forging a connection between secular action and democratic struggles, and are seeking the ways and means for realizing it. Among them is a possible collaboration between voluntary organizations and secular political parties in a constructive programme of creating secular communities.

The collaboration and consolidation of anti-communal forces is predicated on a major change in the perspective of secular political parties. To most of them, secularism is only a platform for electoral alliances and not an ideology around which continuous social mobilization is necessary. Even a genuine belief and commitment are lacking in some of them, which accounts for the quick changes in allegiance from the secular to the communal grouping witnessed in recent times. Unless the secular forces create an active and articulate social base, as Hindutva has done over the years, but depend only upon the alliances of political parties with uncertain commitment, their chances of countering communalism are not likely to be very bright.

III

Why and how communalism has managed to gain so much support in Indian society has been the subject of several inquiries and considerable theorization. Its roots have been traced to the excrescence of tradition, the manipulation of colonial power, the pathology of nationalism, the weakness or infirmity of modernity, and so on. The concern here is not so much about its origins, but about its meaning to the future of Indian society, particularly its implications for the secular and democratic character of its political institutions which have already been subjected to considerable strain by the politics of Hindutva. The Indian society, it appears, is forced to make a choice, once again, about its polity and identity.

Earlier it did so in 1950. At that time despite the human tragedy that Partition entailed, the secular convictions were strong enough to favour a secular–democratic republic. Today the secular–communal divide is sharper and there are far more active adherents to the communal cause, though the secular commands an as yet immobilized majority in civil society. The decision of 1950 was preceded by a national debate as represented by the deliberations in the Constituent Assembly. Whether the principles which informed that decision will continue to hold has become a paramount question before the nation. And if they do not, what will it portend for the future of Indian democracy?

K.N. Panikkar

Index

Hindu(s), xiii, xviii, 1-4, 8-9,
20, 22, 24, 26-27, 53, 125,
172-75, 177-78, 181, 186-87,
207;
  communalization, vii, xi, xix,
  xxi, xxiii-xxiv, xxvi, 136,
  237;
  law codification, 52-53, 57;
  Muhammadans, 85;
  muslim conflicts, xii, 92, 94;
  unity, 175;
  personal law, 57;
  religious endowments, 54;
  sikh violence, 190-91, 220;
  system of education, xxi;
  tolerance, xxii; women, 140,
  147-50, 153-55, 199
Hinduism, x, xv, xix, 9-10, 22,
25-26, 34-35, 40-41, 76, 81,
89-90, 97, 169, 182, 208;
  brahmanical, 138;
  politicization, 58;
  puranic, 23;
  reconversion to, 78, 81, 92
Hindutva, xxiv, 1-2, 28-31, 40,
76, 80, 100, 126-28, 208-09,
232-34, 237;
  social and political
  acceptability, xxx, 117
Hindu Adoption and
Maintenance Act, 1956, 70*n*
Hindu Chetna, 140
Hindu Code Bill, 52, 57
'Hindu, Hindi, Hindustan',
176
Hindu-Hitarthi Vidyalaya, 87
Hindu Jagaran Manch, 220
Hindu Mahasabha, 104*n*

Hindu Manch, 78
Hindu Marriage Act, 1955, 70*n*
Hindu Minority and
Guardianship Act, 1956, 70*n*
Hindu Rashtra, 155, 157-58
Hindu Right, 96
Hindu Sangathan, 92
Hindu Succession Act, 1956,
70*n*
Hindustan Times, 194
Hukum Chand, 70*n*
Hum Aap, 218
Hum Aapke Hain Koun . . .!,
206
Hunas, 5, 7
Husain, M.F. xxxv*n*
Hyderabad, Nizam of, 51

Ijma (consensus), 37
imperialism, 113, 116, 137
Indegenism, xxv
India(n): adjustment
strategies, failure, 120-21;
communalism, xi, xiv, 163;
cultural and social diversity,
vii, 35;
Christianity, 41;
employment generation,
120-22;
fundamentalist tendencies
and violence, 117-29;
Islam, spread of, xvii;
media and public sphere,
167-70;
Muslims 41;
partition, viii, 45, 47, 51;
Persian contacts, 5;
political history, xii;